# Exchange Rate Policies
in the Nordic Countries

# Exchange Rate Policies in the Nordic Countries

*Edited by*

**Johnny Åkerholm and Alberto Giovannini**

## Centre for Economic Policy Research

The Centre for Economic Policy Research is a network of over 200 Research Fellows, based primarily in European universities. The Centre coordinates its Fellows' research activities and communicates their results to the public and private sectors. CEPR is an entrepreneur, developing research initiatives with the producers, consumers and sponsors of research. Established in 1983, CEPR is a European economics research organization with uniquely wide-ranging scope and activities.

CEPR is a registered educational charity. Institutional (core) finance for the Centre is provided through major grants from the Economic and Social Research Council, under which an ESRC Resource Centre operates within CEPR; the Esmée Fairbairn Charitable Trust; the Bank of England; 14 other central banks and 30 other companies. None of these organizations gives prior review to the Centre's publications, nor do they necessarily endorse the views expressed therein.

The Centre is pluralist and non-partisan, bringing economic research to bear on the analysis of medium- and long-run policy questions. CEPR research may include views on policy, but the Executive Committee of the Centre does not give prior review to its publications, and the Centre takes no institutional policy positions. The opinions expressed here are those of the authors and not those of the Centre for Economic Policy Research.

Published by the Centre for Economic Policy Research
25–28 Old Burlington Street, London W1X 1LB, UK

© Centre for Economic Policy Research, 1994

*British Library Cataloguing in Publication Data*
*A Catalogue record for this book is available from the British Library*

ISBN: 1 898128 11 1

# Contents

v

## 6   The Struggle to Turn the Swedish Krona into a Hard Currency        133
**Lars Hörngren and Hans Lindberg**

## 7   Disinflation Experience in Finland Compared with Other OECD Countries        173
**Palle S. Andersen**

## 8   The Currency Band and Credibility: The Finnish Experience        231
**Olli-Pekka Lehmussaari, Antti Suvanto and Laura Vajanne**

# List of Tables

# List of Figures

# Preface

This volume contains a selection of the papers presented at the conference on 'Exchange Rate Policies in the Nordic Countries', jointly sponsored by the Centre for Economic Policy Research and the Bank of Finland. The conference was part of the CEPR research programme in International Macroeconomics, and was hosted by the Bank of Finland in Helsinki on 21–22 September 1992.

We would like to thank Richard Portes for his encouragement in this project, as well as the staff of CEPR who, in the various stages of the conference and the preparation of this volume, have lent their valuable support. Special thanks go to Kate Millward and the Publications Department for the high-quality work and the energy with which they completed this volume.

*Johnny Åkerholm and Alberto Giovannini*
1 July 1994

# List of Conference Participants

Johnny Åkerholm *Bank of Finland/Suomen Pankki*
Palle S. Andersen *Bank for International Settlements, Basle*
Torben M. Andersen *Universiteit van Aarhus and CEPR*
Eduard J. Bomhoff *Erasmus University*
William Branson *Princeton University and CEPR*
Angel Calderon *El Colegio de México*
Zhaohui Chen *London School of Economics*
Susan M. Collins *Georgetown University, The Brookings Institution and CEPR*
Bernard Delbecque *Université Catholique de Louvain and International Monetary Fund*
Hans Denkov *Danmarks Nationalbank*
John Driffill *University of Southampton and CEPR*
Alberto Giovannini *Columbia University and CEPR*
Pertti Haaparanta *Helsinki School of Economics and Business Administration*
Seppo Honkapohja *University of Helsinki and CEPR*
Lars Hörngren *Sveriges Riksbank*
Olli-Pekka Lehmussaari *Bank of Finland/Suomen Pankki*
Hans Lindberg *Sveriges Riksbank and Institute for International Economic Studies, Stockholm*
Gabriela Mundaca *Norges Bank*
Marie-José Nadal *Banque de France*
Peter Erling Nielsen *University of Copenhagen*
Maria Perez Jurado *Banco de España*
Pentti Pikkarainen *Bank of Finland/Suomen Pankki*
Richard Portes *CEPR and Birkbeck College, London*
Kari Puumanen *Bank of Finland/Suomen Pankki*
Jan F. Qvigstad *Norges Bank*
Alan Sutherland *University of York and CEPR*
Antti Suvanto *Bank of Finland/Suomen Pankki*
Lars E. O. Svensson *Institute for International Economic Studies, Stockholm and CEPR*
Niels Thygesen *University of Copenhagen*
Laura Vajanne *Union of Bank of Finland*
Jouko Vilmunen *Bank of Finland/Suomen Pankki*
Charles Wyplosz *INSEAD, Fontainebleau and CEPR*
Joseph Zeira *Hebrew University of Jerusalem*

# Foreword

The timing of this conference was ideal for discussants, hopeless for authors. The events then taking place in the Exchange Rate Mechanism of the EMS provided an extraordinary background to our analyses and debates. Those participants with policy responsibilities may at least have found some relief in the intellectual atmosphere of the meetings.

The ERM crisis was of course directly relevant to the exchange rate policies of all the Nordic countries, and each of their economies was directly affected by it. The period since September 1992 has seen highly significant further developments, the latest being agreement in the negotiations for the accession of Finland, Sweden and Norway (as well as Austria) to the European Union. Whereas the French referendum on Maastricht was the day before our conference began, the Nordic referendums on accession will take place shortly after this book appears. The results will affect exchange rates, exchange rate policies, and many other aspects of the economies of these countries and the EU. The papers in this volume illuminate the choices and their consequences.

CEPR is very grateful to the Bank of Finland for its warm hospitality and financial support of this conference. We look forward to continued collaboration.

*Richard Portes*
July 1994

# 1

# Introduction

## Johnny Åkerholm
*Bank of Finland/Suomen Pankki*

## Alberto Giovannini
*Columbia University and CEPR*

This volume contains a number of research papers presented at a conference held in Helsinki on 21–22 September, 1992. The conference, sponsored by the Bank of Finland and organized jointly with CEPR, was originally designed to assess a rather important development in the monetary history of Europe: the substantial convergence of exchange rate regimes and policy stances by almost all countries. Central banks as far away as the Bank of Finland and the Banco de Portugal adopted in essence the same policy: pegging their exchange rate to the group of the ERM countries or, more specifically, to the Deutschemark.

Since the time of the conference, this regime has almost completely unfolded. Ex post facto, the unfolding of a fixed exchange rates regime with imperfect credibility but perfect capital mobility might appear a warranted development, so much so that the choice to peg exchange rates might be considered a serious policy mistake. This view—which seems to be the common wisdom of the day—does not take into account that in 1992 Europe got as close as it ever did to perfecting the conditions to set up a monetary union. Indeed, we have just witnessed the passing, through a democratic process that involved either qualified parliamentary majorities or national referendums, of a constitutional law that envisages monetary union before the end of the century. On the one hand, policy-makers might have well underestimated the might of foreign exchange markets. On the other hand, though, their trust to the process of continuous monetary integration in Europe was also well justified.

Hence, we do not think that simply stating that the ERM and exchange rate pegging were a mistake disposes of the problems of European monetary policy in the 1980s and 1990s. Instead, we believe it is useful to go back and understand the motivations that countries had to embark in certain stabilization programmes of which the exchange rate regime was an important element, and to improve our understanding of the problems that such countries have encountered in this process.

The chapters in this book cover a number of topics which are related to the adoption of fixed exchange rates and the empirical regularities which they seem to be associated with. In particular, the chapters study, among other things, the determinants of the choice of an exchange rate regime, the meaning of exchange rate overvaluation, the working of target zones, the motivations and effects of strong-currency policies, and, finally, the policies accompanying exchange rate stabilizations.

The focus of the volume is the Nordic countries. These countries, despite their diversity, share a number of characteristics which justify their grouping in this volume: they are all small open economies, they all have undergone substantial capital account liberalizations, albeit at different times, and they all trade intensely with continental Europe. Of course, they all geared their monetary policies to the policies of the continent.

This introductory chapter contains three remaining sections. In section 1.1 we put the recent monetary history in Denmark, Finland, Norway and Sweden into perspective. The objective is to identify the motivation of certain regime shifts (in particular the recent shift towards fixed rates vis-à-vis continental Europe) and to provide a chronicle of the most recent events, to facilitate the reading of the papers in the collection.

Section 1.2 identifies some key policy questions, relating both to the choice of fixed exchange rates, and the phenomena that this choice gave rise to, before and after the collapse of fixed rates. Finally, section 1.3 contains a discussion of the prospects for monetary policy and international monetary arrangements in the EFTA countries and, by extension, in the whole of Europe.

## 1.1 Exchange Rate Policies in Nordic Countries in Perspective

Table 1.1 summarizes the history of exchange rate arrangements in the Nordic countries. In the second post-war period, these countries have followed policies similar to those of other industrial countries. After the collapse of the Bretton Woods regime, all Nordic countries maintained fixed exchange rates arrangements. Denmark, Norway and Sweden participated in the European 'Snake', starting in 1972. Finland did not officially adhere to any fixed exchange rate arrangement, but in practice the Bank of Finland pegged the exchange rate of the markka to a trade-weighted basket of currencies.

**Table 1.1** Exchange rate arrangements in the Nordic countries

| Year | Denmark | Finland | Norway | Sweden |
|------|---------|---------|--------|--------|
| 1950–73 | Fixed exchange rates under Bretton Woods regime | | | |
| 1972–3 | Snake | Peg to a basket (unofficial) | Snake | Snake |
| 1977 | | Official peg to trade-weighted basket | | Peg to trade-weighted basket |
| 1979 | EMS | | | |
| 1990 | | | Peg to ECU | |
| 1991 | | Peg to ECU | | Peg to ECU |
| 1992 | | Float | Float | Float |

In 1977, Sweden left the Snake, to be followed by Norway the following year. Both countries pegged to a currency basket. The basket peg was officially introduced in Finland with a law in 1977. Denmark joined the EMS in 1979.

Throughout the 1970s and 1980s, Nordic countries have used exchange rate management quite actively as a means of external adjustment. Exchange rate devaluations, however, inevitably became progressively harder to manage during the 1980s, as capital accounts were liberalized.

The 1980s were also an important decade for Nordic countries, as the coexistence of EFTA (to which Norway, Finland and Sweden belong) with the EC (to which Denmark belongs) was tested by the rapidly increasing integration of the latter, and the growing awareness that the former had little justification as a trading block; EFTA countries are, individually, much more integrated with the EC than with themselves. The EFTA–EC dilemma was solved by pursuing more actively trade integration between the two areas.

Hence, while the experience of Denmark differs from that of Finland, Sweden and Norway—since the former has been a member of the ERM of the EMS—the policies of the four countries have been converging. This convergence of policies was a reflection of the planned increased integration between EFTA and the EC, and the economics underlying that policy strategy.

In summary, the exchange rate policies in the Nordic countries over the last decade are underpinned by the process of integration of those countries with the rest of Europe, and by the traditional aversion towards floating exchange rates in Europe. The latter, in the absence of definitive economic theory and evidence linking exchange rate regimes to country characteristics such as openness and regional trade integration (on this important topic, see chapter 3), is usually explained by the perception of excessive terms of trade volatility associated with floating nominal exchange rates, and by the belief that such excessive volatility disrupts trade and economic activity; both propositions still have not found convincing logical proof or evidence in their favour. Indeed, small open economies like the Nordic countries are vulnerable to large changes of terms of trade which often originate exogenously. In such circumstances, fixed exchange rates become harder to maintain. For example, in the 1980s Norway experienced large changes in its terms of trade, largely oil-related. In the latter part of that decade, Finland saw a more than 20% increase in its own terms of trade as that country, with an energy-intensive productive structure, benefited from the fall in oil prices and the markets for forest-based products boomed.

As we mentioned above, exchange rate pegging was abandoned by all Nordic countries except one: Denmark. On 8 September, 1992 the Finnish markka was let free of the ECU peg. On 19 November the Swedish krona was allowed to float freely. On 10 December the Norwegian krone was also floated.

## 1.2    The Questions

As discussed above, the traditional justification for the superiority of pegged exchange rates in Europe has been that under pegged exchange rates non-fundamental exchange rate volatility, with the attendant volatility of terms of trade, is eliminated. With capital controls, at least to some extent the nominal exchange rate target can be decoupled from other targets of the monetary authority, and in particular from interest-rate targets. This was possible until the early 1980s.

At the time of the elimination of capital controls the policy focus of pegged exchange rates shifted away from the stability of the terms of trade. Policy-makers and commentators alike all started discussing the use of pegged exchange rates to facilitate disinflation. The argument went that pegged rates represented a superior 'commitment technology', making disinflation efforts more credible, and hence less costly.

Where did the focus on inflation stabilization come from? Throughout the 1970s and part of the 1980s, the typical policy pattern has been the use of exchange rate devaluations to bolster international competitiveness, followed by domestic incomes policies to prevent the devaluation of the exchange rate to generate inflationary pressures. This pattern, of course, is identical to that of the IMF-style stabilization programmes of the traditional kind, of which there are numerous examples, most notably in Latin America.

The failure of such experiences led to a gradual shift in focus. In the late 1970s countries such as Chile, Argentina and Uruguay all embarked in 'new style' stabilization programmes, where the exchange rate peg was regarded as the main instrument to bring down inflation. Almost exactly at the same time, Finland attempted to break the inflation–devaluation spiral by placing a heavier emphasis on the exchange rate.

A sharper focus on the exchange rate was required by increased capital mobility. With high capital mobility, if investors do not regard a given exchange rate target sustainable, they give rise to high domestic interest rates, which in the absence of a devaluation translate in high ex-post real interest rates. Indeed, there is mounting evidence that ex-post real interest rates are high even in the cases when devaluations occur.

In essence, during the 1970s exchange rate pegs were viewed as a device to stabilize in the short run—but also to manage in the medium run—terms of trade. The failure of this device, perhaps caused by increased international capital mobility, made exchange rate pegs the central focus of anti-inflation policies.

The experience of exchange rate based stabilization has been studied extensively, in a literature that goes under the heading of 'the capital inflow problem'. The empirical regularities that have been studied in this literature include the ultimate failure of the exchange rate peg. Such failure is explained, in the literature on the capital inflow problem, by the failure of inflation to come down quickly enough to ensure the sustainability of the nominal exchange rate peg. This last phenomenon has found different interpretations: according to some, inflation is sluggish because of price stickiness; according to others, the fundamental problem is the credibility of the regime change (the pegging of the exchange rate); and finally, a third set of theories associates the failure of the peg with the presence of real shocks, or expectations of real shocks, like extraordinary taxation.

The experience of European and Nordic countries has enriched the analysis of pegged exchange rates in an important direction: it is arguable that, in some cases, exchange rate devaluations have been triggered not by fundamental disequilibria such as real exchange rate misalignments, but by self-fulfilling speculative pressures. In this respect, the case of the Nordic countries illustrates a variety of channels through which speculative pressures may force such devaluations.

With free capital movements, expectations of exchange rate devaluations, that is speculative pressures, are reflected in high money-market interest rates. Such high interest rates have different effects in different countries. For example, in Sweden, high interest rates depressed the real-estate market, and as a result sent shock waves to the banking industry, which in that country holds substantial real-estate assets. In Finland, high interest rates hit an economy which was already depressed by the shortfall in exports to the former Soviet Union.

Hence, the recent monetary history in the Nordic countries provides a rich case study of the motivations for exchange rate pegging, as well as an illustration of the weaknesses of pegged exchange rates regimes. The post-devaluation experiences also raise a number of important questions, to which in our view there are still no satisfactory answers. These questions have to do with the slow reactions of macroeconomic variables to large nominal exchange rate movements. In particular, we have seen that both long-term interest rates and inflation have been slow to change much after the devaluations of the markka and the Swedish krona. In the case of prices, the lack of response might be, at least in part, due to the increase in uncertainty (volatility) associated with the switch to floating exchange rates, making price setters reluctant to fine tune to any change in the exchange rate. In the case of long-term interest rates, their failure to adjust is even more difficult to explain. On the one hand, the event of a devaluation should make the likelihood of future devaluations smaller, and should have at least a marginal impact on long-term rates. On the other hand, the event of a devaluation triggers expectation of inflation and future devaluations, which are known to affect long-term rates. Indeed, once again the Finnish experience well illustrates this trade-off. After the November 1991 devaluation of the markka, long-term interest rates clearly jumped upwards. In that country, capital outflows have persisted even after the nominal exchange rate had depreciated by some 40%.

## 1.3    The Prospects

The dramatic experience of the past year is bound to influence in a profound way the future exchange rate strategies of the Nordic countries. In the past months the awareness of the dangers of less than fully consistent (and therefore credible) monetary policies were fully revealed. While the credibility of exchange rate pegs was certainly enhanced by the Nordic countries' commitment to increased European integration, the numerous uncertainties and ambiguities surrounding the project of monetary union had extremely disruptive effects in the foreign exchange markets.

Interestingly, the extreme disruptions of the summer of 1993 did not change two basic policy attitudes, both in the Nordic countries and elsewhere: (i) the preference for pegged exchange rates, and (ii) the preference for free international capital movements. Isolated calls for restrictions in international capital movements have been met with criticism from the academic community as well as scepticism from the policy community. It is well understood by now that the solution to unstable international financial markets has to be found in a set of policies aimed at achieving confidence and stability, and not in stratagems that prevent international financial markets to do their work.

Despite this broad commitment to pegged exchange rates and free capital flows, however, the Nordic countries outside the ERM are reluctant to re-enter such an arrangement, in a condition of substantial uncertainty, in part caused by a vacuum of policy leadership from the main EC countries. In the meantime, floating exchange rates, while difficult to manage, remain the stable solution.

# 2

# Equilibrium Real Exchange Rates

## Alberto Giovannini
*Columbia University and CEPR*

## 2.1    Introduction

Understanding the behaviour of the real exchange rate is one of the
biggest headaches of policy-makers. The following uneasy statement of
President Carter at the worst time of the dollar slide in 1978, despite its
intentions, reveals the ignorance in which policy-makers are often forced
to take decisions:

> I've spent a lot of time studying about the American dollar its value in
> international monetary markets, the causes for the recent deterioration as it
> relates to other major currencies. I can say with complete assurance that the
> basic principles of monetary values are not being adequately assessed on the
> current international money market. (President Jimmy Carter, 2 March 1978,
> cited in Bartley (1992), p.77.)

Paul Volcker recognizes explicitly our ignorance on equilibrium real
exchange rates when he recalls:

> Clearly, the founders of the Fund were unable to devise any hard-and-fast
> rules about when a country was justified in devaluing, when, in the Fund
> jargon, it was in 'fundamental disequilibrium'. Per Jacobssen, who became
> IMF managing director in the early 1960s after a long career in European
> Central banking, said he could not define 'a pretty girl, but you can recognize
> one when you meet one'. [He spoke before the feminist revolution.] (Volcker
> and Gyohten (1992), p.14.)

Understanding the behaviour of the real exchange rate is also one of
the biggest challenges for economic theory. The real exchange rate,

whichever definition one relies on, is a relative price. As such, we expect it to respond to those real shocks that affect the demand for and supply of those goods whose prices it measures. At the same time, however, the real exchange rate appears to be affected by monetary phenomena.[1]

Hence the core of the problem for economic theory and economic policy is identifying real and monetary determinants of the real exchange rate. This problem is different, depending on the exchange rate regime. Under floating exchange rates, it is often asked whether large movements of relative prices can be ascribed to monetary 'surprises', or are equilibrating responses to other types of shocks, typically fiscal policy shocks. The debates on the dollar exchange rate in the 1980s was a good illustration of the complexity of this problem; was the appreciation from 1980 to 1985 caused by the turnaround in monetary policy started by Paul Volcker in 1979, or was it to be ascribed to the fiscal expansion that took place in the same period? The difficulty of identifying real and monetary determinants of real exchange rates under floating is compounded by the difficulty of describing the behaviour of expectations. Hence, for example, the prolonged appreciation of the dollar could be due to a slow convergence of expectations about US monetary policy to the actual change in the Fed's policy stance.

Under managed exchange rates, the real exchange rate questions that have attracted most attention from observers and policy-makers alike are those associated with the so-called 'capital inflow problem'. Many countries, in different parts of the world, have supported stabilization programmes with an exchange-rate policy aimed either at slowing down the rate of depreciation relative to some reference currencies, or at pegging the nominal exchange rate altogether. This policy was often accompanied by a substantial liberalization of international capital flows. Typically, the impact of these policies is a large increase in capital inflows, partly to finance current account deficits and partly resulting in an accumulation of foreign exchange reserves. At the same time, inflation exceeds the rate of depreciation of the currency, and ex post facto real interest rates exceed those in foreign countries.[2] In the literature on the capital inflow problem it is often asked whether the phenomena listed above are in any way suggestive of the presence of 'disequilibria' or other distortions that require government intervention. The question is thus whether the real exchange rate that is observed after the nominal exchange rate is pegged and capital flows are liberalized is 'overvalued', and whether a nominal exchange rate depreciation can correct such overvaluation.

This paper concentrates on real exchange rate problems in regimes of managed exchange rates. The problems of real exchange rates under a managed exchange-rate regime are, of course, central in most European countries today. The plan for monetary union as being currently pursued by European governments envisages a period during which nominal exchange rates are to be kept stable, and inflation rates have to converge. The experience between the two most recent realignments (December 1986 and September 1992) has been one of slow convergence of inflation rates. In particular, in countries like Italy and Spain[3] the slow convergence was caused by a faster inflation of non-traded goods prices relative to traded goods prices. According to one definition, the real exchange rate appreciation is an increase in that relative price. In that sense, the competitiveness problem of countries like Italy and Spain has been discussed in terms of the differential dynamics of prices in these two sectors.[4]

The paper illustrates the difficulties of identifying the sources of real exchange rate fluctuations, with the use of a two-sector model of an open economy. Among the monetary determinants of the real exchange rate under managed exchange rates I discuss expectations of nominal exchange rate changes, which have real effects to the extent that money is non-neutral. Among the real determinants of real exchange rates, I discuss productivity movements, exogenous and endogenous, as well as real wage shocks and shocks to government spending.

## 2.2    The Traditional Model of the Real Exchange Rate

The traditional model of the real exchange rate is the two-sector model of Salter (1959) and Swan (1960). The version described below is developed, and discussed more in detail, by De Gregorio et al. (1992). The essential feature of the model is the presence of a non-competitive non-traded goods sector. The traded goods sector is also non-competitive although, facing a given world price for its output, it effectively behaves competitively.

Consider first the non-traded goods sector. It is composed of $n$ firms, each producing a differentiated good with an identical technology. The demand for non-traded goods is the solution of a period-by-period optimization problem of consumers of the following type:

$$\min_{\{c^N(i)\}^n_{i=1}} \sum_{i=1}^{n} c^N(i)p^N(i) \equiv \phi I \qquad (2.1)$$

subject to:

$$\left( \frac{1}{n^{1/\theta}} \sum_{i=1}^{n} c^N(i)^{\frac{\theta-1}{\theta}} \right)^{\frac{\theta}{\theta-1}} \geq \bar{c}^N \qquad (2.2)$$

where the notion is straightforward. The assumption in equation (2.1) is that a fraction $\phi$ of total expenditure $I$ every period is devoted to the purchase of non-traded goods. In other words, the utility function is Cobb–Douglas over tradables and the index of non-tradables specified in equation (2.2). The first-order conditions for this problem yield to the familiar isoelastic demand functions:

$$c^N(i) = \frac{\phi I}{np^N} \left(\frac{p^N(i)}{p^N}\right)^{-\theta}$$

(2.3)

where the aggregate price index consistent with the postulated utility function is:

$$p^N = \left(\frac{1}{n}\sum_{i=1}^{n} p^N(i)^{1-\theta}\right)^{\frac{1}{1-\theta}}$$

(2.4)

The production function, identical for all firms in the non-traded sector, is:

$$y^N(i) = a_N(l^N(i) - F), \; l^N(i) \geq F$$

(2.5)

where $l^N(i)$ is employment by firm $i$ and $y^N(i)$ is output. $F$ represents the fixed amount of labour that is needed to undertake production in each firm.

Given isoelastic demand by the private sector, firms set prices applying a constant mark-up over marginal costs:

$$p^N(i) = \frac{\theta}{\theta - 1} \frac{W}{a_N}$$

(2.6)

where $W$ is the wage rate. This equilibrium price is plugged into equation (2.3) to obtain the consumption of each good $i$, since all firms are identical. Equilibrium private consumption of good $i$ is, therefore:

$$c^N(i) = \phi I \frac{\theta - 1}{\theta} \frac{a_N}{nW}$$

(2.7)

Firms in the non-traded sector sell their output also to the government. The price they charge to the government, however, equals the marginal cost. In other words, firms charge their entire overhead to their private sales. Hence, the profit of each firm equals the difference between price and marginal cost times the private sales, minus the fixed cost, plus the subsidy they receive from the government:

$$\frac{W}{a_N} \left(\frac{1}{\theta-1}\right) \phi I \left(\frac{\theta-1}{\theta}\right) \frac{a_N}{nW} - WF + \frac{S}{n} \tag{2.8}$$

The assumption in equation (2.8) is that the government chooses the total amount of a subsidy to the non-traded sector, which is distributed lump-sum and equally to all firms in business. Setting profits equal to zero, and after some simplification, we obtain the equilibrium number of firms:

$$n = \left(\frac{\phi I + \theta S}{\theta}\right) /(WF) \tag{2.9}$$

Total output of each firm equals the sum of private consumption and government consumption:

$$y^N(i) = \frac{\phi I}{n} \frac{(\theta-1)a_N}{\theta W} + G/n \tag{2.10}$$

Demand for labour by each firm is obtained by substituting total output into the production function, and solving:

$$l^N(i) = F + \left(\frac{WF\theta}{\phi I + \theta S}\right)\left[\frac{\phi I(\theta-1)}{W\theta} + \frac{G}{a_N}\right] \tag{2.11}$$

Finally, total demand for labour is obtained by multiplying $n$ demand for labour by individual firms:

$$nl^N(i) = \left(\frac{\phi I + \theta S}{W\theta}\right) + \left[\frac{\phi I(\theta-1)}{W\theta} + \frac{G}{a_N}\right] \tag{2.12}$$

Equation (2.12) shows that the total demand for labour by the non-traded sector is affected both by the subsidy and government spending, though through different channels. An increase in the subsidy increases the number of firms, although it decreases the total output of each firm. This means that output is produced less efficiently by each firm, and as a result demand for labour from the non-traded sector is higher. An increase in government spending, by contrast, does not change the equilibrium number of firms since it does not affect profits (firms charge marginal cost to the government). It does increase labour demand through the increase in output.

Equation (2.12) illustrates an important feature of the two-sector model, little appreciated in the literature: the demand for labour from the non-traded goods sector depends in many ways on government activities. Government spending on goods and services (an effect recently emphasized by Froot and Rogoff (1991) is only part of the story. In the model of this paper, increases in the demand for labour from the non-traded sector may come also from inefficient production, which is subsidized by the government.

The traded goods sector is simplified. There is one representative firm, with a decreasing-returns-to-scale production technology. The production function is:

$$y^T = a_T l^{T\alpha}, \quad \alpha < 1 \tag{2.13}$$

Setting the marginal productivity of labour equal to the product wage, we obtain equilibrium output supply:

$$y^T = a_T^{\frac{1}{1-\alpha}} \left( \frac{\alpha p^T}{W} \right)^{\frac{\alpha}{1-\alpha}} \tag{2.14}$$

Finally, substituting this equation into (2.13) and solving for *l* we get the demand for labour in the traded goods sector.

The core of the model is the labour market. Notice that labour supply does not enter the utility function. An attractive specification of the labour market, used by De Gregorio et al. (1992), postulates a union with monopoly power, whose bargaining schedule—relation between wage and employment—is an increasing function of employment. The intersection of the union's bargaining schedule and the total demand for labour from the two sectors (derived above) determines equilibrium employment and the wage rate in the economy.

The illustration of the two sector model above has left out the discussion of the determinants of spending and the current account, which are essential in order to solve it. These dynamic aspects, described in detail by De Gregorio et al. (1992) do not add significantly to the main catalogue of the determinants of the real exchange rate, and are left out in this discussion. The discussion of the basic model is concluded with a catalogue of the possible exogenous causes of fluctuation of the real exchange rate.

### 2.2.1  *Government Spending*

As mentioned above, these shocks increase output in the non-traded goods sector, and the real wage rate. As a result, output in the tradable sector decreases, and at the same time the average labour productivity in that sector goes up. However, the model distinguishes between government purchases of goods and services and subsidies to firms in the non-traded sector. While in the former case the increase in demand for labour comes from an IS-like effect (increase in aggregate demand) in the latter case the increase in labour demand is caused by inefficient production decisions, caused by the transfer.

### 2.2.2   *Productivity Shocks*

Productivity shocks have been the focus of the traditional literature on purchasing power parity and of analyses of real exchange rate fluctuations (for the former, see Samuelson (1964) and Balassa (1964), and for the latter, see Hsieh (1982). Consider an increase in total factor productivity in the traded goods sector. Other things being equal, these shocks increase profits there, and bring about an increase in labour demand, with an attendant increase in the real wage rate. The real exchange rate increases too.

### 2.2.3   *Wage Shocks*

In the model, wage shocks can produce the effects that are often discussed in the models of Barro–Gordon. In the model described in this paper there are no nominal variables. The effects of expectations about inflation and the nominal exchange rate, however, can be easily illustrated. Suppose nominal wages were to be set, by unions and employers, to prevail for more than one period. Union nominal wage demands would depend on expectations of inflation and exchange-rate depreciation. These expectations will be reflected in shifts in the wage bargaining schedule of the union. The higher the expected rate of inflation, the larger the upward shift in the wage bargaining schedule. If the nominal exchange rate does not accommodate these inflation expectations, the shift in the wage bargaining schedule persists, and gives rise to a sort of exogenous real wage increase. The increase in the real wage brings about a fall in employment in the tradable sector, and an increase in the relative price of non-traded goods.

This informal description of the effects of exogenous shocks helps to stress a fundamental problem in the analysis of equilibrium real exchange rates; for all the exogenous shocks considered, the effects on the relative price on non-tradables and on the average labour productivity in the tradable sector are identical. In other words, studying the behaviour of these two variables does not help to identify the source of fluctuation of the real exchange rate. The implication for policy is straightforward:

difficulties in identification of the appropriate response to it. In the following section I discuss briefly extensions of the basic model which make the policy-maker's job even more intractable.

## 2.3    Extensions of the Basic Model

One set of simplifying assumptions of the model in the previous section regard the behaviour of productivity. Total factor productivity is exogenous, while labour productivity in the tradables sector is a function of employment, since the production function has decreasing returns to labour. In this section I sketch the effects of releasing these two assumptions. I consider, first, the phenomenon of efficiency wages, and, next, the possibility of endogenous managerial effort.

### 2.3.1    Efficiency Wages

Efficiency wage models assume a positive relation between real wages and productivity. Without inquiring about the source of this positive relation, consider the optimization problem of the firm in the tradable sector. The assumption, consistent with the analysis above, is that the firm behaves competitively in the labour market. As before, it faces a given price for its output, determined in international markets. With labour productivity positively affected by the real wage, the production function is now:

$$y^T = a_T \left[ \left( \frac{W}{p^T} \right)^\beta l^T \right]^\alpha, \quad \alpha < 1 \tag{2.15}$$

where the real wage enters as a labour-augmenting productivity factor. From the first-order condition, and after solving into the production function, we have:

$$y^T = a_T^{\frac{1}{1-\alpha}} \; \alpha^{\frac{\alpha}{1-\alpha}} \left( \frac{p^T}{W} \right)^{\alpha \left( \frac{1-\beta}{1-\alpha} - \beta \right)} \tag{2.16}$$

Equation (2.16) suggests that, if labour productivity depends on the real wage, the sensitivity of output in the traded goods sector to the real wage and—since in this model there is a one-to-one relation between the real wage and the real exchange rate—to the real exchange rate decreases. The higher the sensitivity of productivity to the real wage, the lower the sensitivity of tradable outputs to the real exchange rate. In this model the balance of income and spending is directly proportional to the flow of output of tradables. Hence, in the presence of efficiency wages, large fluctuations of the real exchange rate have less of an effect on the balance of income and spending—and thus on external balance. In other words, large fluctuations of the real exchange rate are not indicators of serious 'disequilibria'.

### 2.3.2 *Managerial Effort*

The discussion of efficiency wages has shown one way to endogenize, in part, the productivity performance. The exercise represents a radical departure for the traditional Balassa–Samuelson analysis of real exchange rates, where productivity shocks are exogenous. In other words, according to the traditional analysis, the direction of causality is from shocks in total factor productivity to the real exchange rate, through the impact of these shocks on labour demand and real wage. By contrast, we are now considering the possibility that shocks in the real exchange rate or the real wage—like, for example, the exogenous wage shocks discussed in the previous section—cause fluctuations in total factor productivity.

Another channel through which productivity can respond endogenously to cost shocks is the behaviour of firms' managers. The literature on 'X-efficiency', for example, shows how competition from international trade leads firms' managers to expend more effort to achieve a more efficient combination of productive resources (see Balassa (1975), Corden (1970, 1974) and Horn et al. (1992)). Alternatively, a risk averse firm manager or owner might find that the marginal utility of profits from innovation when the firm is hit by a negative cost are higher than in the case the firm is 'ahead' of the competition.

Rather than exploring the analytics of these alternative hypotheses in detail, I limit myself, in this paper, to a brief exploration of the evidence on the relation between the real exchange rate and factor productivity.

## 2.4 Some Empirical Evidence

In this section, I use data on Italy to illustrate some evidence on the relation between the real exchange rate and productivity. The data used in this section is sectoral national income data, ranging from 1960 to 1988, and estimates of the capital stock by sector, also during the same period.[5]

I compute total factor productivity and average labour productivity for the tradables sector (defined as all sectors minus services and government), the non-tradables sector, including all market services, and a few sectors among the traded goods: energy, textiles and clothing, machinery and motor vehicles. The real exchange rate is defined as the price of non-tradables in terms of tradables.

Figure 2.1 plots the real exchange rate. The figure shows a constant real appreciation from 1960 to 1988, interrupted in 1969 and 1974–5. For all tradable goods, not surprisingly, total factor productivity also constantly grows (although it is not reported here).

In the previous section I have argued that one of the most difficult problems in interpreting the behaviour of real exchange rates is the identification of the causes of their fluctuations. If a real appreciation is due to productivity growth in the tradables' sector it certainly should not raise any concerns about competitiveness or 'overvaluation'. Some evidence on the *causal* relation between real exchange rates and productivity can be obtained by looking at their *temporal* relation. The identification of causality with temporal precedence is of course a bold assumption. In this context, such assumption is probably justified by the fact that adjustment costs in employment and production decisions make them respond to shocks with a lag.

Table 2.1 reports the results of cross-section–time-series regressions of (changes in) total factor productivities on (changes of) the real exchange rate, and vice versa. I use both average labour productivity, defined as value added divided by employment for each sector, and total factor productivity. The latter is computed by subtracting from the log of the value added a linear combination (with weights summing to 1) of

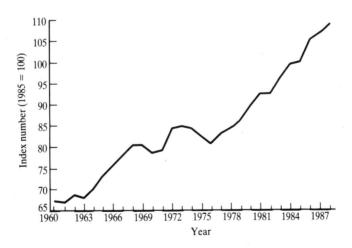

**Figure 2.1**   Italy's relative price of tradables

**Table 2.1**   The relation between the real exchange rate and productivity

| Regression equation | Coefficient | Standard Error |
|---|---|---|
| DTFP on DRXR (−1) | −0.0247 | 0.5105 |
| DALP on DRXR (−1) | 0.8581 | 0.2589 |
| DRXR on DTFP (−1) | 0.0000 | 0.0002 |
| DRXR on DALP (−1) | 0.0004 | 0.0005 |

*Notes*: DRXR: log-difference of the relative price of non-tradables in terms of tradables.
DTFP: log-difference of total factor productivity.
DALP: log-difference of average labour productivity.
Sample: 1962 to 1988.
The sectors included in the regressions are: energy, textile and clothing, machinery and motor-vehicles, and total traded goods, defined as all sectors less public sector and marketable services. Regressions are run with the 'seemingly unrelated' method, constraining coefficients to be the same across equations.

employment and the stock of machinery capital. The weights are computed, period by period, as the share of the wage bill in value added for labour, and the complement to 1 of that number for capital.

Table 2.1 shows that, for the sectors chosen, the relation between productivities and the real exchange rate is not very strong. The only reliable correlation has been found in the case of average labour productivity; the latter is significantly affected, with a lag, by the relative price of non-tradables. An increase in the relative price of non-tradables brings about an increase in average labour productivity. This is the implication of the traditional two-sector model: an increase in the real exchange rate, whatever its causes, other things equal brings about a shrinkage of the tradables sector, a fall in employment there, and an increase in marginal and average labour productivity (because of decreasing returns to labour).

Notably, the regressions do not show any relation between total factor productivity and the real exchange rate. The traditional model suggests that an exogenous increase in total factor productivity in the tradables sector produces excess demand in the labour market and, as a result, an increase in the relative price of non-tradables. This is not detected in the data. At the same time, the estimates do not show any indication of reverse causality: total factor productivity is not significantly correlated with lagged changes in the real exchange rate.

More detail on the relation between the real exchange rate and total factors productivity is obtainable from Figure 2.2. The figure reports the rate of growth of total factor productivity in the tradable sector and the rate of change of the real exchange rate. From 1961 to 1973 fluctuations in productivity seem to mimic, with a 1 year lag, those of the real

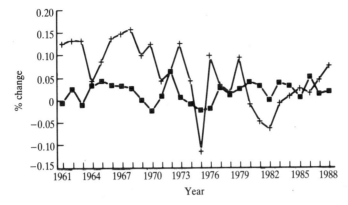

**Figure 2.2** Tradable goods productivity (+) and real exchange rate (■)

exchange rate. After 1973, however, no regular pattern is observed. Hence, the relation between real exchange rate movements and productivity suggest that increases in costs (appreciation of the real exchange rate) led to improvements in productivity—a phenomenon consistent with the reverse-causality view of real exchange rate described in the previous section.

## 2.5 Concluding Observations

This paper has discussed some determinants of equilibrium real exchange rates. In the introduction, I mentioned that the focus of this paper is managed exchange rates: while the model does not contain any real variables, it is easy to use it to discuss exchange rate expectations failing to converge. If nominal wages are determined in centralized bargaining, and they are affected by expectations of exchange rate devaluations and inflation, a failure of those expectations to materialize brings about a shock in the real exchange rate, with effects discussed in the theoretical section.

This simple story of failed convergence, however, is considerably complicated by the possibility that productivity responds endogenously to shocks. Under that hypothesis, the concept of equilibrium real exchange rate becomes even less reliable.

The last section of the paper contains an analysis of the Italian data on the relation between productivity and the real exchange rate. While average labour productivity increases in response to past changes in the real exchange rate, the relation between total factor productivity and the real exchange rate does not seem to be stable. An informal analysis of the data, however, suggests that until the early 1970s, changes in the real exchange rate help predict changes in total factor productivity, but not vice versa. This is prima facie consistent with the hypothesis of endogenous productivity response and not with the traditional model, which stresses the direction of causality from total factor productivity to the real exchange rate.

## Notes

This paper was conceived while I was a consultant to the IMF European Department. I have benefited from discussions with Massimo Russo and Roberto Perotti. The work I have carried out with José De Gregorio and Thomas Krueger is behind many of the ideas expressed here.
1. The best illustration of the potential influence of monetary phenomena on real exchange rates is the plot of real exchange rates in the postwar period. Dornbusch and Giovannini (1990) present plots of percent changes in the ratio of wholesale price indices, corrected by the spot exchange rate, of the United States relative to Germany, the United Kingdom, Japan and Canada. They show that the volatility of real exchange rate changes hugely across periods, increasing dramatically during floating-rate regimes.
2. For a survey of the experience in Latin America countries, see Calvo et al. (1992).
3. Spain joined the exchange rate mechanism of the European monetary system in June 1989.
4. For a clear description of the problem in the case of Italy, see Barca and Visco (1992).
5. In Italy there has been a change in national income accounts which affects the data after 1970. The data set used in this paper contains a set of series for which reconciliation of the pre- and post-1970 periods has been carried out. These series were computed by Prometeia, Bologna. Estimates of the capital stock by sector are taken from Annunziato et al. (1992).

## References

Annunziato, P., Manfroni, P. and Rosa, G. (1992), 'La stima del capitale per settore ed area geografica e alcuni indici de produttività'. Mimeo, Confindustria.

Balassa, B. (1964), 'The purchasing power parity doctrine, a reappraisal', *Journal of Political Economy*, **72**, 584–96.

Balassa, B. (1975), 'Trade, protection, and domestic production: A comment', in P. Kenen (ed.), *International Trade and Finance: Frontiers for Research*, Cambridge University Press, Cambridge.

Barca, F. and Visco, I. (1992), 'L'economia italiana nella prospetiva europea: teriario protetto e dinamica dei salari nominali. Banca d'Italia, *Temi di Dicussione*, n.175 (July).

Bartley, R.L. (1992), *The Seven Fat Years*, The Free Press, New York.

Calvo, G.A., Leiderman, L. and Reinhart, C.M. (1992), 'Capital Inflows and the Real Exchange Rate Appreciation in Latin America: The Role of External Factors', IMF Working Paper, July.

Corden, M.W. (1970), 'The efficiency effects of trade and protection', in I.A.

McDonald and R.H. Snape (eds), *Studies in International Economics*, North Holland, Amsterdam.

Corden, M.W. (1974), *Trade Policy and Economic Welfare*, Oxford University Press, London.

De Gregorio, J., Giovannini, A. and Krueger, T. (1992), 'The boom of non-tradeable prices in Europe: evidence and interpretation'. Mimeo, International Monetary Fund.

Dornbusch, R. and Giovannini, A. (1990), 'Monetary policy in the open economy', in B. Friedman and F. Hahn (eds), *Handbook of Monetary Economics*, North Holland, Amsterdam.

Froot, K. and Rogoff, K. (1991), 'Government consumption and the real exchange rate: The empirical evidence'. Mimeo, Harvard University.

Horn, H., Lang, H. and Lundgren, S. (1992), 'Managerial effort incentives, X-inefficiency, and international trade'. Mimeo, Institute for International Economic Studies, University of Stockholm.

Hsieh, D.A. (1982), 'The determination of the real exchange rate', *Journal of International Economics,* **12**, 355–62.

Salter, W. (1959), 'Internal and external balance: The role of price and expenditure effects', *Economic Record*, **35**, 226–38.

Samuelson, P.A. (1964), 'Theoretical notes on trade problems', *Review of Economics and Statistics*, **46**, 145–54.

Swan, T. (1960), 'Economic control in a dependent economy', *Economic Record*, **36**, 51–66.

Volcker, P. and Gyohten, T. (1992), *Changing Fortunes*, Random House, New York.

# Discussion

## Eduard J. Bomhoff
*Erasmus University*

Giovannini's paper deals with real exchange rates in the European monetary system. He notes correctly that substantial variation in these real exchange rates has been observed, both in the early years of the system, when nominal exchange rates were adjusted quite frequently, and in more recent years, when no realignments occurred between 1987 and September 1992. His paper sketches a theoretical model which emphasizes the distinction between production of tradables and non-tradables. The model is quite similar to that in Froot and Rogoff (1991) and leads to very similar conclusions. Both models stipulate that the law of one price holds for the tradable sector, but that real exchange rates are computed using national price indices that reflect movements in both prices of tradables and prices of non-tradables. Productivity trends differ between the two sectors, but a single labour market equalizes wages between the two sectors.

Both Froot and Rogoff and Giovannini note that within the context of this type of model, a permanent rise in government spending raises the real exchange rate. Government predominantly absorbs non-tradables, forcing the economy to adjust its output mix towards more non-tradables and fewer tradables, which it does by a real exchange rate change that reduces the foreign demand for tradables. Both models also note that an unanticipated but permanent rise in productivity in the traded goods sector has the same effect of causing an appreciation of the domestic currency. Several observers have pointed to the secular appreciation of the Japanese yen as evidence of the tendency of a real exchange rate to strengthen in the case of a country that experiences very high growth of productivity in its tradables sector.

Giovannini contributes to the literature by estimating a cross-section–time-series reduced form for the Italian economy using annual data on the real exchange rate and on productivity increases in four different sectors of the Italian economy.[1] He finds a statistically significant coefficient if average labour productivity is regressed on last year's exchange rate but notes that this result leaves open questions about cause and effect.

The paper does not contain statistical tests of the hypothesis that increases in the size of the Italian government sector have been a cause of the tendency of the lira to appreciate in real terms. Dornbusch (1991) has noted that it is difficult to determine whether increased government spending is, in fact, the driving force behind the appreciation of the lira, since the productivity effect will tend to increase the *real* price of non-tradables in terms of tradables so that constant real spending on government goods would show up in the data as an increase in government's share of *nominal* spending. Dornbusch shows, in fact, that for Italy the nominal spending share of government in GDP is very closely related to the level of productivity in manufacturing, making it impossible to disentangle without further analysis the relative importance of increases in productivity in the Italian manufacturing sector and changes in the ratio of nominal government spending to nominal GDP in Italy. Giovannini correctly notes that 'difficulties in identifying the sources of an overvaluation problem imply difficulties in identification of the appropriate response to it'. The preliminary question arises, to which extent one should speak of a 'problem'. Why is it damaging to Italy or its EMS partners that the lira has exhibited a tendency towards appreciation during the period since 1979 which economists have not been able to fully understand? Giovannini's paper does not address this question, but it is pertinent to the agenda of the Conference. One possible answer could be that the less we understand about sources of longer term movements in real exchange rates, the harder it will be for policy-makers when they have to meet to consider devaluations and revaluations in the system to make a proper estimate of the amount of devaluation and revaluation that is required. This may be a relevant consideration during the period of fixed but adjustable exchange rates. If and when the decision is taken to no longer change the exchange rate between the lira and its EMS partners in preparation for the future introduction of a single currency, the question has to be reformulated as follows: which damage is done to either Italy or its EMS partners if the Italian region within a European common currency area has the tendency to require a somewhat higher rate of inflation than the other European regions? The standard answer to this question would be that damage is done to Italy's European partners if one or more of these trading partners are forced to experience a negative rate of inflation. The same argument has indeed been made in the past as a possible reason for caution on the part of Germany's trading partners in case their currencies would have to depreciate in real terms whilst at the same time German dominance in the EMS delivered approximately zero inflation in that country. For, under such a circumstance, a certain degree of deflation would be required in one or more of Germany's trading partners, and that would be damaging to these economies, if one believes in negative aggregate effects of decreases in the general price level, either because real rates of interest may be higher than they otherwise would be given the zero floor on nominal interest rates, or because of unintended wealth transfers from debtors to creditors that might have aggregate effects. In the case of Italy it would at the present time seem far-fetched to seriously consider the risk that in a future EMS inflation in Italy will be approximately equal to zero whilst simultaneously Italy's trading partners would require structural real depreciation with respect to the lira.

## Note

1. To be precise, the regressions relate to three sectors and to the aggregate for the traded goods sector, which is approximately equivalent to estimating the relationship for four different sectors.

## References

Dornbusch, R. (1991), 'Comment on K.A. Froot and K. Rogoff', in *Macroeconomics Annual*, NBER, pp. 317–22.

Froot, K.A. and Rogoff, K. (1991), 'The EMS, the EMS and the transition to a common currency', in *Macroeconomics Annual*, NBER, pp. 269–317.

# Discussion

## Joseph Zeira
*Hebrew University of Jerusalem*

## Introduction

Macroeconomic analysis of open economies made great progress in the 1970s and early 1980s. The major theoretical developments in macroeconomics at the time, namely the monetary model, rational expectations and the intertemporal optimization, were successfully applied to analysis of open economies and exchange rates.[1] This progress has been fuelled not only by theoretical developments in other areas, but by the economic events as well. The integration of international capital markets and the increasing use of floating exchange rates, have changed the way open economies operate, and have posed new challenges for economists.

The new experience of greater capital mobility and greater exchange rate flexibility has encouraged analysis on the one hand, but has also discouraged it on the other hand, as the new experience has rejected much of the new theories developed in the 1970s and early 1980s. Exchange rates have proved to be much more volatile than theory predicts (Dornbusch and Giovannini, 1990). Furthermore, theory has also failed in predicting consistent patterns of exchange rate dynamics (Levich, 1985; Meese, 1990). Hence, the progress achieved in exchange rate theory is still short of giving us a satisfactory explanation of recent experience and of the observed stylized facts.

In the following comments I suggest one way to get theory and facts closer, by applying some recent developments in macroeconomic theory into the analysis of open economies. The paper by Giovannini is a good example in this direction, as it uses an imperfect competition model to analyse the issue of real exchange rates. In the following comments I supply more examples of such applications from various areas: imperfect competition, endogenous growth, imperfect information, imperfect capital markets and income distribution.

## Imperfect Competition

Models of imperfect competition have recently been applied to many areas in economics, mostly to industrial organization, international trade, technology creation and macroeconomics. One of the major macroeconomic applications of imperfect competition to macroeconomics has been to models of 'sticky prices', since the best framework to analyse price setting by individual sellers or buyers is a model of monopolistic competition.[2] Price rigidity is highly relevant for the analysis of exchange rates and mostly for comparison of exchange rate regimes, since if prices and wages are fully flexible, money is neutral and the real economy is independent of the exchange rate regime.

The theory of monopolistic competition can be applied not only to nominal exchange rates but to real exchange rates as well, as shown in the paper by Giovannini. This paper demonstrates, among other things, that the equilibrium real exchange rate is affected, by the elasticity of substitution between producers of non-traded goods. In monopolistic competition, this elasticity affects the mark-up, and hence the real exchange rate. In other words, the more competitive domestic markets are, the lower the real exchange rate is.[3]

## Endogenous Growth

Recent years have seen renewed interest in issues of economic growth and development, as reflected in Romer (1986, 1990), Lucas (1988), Stokey (1988), Grossman and Helpman (1992) and many others. This research is inherently related to international economics, since one of its key issues is understanding international differences in growth experience.[4] Furthermore, this new research on economic growth can be applied to issues of real exchange rates as well.

Note first that real wages can be interpreted as real exchange rates. Labour is a non-traded good and hence its relative price is a component of the real exchange rate. Furthermore, non-traded goods are usually more labour-intensive, and hence real wages are highly correlated with real exchange rates. A developed economy adopts new technologies, and that raises real wages both directly, through labour productivity, and indirectly, through capital accumulation. Hence, output per capita and the real exchange rate should be positively correlated.

But causality between growth and real exchange rates can go in both ways. A major type of technological innovation is labour-saving innovations, namely machines which replace workers. An economy adopts such innovations only if wages are relatively high. Thus, high real wages are not necessarily detrimental to economic development, but can encourage it by creating incentives for labour-saving technological innovations. This idea has already been widely discussed in the 1960s and the 1970s, following Habakkuk (1962), who has claimed that the United States has grown faster than the United Kingdom in the 19th century due to higher real wages.[5] A modern formalization of this idea appears in Zeira (1994).

Hence, real exchange rates and economic growth are highly correlated and the causality goes in both ways. Growth raises the price of non-traded goods, and this creates incentives to expand the traded sector even further.

## Imperfect Information

Information theory can be applied to many open economy issues. Current examples include the peso problem, exchange rate bands and similar issues, in which information on future exchange rate policy affects the behaviour of exchange rates in the present.

This section presents an additional example of how imperfect information affects the dynamics of real exchange rates. It is shown that missing aggregate information, and the resulting learning process, contribute to exchange rate volatility. This idea appears in Zeira (1993), and is explained here through a simple example.

Consider a growing economy, in which the traded sector grows faster than the non-traded sector. As a result, the real exchange rate appreciates, as described in the previous section. Assume that the duration of this growth period is unknown in advance. We next show that as a result, the real exchange rate overshoots. Denote by $Q_t$ the long-run real exchange rate, which rises during the growth period. Assume that:

$$Q_T = Q_0 + \alpha T \tag{1}$$

where $T$ is the end of the growth period. $T$ is unknown in advance, and becomes known only when reached. Assume that all the prior information on $T$ is that it is bounded from above by $T^*$. Hence, the prior distribution on $T$ is uniform between 1 and $T^*$. For the sake of simplicity assume that the discount rate is zero. Hence, the (short-run) equilibrium real exchange rate $q_t$ must satisfy:

$$q_t = E_t q_{t+1} \tag{2}$$

By applying the Bayesian learning rule to condition (2), we get that in period $t$, as long as $T$ is not reached, the short-run and long-run prices are related by:

$$q_t = Q_{t+1} \frac{1}{T^* - t} + q_{t+1} \frac{T^* - t - 1}{T^* - t} \tag{3}$$

Note, that in period $T^* - 1$ the public realizes that in next period growth ends, and hence: $q_{T^*-1} = Q_{T^*}$. We can therefore calculate recursively the real exchange rate as long as $T$ is not reached:

$$q_t = Q_{t+1} + \alpha \frac{T^* - t - 1}{2} \tag{4}$$

Hence, the short-run real exchange rate is higher than the long-run one. When growth ends and $T$ is reached, the real exchange rate falls to its long-run value $Q_T$. The intuition behind this result is straightforward. As long as $T$ is not reached, there are chances for further growth and higher long-run real exchange rates, and the short-run real exchange rate reflects these expectations and is therefore higher. When $T$ is finally reached, the public realizes that there will be no more growth and hence the price falls. This simple example shows, that missing aggregate information can cause severe and long overvaluation of the real exchange rate, as we indeed observe in many exchange markets.

## Imperfect Capital Markets

Most standard models of open economies assume not only that capital is fully mobile, but that capital markets are perfect.[6] Recently, there is a growing literature on macroeconomics with imperfect capital markets. Theoretically, this literature applies models of imperfect credit markets, due to asymmetric information, into macroeconomic models and analyses the effects of such imperfections on issues like business cycles and economic growth.[7] Empirically, this literature has concentrated mostly on tracing credit constraints in firms' investment behaviour.[8]

If imperfect capital markets matter for the macroeconomy, they matter for the open economy as well. A recent recognition of that appears in Lucas (1990), who asks why capital does not flow from rich to poor countries, and claims that imperfect capital markets are part of the answer. Another example for the relevance of capital markets imperfections is the issue of LDC debt. The literature on it usually models developing countries as individual (sovereign) borrowers in international markets, who face credit constraints.

But imperfect credit markets play an important role even in developed countries, where borrowing and lending are decentralized. Since borrowing can be constrained, and since the current account is the difference between lending and borrowing, it is affected by the state of credit in the economy as well, as shown in Zeira (1991). Hence, imperfect capital markets affect important open economy issues, like the current account and the real exchange rate.

## Income Distribution

Recent years have seen renewed interest in income distribution and in its macroeconomic effects. The research on these topics has concentrated on the relationship between distribution and growth. This research has clear international perspectives, as it is part of the effort to explain international differences in growth patterns.[9]

Issues of income distribution can help in explaining the real exchange rate as well. Assume, for example, that the traded good sector uses skilled labour, which requires investment in human capital, while the non-traded good sector uses non-skilled labour. As shown in Galor and Zeira (1993), if capital markets are imperfect, inherited wealth determines the amount of individual investment in human capital. Thus, the wealth distribution determines the aggregate amount of investment in human capital and as a result the size of the two sectors: traded and non-traded. It therefore determines also the relative price of the two goods, namely the real exchange rate. Income distribution is therefore strongly related to the real exchange rate.

## Summary

In these comments I have given some examples to how recent developments in economic theory can be applied to the analysis of the open economy and of real exchange rates. These extensions of the standard theory of the open economy are important for two main reasons. First, they enrich our understanding of open economies and allow us to account for some phenomena, which cannot be explained by standard theory. Second, these applications extend the theory in important realistic directions. As we all know, capital markets are imperfect, income is not equally distributed, vital information is missing, and markets are not perfectly competitive. These two reasons apply to the paper by Giovannini as well, and make it an important contribution to the theory of exchange rates.

# Notes

1. For a quick survey of these applications see Frenkel and Mussa (1985) and Obstfeld and Stockman (1985).
2. See Mankiw and Romer (1991) for a survey of this line of research.
3. In these comments, as in Giovannini's paper, the real exchange rate is the relative price of the non-traded good in terms of the traded good.
4. This is true even if some of the seminal works in this literature, like Romer (1986) and Lucas (1988), use closed economy models. The open economy aspects of growth and development become more evident in Lucas (1990) and Grossman and Helpman (1992).
5. See David (1975) for a thorough discussion.
6. Note, that these are two independent assumptions. Perfect capital mobility means that capital markets are fully integrated, while the other assumption means that there is perfect competition in these markets.
7. The effects of capital market imperfections on output fluctuations are analysed in Mankiw (1986), Bernanke and Gertler (1989, 1990), Sussman (1991) and others. The effects of such imperfections on growth are analysed in Tsiddon (1992), Galor and Zeira (1993), Azariadis and Smith (1992) and others.
8. See works by Gertler and Gilchrist (1991), Chirinko and Schaller (1992), Oliner and Rudenbusch (1992), Whited (1992) and many more.
9. This research includes Loury (1981), Galor and Zeira (1993), Banerjee and Newman (1991), Benabou (1993), Glomm and Ravikumar (1992), Durlauf (1992), Persson and Tabellini (1991), Alesina and Rodrick (1991), Atkeson and Lucas (1992) and Perotti (1993).

# References

Alesina, A. and Rodrick, D. (1991), 'Distributive Politics and Economic Growth', Mimeo.

Atkeson, A. and Lucas Jr, R. E. (1992), 'On efficient distribution with private information', *Review of Economic Studies*, **59**, 427–53.

Azariadis, C. and Smith, B. D. (1992), 'Adverse Selection in a Neoclassical Growth Model', Mimeo.

Banerjee, A. and Newman, A. F. (1991), 'Risk-bearing and the theory of income distribution', *Review of Economic Studies*, **58**, 211–35.

Benabou, R. (1993), 'Workings of a city: location, education, and production', *Quarterly Journal of Economics*, **108**.

Bernanke, B. and Gertler, M. (1989), 'Agency costs, collaterall, and business fluctuations', *American Economic Review*, **79**, 14–31.

Bernanke, B. and Gertler, M. (1990), 'Financial fragility and economic performance', *Quarterly Journal of Economics*, **105**, 87–114.

Chirinko, R. S. and Schaller, H. (1992), 'Why does liquidity matter in investment equations?', Mimeo.

David, P. A. (1975), *Technical Choice, Innovation and Economic Growth*, Cambridge University Press, London.

Dornbusch, R. and Giovannini, A. (1990), 'Monetary policy in the open economy', in B. Friedman and F. Hahn, (eds), *Handbook of Monetary Economics*, North Holland, Amsterdam.

Durlauf, S. N. (1992), 'A theory of persistent income inequality', Mimeo.

Frenkel, J. and Mussa, M. (1985), 'Asset markets, exchange rates and the balance of payments', in R. Jones and P. Kenen (eds), *Handbook of International Economics*, Volume II, North Holland, Amsterdam, pp. 679–747.

Galor, O. and Zeira, J. (1993), 'Income distribution and macroeconomics', *Review of Economic Studies*, **60**, 35–52.

Gertler, M. and Gilchrist, S. (1991), 'Monetary policy, business cycles and the behavior of small manufacturing firms', Mimeo.

Glomm, G. and Ravikumar, B. (1992), 'Public vs. private investment in human capital: Endogenous growth and income inequality', *Journal of Political Economy*, **100**, 818–34.

Grossman, G. M. and Helpman, E. (1992), *Innovation and Growth in the Global Economy*, MIT Press, Cambridge, MA.

Habakkuk, H. J. (1962), *American and British Technology in the Nineteenth Century*, Cambridge University Press, Cambridge.

Levich, R. (1985), 'Empirical studies of exchange rates: price behavior, rate determination and market efficiency', in R. Jones and P. Kenen (eds), *Handbook of International Economics*, North Holland, Amsterdam, pp. 979–1040.

Loury, G. C. (1981), 'Intergenerational transfers and the distribution of earnings', *Econometrica*, **49**, 843–67.

Lucas Jr, R. E. (1988), 'On the mechanics of economic development', *Journal of Monetary Economics*, **22**, 3–42.

Lucas Jr, R. E. (1990), 'Why doesn't capital flow from rich to poor countries?' *American Economic Review*, **80**, 92–6.

Mankiw, N. G. (1986), 'The allocation of credit and financial collapse', *Quarterly Journal of Economics*, **101**, 455–70.

Mankiw, N. G. and Romer, D. (1991), *New Keynesian Economics*, MIT Press, Cambridge, MA.

Meese, R. (1990), 'Currency fluctuations in the post-Bretton Woods era', *Journal of Economic Perspectives,* **4**, 117–34.

Obstfeld, M. and Stockman, A, (1985), 'Exchange rate dynamics', in R. Jones and P. Kenen (eds), *Handbook of International Economics*, North Holland, Amsterdam, pp. 917–77.

Oliner, S. D. and Rudenbusch, G. D. (1992), 'The transmission of monetary policy to small and large firms', Mimeo.

Perotti, R. (1993), 'Political equilibrium, income distribution and growth', *Review of Economic Studies*, **60**, 755–76.

Persson, T. and Tabellini, G. (1991), 'Is inequality harmful for growth?' Mimeo.

Romer, P. M. (1986), 'Increasing returns and long-run growth', *Journal of Political Economy*, **94**, 1002–37.

Romer, P. M. (1990), 'Endogenous technological change', *Journal of Political Economy*, **98**, S71–102.

Stokey, N. L. (1988), 'Learning by doing and the introduction of new goods', *Journal of Political Economy*, **96**, 701–17.

Sussman, O. (1991), 'On market imperfections and spontaneous fluctuations', Mimeo.

Tsiddon, D. (1992), 'A moral hazard trap to growth', *International Economic Review*, **33**, 299–321.

Whited, T. M. (1992), 'Debt, liquidity, and corporate investment: evidence from panel data', *Journal of Finance*, (forthcoming).

Zeira, J. (1991), 'Credit rationing in an open economy', *International Economic Review*, **32**, 959–72.

Zeira, J. (1993), 'Informational overshooting, booms and crashes', Mimeo.

Zeira, J. (1994), 'Workers, machines and economic growth', Mimeo.

# 3

# Country Characteristics and the Choice of the Exchange Rate Regime: Are Mini-skirts Followed by Maxis?

## Seppo Honkapohja
*Academy of Finland, University of Helsinki and CEPR*

## Pentti Pikkarainen
*Bank of Finland/Suomen Pankki*

## 3.1    Introduction

Why have the Nordic countries—Finland, Norway, Sweden and Iceland—pegged their currencies to a basket? On 8 September 1992 the Bank of Finland decided to float the Finnish markka, which was pegged to the ECU. The Bank of Finland has announced that the float of the markka is temporary and Finland will restore the basket peg regime when the economic situation so permits. Is the basket peg system a natural choice for Finland? In September 1992 the United Kingdom, Italy and Spain and in November 1992 Sweden were not able to resist the speculative attacks on their currencies: the UK pound sterling, the Italian lira and the Swedish krona are floating now and the Spanish peseta was devalued with respect to other EMS currencies. Although the UK and Italian governments are planning to restore their EMS memberships, would they be better off with a floating exchange rate regime rather than rejoining the EMS? Why do Switzerland, a 'small open economy', and the United States, a large industrialized nation, let their currencies float freely? Do developing countries typically restrict movements in their exchange rates rather than let their currencies float?

These are some of the issues we want to address in this study. The choice of the exchange rate regime is one of the most fundamental but also one of the most controversial issues in international monetary economics. If one accepts the extreme monetarist or new classical view that 'money does not matter', one should also agree with the view that the exchange rate regime of a country does not matter.[1] For many economists and laymen this is too extreme a statement to concur with. If one agrees with the view that the exchange rate regime does matter, one must accept some kind of non-new classical argument: there exist some imperfections or rigidities in the economy which make monetary policy effective or money non-neutral, at least in the short run, and as a consequence also the exchange rate regime matters. There could exist several types of imperfections or rigidities which create a role for monetary policy or the international monetary standard: wages adjust slowly; adjustment in the financial markets, in particular the foreign exchange market, is much faster than in the goods market, etc.[2] In this paper we accept the view that the exchange rate regime may—but does not necessarily—matter.

One may discuss the choice of the exchange rate regime from several theoretical view points: there exists a vast literature under the title of optimal currency areas; one may study the microeconomic consequences of alternative exchange rate systems; recently the properties of alternative exchange rate arrangements have been studied from the point of view of credibility.[3] Also, as mentioned above, one may study the issue from the point of view of different schools of economic thought, i.e. the ongoing debate between monetarists and Keynesians. It is also possible that the choices do not reflect any rationalization provided by economists but rather the choice is like a fad: during the Bretton Woods era some economists criticised the existing international monetary system and advocated more flexible arrangements; after some experience with a more flexible international monetary standard many arguments, theoretical and empirical, against floating have been put forward. If one wants to be fatalistic, one could say that the history of the international monetary standard is like any other fashion: mini-skirts are followed by midis, which are followed by maxis, and so on. It is also argued (see, for instance, Feldstein (1992)) that the choice of the exchange rate regime is based more on political pressure than on economic rationalization.

During the last 10 years or so flexible exchange rate arrangements have gained popularity (Table 3.1). The percentage of countries that peg to a single currency has decreased substantially from 40.0 to 26.1%. Meanwhile the regime of free floating has become more popular: the percentage of countries in this regime has increased from 7.6 to 21.7%. Although the proportion of countries that peg to a single currency has decreased substantially, the popularity of pegging to a currency composite has remained very stable at the level of about 24%.[4]

Part B of Table 3.1 shows how countries have moved from one exchange rate system to another during the last 10 years. Eighty seven (60.8%) nations have not changed position. While 46 (32.2%) economies have moved towards a more flexible exchange rate system, only 10 (7.0%) nations have adopted a more rigid exchange rate arrangement.

The purpose of the paper is to study empirically how different country

**Table 3.1**  Exchange rate arrangements in 1982 and 1992

A.  Number of countries with alternative exchange rate arrangements

|         | 1982          | 1992          |
|---------|---------------|---------------|
| Group A | 58 (40.0%)    | 41 (26.1%)    |
| Group B | 36 (24.8%)    | 37 (23.6%)    |
| Group C | 17 (11.7%)    | 14  (8.9%)    |
| Group D | 23 (15.9%)    | 30 (19.1%)    |
| Group E | 11  (7.6%)    | 34 (21.7%)    |
| Total   | 145           | 157           |

*Note*: 1982: as of 31 March; 1992: as of 31 March. Group A: pegged to a single currency. Group B: pegged to a currency composite. Group C: flexibility limited in terms of a single currency or group of currencies. Group D: adjusted according to a set of indicators or other managed floating. Group E: independently floating. Although Switzerland is not included in the IMF classification tables, Switzerland is included here into the group of independently floating countries.

B.  Changes in country positions from 1982 to 1992

|         | Group A | Group B | Group C | Group D | Group E |
|---------|---------|---------|---------|---------|---------|
| Group A | 36      | 4       | 0       | 7       | 10      |
| Group B | 0       | 24      | 0       | 9       | 2       |
| Group C | 0       | 0       | 12      | 2       | 3       |
| Group D | 1       | 4       | 1       | 8       | 9       |
| Group E | 1       | 0       | 1       | 2       | 7       |

*Note*: Groups in the column indicate the position of a country in 1982, and in the row the position of a country in 1992. The diagonal elements indicate how many countries have stayed in the same group. Thus, for instance, 36 countries have stayed in group A and 4 countries have moved from group A to group B. Burma and Upper Volta are omitted.

characteristics are associated with the choice of a country's exchange rate system. In section 3.2 we discuss some theoretical hypotheses. The data are introduced in section 3.3. The data consist of 140 countries, both developing and industrialized nations, and are far more comprehensive than the data analysed in the previous empirical studies.[5] The data allow us to put monetary integration in Europe and the exchange rate regime choices in the Nordic countries into a global perspective. In section 3.4 we study whether the means and medians of the country characteristics differ in alternative exchange rate regimes. In section 3.5 we estimate logit and probit models to explain the choices in terms of the country characteristics.

## 3.2    The Hypotheses

As mentioned in the introduction, one cannot analyse the choice of the exchange rate regime in a comprehensive way using a single theoretical model. In this section we draw from several branches of the literature to build an empirical model for explaining how some country characteristics may be associated with the choice of a country's exchange rate system.

1. *The size of a country.* One may assume that small economies are typically price takers in the world market whereas large countries have some influence over the prices of traded goods. Moreover, the pattern of production and the foreign trade sector are often more diversified in large countries than in small economies. As a consequence, changes in individual commodity markets will offset each other, making a floating exchange rate regime a more likely choice for large countries. In a small undiversified country it may be necessary to offset fluctuations in export receipts to alleviate the impact of price fluctuations on the domestic price level. Thus, we expect large countries to be floaters and small economies to typically restrict exchange rate fluctuations. In this study the size of the economy is measured by GDP.

2. *Degree of economic development.* We would expect that the lower the level of a country's economic development, the less developed and less efficient would be its goods, factor and capital markets. The more developed a country, the better it is able to cope with fluctuating exchange rates. One can also show that restrictions on the movements of exchange rates are a kind of substitute for developed capital markets. For instance, if in the basket peg system the exchange rate authorities hold the value of the currency index constant and there are no forward currency markets, the currency index system is a partial substitute for forward currency markets (Pikkarainen, 1991a, b). Thus, we would expect developing countries to restrict exchange rate fluctuations but advanced industrialized nations to be floaters. GDP per capita (GDPCAP) is used as a measure of the level of economic development.

3. *Openness of the goods producing sector of a country.* The more open the country, the more vulnerable it is to changes in economic developments in its foreign trading partners. The openness of the economy may also correlate negatively with the size and the degree of diversification of production and international trade of the economy: small countries tend to be more open and less diversified. Accordingly, we would expect that the more open the country, the more likely it is to restrict exchange rate fluctuations. Closed economies tend to be floaters. The openness of the goods producing sector of the economy is measured by the ratio of foreign trade (imports plus exports) to GDP (OPEN).

4. *Degree of international financial integration.* One may look at the

implications of the openness of capital markets from several points of view. On the one hand, from the point of view of insulation from different types of shocks and effectiveness of stabilization policies, the properties of alternative exchange rate regimes depend on the source of shocks. From this point of view it is difficult to put forward clear-cut hypotheses for the choice of the exchange rate regime. On the other hand, the higher the degree of a country's international financial integration, the more likely it is to have well-developed financial markets and the easier it is for agents to cover risks due to fluctuations in exchange rates. Thus, from this point of view we would expect countries with open capital markets to tend to be floaters and those with several restrictions on international capital movements to tend to also restrict the volatility of exchange rates. In this study the openness of capital markets is measured by the ratio of foreign assets of the banking system to the money supply (FIN).[6]

5.   *Diversification of foreign trade.* Here we distinguish between two features: the geographical and commodity concentration of foreign trade. Countries with well-diversified exports will experience greater stability in foreign exchange earnings and may consequently opt for a more flexible exchange rate regime. Countries with less diversified trade tend to restrict exchange rate movements. The geographical concentration of foreign trade is measured by the percentage share of the three largest export destinations (DIVGEO) and the commodity concentration by the Hirschmann concentration index of exports (DIVCOM). Note that the greater the value of these measures the less diversified is a country's exports.

6.   *Fluctuations in the terms of trade.* Fluctuations in the terms of trade are likely to be greater the greater are fluctuations in the real exchange rate. Due to the insulating property of floating exchange rates with regard to foreign price disturbances, higher real exchange rate variability may lead a country to opt for a flexible exchange rate arrangement. Fluctuations in the terms of trade are measured by the coefficient of variation of the terms of trade (TERMS).

Following Edison and Melvin (1990) and the previous empirical literature we dub the hypotheses presented above the 'conventional view' or the 'conventional wisdom'. In the empirical and theoretical literature on the choice of the exchange rate regime other hypotheses are also put forward. McKinnon (1979) discusses the implications of convertibility of a currency. While countries with fully convertible currencies have the option of pegging or not pegging, those with exchange rate controls and restrictions on making foreign payments are compelled to restrict exchange rates. To take into account the effects of the convertibility of a currency we introduce a dummy variable (INCONV), which obtains the value of 1 for the countries with inconvertible currency and the value of 0 otherwise.

Kenen (1969) and Giersch (1973) suggest that small, open, and undiversified economies can derive greater benefits from exchange rate flexibility than large, closed, and diversified countries. They argue that export diversification reduces the necessity to change the exchange rate frequently. A corollary to this argument is that an undiversified and, therefore most likely, a small economy will be better off with a flexible exchange rate system. The empirical results in Dreyer (1978) give some support for this hypothesis: countries with high export diversification tend to restrict exchange rate movements.

It is postulated by Holden et al. (1979) and Melvin (1985) that the greater the difference between a country's inflation rate and that of its trading partners, the more flexible will be its exchange rate policy. Melvin also argues that the greater the domestic money shocks, the more likely the country is to restrict movements in exchange rates. We agree that these factors may affect the choice of the exchange rate regime but there are good grounds for suspecting that they are determined simultaneously with the exchange rate regime. For instance, if the central bank is committed to restricting movements in exchange rates in order to keep inflation low, the country's inflation rate must (in the long run) be very close to those of its trading partners. If the private sector believes that the central bank is able and willing to make this commitment, i.e. the exchange rate regime is perceived to be credible, pricing behaviour reflects this belief. Thus, the rate of inflation clearly depends on the exchange rate regime; inflation and the exchange rate regime are determined simultaneously. Similarly, if the monetary authorities are committed to a target zone exchange rate regime, this is reflected in the money supply process. Hence the conduct of monetary policy depends on the exchange rate regime; the money supply process and the choice of exchange rate regime are determined simultaneously.[7]

The traditional optimal currency area view implies that countries with flexible labour markets should adopt fixed exchange rates rather than float their currencies. We believe that this feature of an economy is also determined simultaneously with the exchange rate system: if a country moves towards a more rigid exchange rate system, the labour market partners will eventually understand the consequences and adopt more flexible practices as regards wage determination and labour mobility. Moreover, it is difficult to obtain a measure of labour market flexibility for the large sample studied here.

The simultaneous determination of the exchange rate regime and factors 1–6 above cannot be fully avoided. The exchange rate regime or conduct of exchange rate policy may affect the economic development (growth) of a country. The pattern of foreign trade, in particular the geographical diversification of trade, may depend on the exchange rate regime. The openness of the capital markets of a country may also be determined simultanously with the exchange rate regime. We believe, however, that factors 1–6 are more like 'fundamentals' which do not depend strongly on the exchange rate regime. Factors like the difference between the domestic and foreign inflation rate and the domestic money supply process depend more clearly on the exchange rate regime, and in order to take into account these features one should estimate a simultaneous equations model.

## 3.3    The Data

We use the IMF's classification to identify the exchange rate system of a country. Accordingly, we specify the following five categories:

A:   country pegs to a single currency,
B:   country pegs to a currency composite,
C:   limited flexibility in terms of a single currency or a group of currencies,
D:   currency is adjusted according to a set of indicators or other managed floating, and
E:   independently floating.

The exchange rate arrangements are according to the situation on 31 December 1991. In category A the majority of the countries peg either to the US dollar or the French franc. In category B some countries peg to the Special Drawing Rights (SDRs); however, the majority of countries have chosen a more individual basket, like the Nordic countries Finland, Iceland, Norway and Sweden. The EMS, including Germany, belongs to group C in the IMF classification.[8]

We take the IMF's classification of countries' exchange rate arrangements as given. It might be, for instance, that the monetary integration in Western Europe has become tighter during the last 10 years or so but we do not have any opportunity to attack this issue very seriously.[9] We do, however, use alternative aggregations of countries and alternate the position of Germany (cf. section 3.5). We also study the effects of inconvertibility of a currency.[10]

The exact construction of the data, the data sources, and the countries included in the study are reported in the Appendix. For GDP, GDPCAP, OPEN, and FIN we use the average of annual observations covering the period 1987–90 to even out the contribution of cyclical fluctuations. Fluctuations in terms of trade is measured by the coefficient of variation of quarterly observations over the longer period of 1980–90 to obtain a more robust estimate than the one which would be obtained using the period 1987–90. DIVGEO is measured by the percentage of three largest export destinations in 1987–8, and DIVCOM by the Hirschmann index of exports for 1988.

Some basic statistics on the data are displayed in Table 3.2. For GDP, GDPCAP, and FIN, the medians differ quite substantially from the respective arithmetic means. This is due to some 'outliers' in the data. The same feature is reflected in the high values of the coefficient of variation for these variables.

The correlation matrix does not indicate any serious multicolinearity, the highest correlation being 0.51 between DIVCOM and TERMS. When we consider the openness of the goods producing sector, large countries tend to be less open than small ones. The openness of the financial sector seems to be uncorrelated with the size of a country. Rich countries, however, tend to be more open than developing nations both in terms of trade and financial integration. Both the commodity and geographical diversification of trade tend to be greater in large economies than in small ones, and greater in rich countries than in poor ones. The

**Table 3.2**  Basic statistics on the data

|        | Min   | Max     | Mean   | Median | SD     | CV    |
|--------|-------|---------|--------|--------|--------|-------|
| GDP    | 107   | 5049525 | 126352 | 5918   | 511165 | 4.046 |
| GDPCAP | 120   | 28529   | 4380   | 1699   | 6542   | 1.494 |
| OPEN   | 0.000 | 3.136   | 0.527  | 0.432  | 0.436  | 0.827 |
| FIN    | 0.000 | 18.209  | 0.798  | 0.218  | 1.978  | 2.479 |
| DIVGEO | 21.8  | 90.5    | 54.5   | 52.3   | 15.9   | 0.292 |
| DIVCOM | 5.6   | 92.8    | 40.9   | 40.5   | 23.1   | 0.565 |
| TERMS  | 0.022 | 0.343   | 0.113  | 0.100  | 0.073  | 0.646 |

*Note*: SD: standard deviation. CV: coefficient of variation.

Correlations

|        | GDP | GDPCAP | OPEN  | FIN   | DIVGEO | DIVCOM | TERMS |
|--------|-----|--------|-------|-------|--------|--------|-------|
| GDP    | 1   | 0.45   | −0.12 | −0.00 | −0.19  | −0.30  | −0.13 |
| GDPCAP |     | 1      | 0.14  | 0.22  | −0.27  | −0.41  | −0.46 |
| OPEN   |     |        | 1     | 0.16  | 0.10   | −0.05  | −0.32 |
| FIN    |     |        |       | 1     | −0.10  | −0.11  | −0.46 |
| DIVGEO |     |        |       |       | 1      | 0.40   | 0.03  |
| DIVCOM |     |        |       |       |        | 1      | 0.51  |
| TERMS  |     |        |       |       |        |        | 1     |

*Note*: GDPCAP: GDP per capita. OPEN: openness of the goods producing sector. FIN: degree of financial integration. DIVGEO: geographic concentration of foreign trade. DIVCOM: commodity concentration of foreign trade. TERMS: fluctuations in the terms of trade. See Appendix for detailed description of the data and data sources.

geographical and commodity diversification of international trade are quite strongly positively correlated with each other. The openness of the goods and financial markets are weakly positively correlated with each other. Fluctuations in the terms of trade tend to be greater in small countries than in large ones, and greater in poor countries than in rich ones. Countries with high volatility in the terms of trade tend to be closed in terms of international trade in goods and assets. Not surprisingly, fluctuations in the terms of trade have been greater in economies with low commodity diversification of international trade than in those with high commodity diversification.

## 3.4 Means and Medians of Country Characteristics in Alternative Exchange Rate Arrangements

In this section we first study the means and medians of the country characteristics when countries are classified according to their current exchange rate practices (*cf.* part A of Table 3.1). We also investigate the means and medians when countries are classified according to whether they have changed the exchange rate system during the last 10 years (*cf.* part B of Table 3.1).

The means and medians of the country characteristics in different categories are displayed in Table 3.3, part A. In part B we present tests for equality of means and medians in the subgroups. The *F*-test and *t*-test assume that the variables are normally distributed in the subgroups. Since in some cases there are good reasons to be suspicious of the normality assumption, we also report the results of the Kruskal–Wallis test and the Mann–Whitney test. Recall that the Kruskal–Wallis test is a generalization of the Mann–Whitney test to more than two groups. The pairwise comparisons in part B are carried out by comparing groups B–E with group A. As in the aggregate data the means and medians differ more from each other for GDP, GDPCAP, and FIN than for OPEN, DIVGEO, DIVCOM, and TERMS.

According to both the *F*-test and the Kruskal–Wallis test the mean or median GDP is not the same in the various subgroups. The mean GDP increases in the order group A, B, D, E with group C having the highest mean GDP. The median GDP increases in the order of group A, B, E, D, and C. The mean and median GDP in group E differ substantially from each other. This is due to the fact that there are some very large economies in group E, like the United States and Japan. Also, Canada, Brazil, Australia, and Switzerland are floaters. The mean or median GDP is highest in group C, which is dominated by the EMS economies. The very small countries tend to peg to a single currency. Those countries

**Table 3.3**   Means and medians of country characteristics in alternative exchange
rate regimes

A.  Means and medians of country characteristics in subgroups

|  | Group A | Group B | Group C | Group D | Group E |
|---|---|---|---|---|---|
| GDP | 7535 | 33787 | 384071 | 65517 | 352667 |
|  | 2019 | 5103 | 200000 | 40625 | 8033 |
| GDPCAP | 1734 | 4501 | 14395 | 2101 | 5228 |
|  | 1071 | 1727 | 16000 | 1375 | 1050 |
| OPEN | 0.527 | 0.505 | 0.701 | 0.518 | 0.482 |
|  | 0.445 | 0.525 | 0.560 | 0.447 | 0.373 |
| FIN | 0.814 | 0.529 | 2.085 | 0.484 | 0.815 |
|  | 0.126 | 0.166 | 2.000 | 0.288 | 0.214 |
| DIVGEO | 60.2 | 52.5 | 45.2 | 53.2 | 55.6 |
|  | 58.5 | 51.9 | 46.7 | 50.0 | 55.0 |
| DIVCOM | 52.6 | 44.5 | 26.5 | 31.9 | 36.2 |
|  | 50.0 | 43.3 | 10.0 | 29.0 | 35.0 |
| TERMS | 0.164 | 0.106 | 0.065 | 0.113 | 0.133 |
|  | 0.194 | 0.083 | 0.048 | 0.110 | 0.105 |

*Note*: For each variable the means are in the upper row and medians in the lower row,
respectively.

B.  Tests for location of distributions
F- *and* t-*tests for equality of means in subgroups:*

|  | F | Group B | Group C | Group D | Group E |
|---|---|---|---|---|---|
| GDP | 0.014 | 0.023 | 0.000 | 0.000 | 0.053 |
| GDPCAP | 0.000 | 0.024 | 0.000 | 0.537 | 0.016 |
| OPEN | 0.658 | 0.790 | 0.173 | 0.941 | 0.696 |
| FIN | 0.144 | 0.582 | 0.145 | 0.584 | 0.998 |
| DIVGEO | 0.045 | 0.047 | 0.006 | 0.116 | 0.328 |
| DIVCOM | 0.001 | 0.122 | 0.001 | 0.000 | 0.003 |
| TERMS | 0.078 | 0.064 | 0.010 | 0.223 | 0.555 |

*Note*: The table displays the marginal significance levels of two-sided tests for equality of
means in the subgroups. F: *F*-test for all the subgroups. Last four columns: *t*-tests for group
A and group $i$, $i$ = B, . . ., E, respectively. The smaller the reported significance level, the
more significant the test statistic is.

*Kruskal–Wallis test and Mann-Whitney test for location of distributions*

|  | KW | Group B | Group C | Group D | Group E |
|---|---|---|---|---|---|
| GDP | 0.000 | 0.0238 | 0.000 | 0.000 | 0.001 |
| GDPCAP | 0.000 | 0.147 | 0.000 | 0.347 | 0.226 |
| OPEN | 0.114 | 0.332 | 0.044 | 0.506 | 0.886 |
| FIN | 0.000 | 0.808 | 0.000 | 0.190 | 0.268 |
| DIVGEO | 0.068 | 0.975 | 0.996 | 0.936 | 0.824 |
| DIVCOM | 0.000 | 0.954 | 0.996 | 1.000 | 0.997 |
| TERMS | 0.141 | 0.898 | 0.987 | 0.797 | 0.756 |

*Note*: The table displays the marginal significance levels of tests for location of distributions.
KW: Kruskal–Wallis test for all the subgroups. Last four columns: one-sided Mann–
Whitney tests for group A and group $i$, $i$ = B, . . ., E, respectively.

which peg to a currency composite are also rather small economies on average. Thus, there is some evidence that small countries tend to restrict exchange rate fluctuations rather than float.

When we consider the level of development, the mean GDPCAP increases in the order group A, D, B, E, and C while the median GDPCAP increases in the order group E, A, D, B, and C. The average level of development is very similar in groups A, B, D, and E. Group E is very heterogenous: it includes, on the one hand, very rich countries, like Australia, Canada, Japan, New Zealand, Switzerland, and the United States, and on the other hand, countries with very low GDP per capita. Group C, the EMS countries, clearly forms the most developed block. This pattern does not support the null hypothesis that developing countries are more likely to restrict exchange rate fluctuations than industrialized nations.

Concerning the openness of the goods producing sector and the degree of international financial integration, it is difficult to argue for any clear pattern in the data when we compare groups A, B, D, and E. It is again group C which stands out; it is the most open one both in terms of the real sector and financial openness. The geographical diversification of foreign trade is lowest in group A but it does not differ significantly from that in group E. Group C countries have the highest geographical diversification of foreign trade. On the other hand, the commodity diversification of international trade displays a somewhat clearer pattern than the geographical one: among groups A, B, D, and E the commodity diversification of trade is lowest in group A and group B follows. Not surprisingly, the commodity diversification of trade is highest in group C.

Fluctuations in the terms of trade have been lowest in group C and highest in group A. The fluctuations have been of very much the same magnitude in groups B, D, and E.

Thus far our observations can be summarized as follows. First, there is some support for the view that small countries tend to restrict exchange rate fluctuations rather than let their currencies float. Second, there is weak evidence that countries with less diversified international trade tend to peg their exchange rate rather than float. This is true, in particular, when we consider the commodity diversification of foreign trade. Third, fluctuations in the terms of trade have been most volatile in the group which pegs to a single currency. Fourth, it is difficult to argue for any clear pattern between the choice of exchange rate system and the level of development and the openness of an economy. Fifth, group C, which is dominated by the EMS economies, stands out as a separate block: it is the one with the highest average GDP and GDP per capita, it is the most open group in terms of financial integration, and it has the most diversified trade. According to our null hypotheses or 'conventional wisdom' countries of this type should be floaters rather than restrict fluctuations in exchange rates. On the other hand, group C is the most integrated one in terms of the real sector and also the one where terms of trade fluctuations have been lowest. This is consistent with our null hypotheses: countries with an open real sector and low volatility of terms of trade tend to restrict fluctuations in exchange rates rather than float their currencies freely.

In Table 3.4 we present the means and medians of the country characteristics when countries are classified according to whether they have changed their exchange rate regime during the last 10 years (*cf.* also part B of Table 3.1). Somewhat surprisingly, it is developing countries which have moved towards more flexible exchange rate practices. Countries with well diversified exports have moved towards more rigid exchange rate arrangements. These observations are opposite to the conventional view discussed in section 3.3.

**Table 3.4** Means and medians of country characteristics for countries which have changed their exchange rate system between 1982 and 1992

A. Means and medians of country characteristics in subgroups

|         | Group R | Group N | Group F |
|---------|---------|---------|---------|
| GDP     | 155295  | 197019  | 30177   |
|         | 64392   | 6338    | 15000   |
| GDPCAP  | 7017    | 6147    | 1875    |
|         | 5460    | 2364    | 866     |
| OPEN    | 0.361   | 0.534   | 0.494   |
|         | 0.374   | 0.500   | 0.347   |
| FIN     | 0.821   | 0.977   | 0.396   |
|         | 0.341   | 0.239   | 0.208   |
| DIVGEO  | 44.6    | 53.7    | 59.0    |
|         | 44.6    | 52.3    | 59.4    |
| DIVCOM  | 19.0    | 40.8    | 46.5    |
|         | 17.2    | 41.4    | 43.5    |
| TERMS   | 0.068   | 0.110   | 0.173   |
|         | 0.066   | 0.100   | 0.113   |

*Note*: Group R: countries which have moved to a more rigid exchange rate arrangement. Group N: no change in the exchange rate system. Group F: countries which have moved to a more flexible exchange rate regime.

B. Tests for location of distributions
F- *and* t-*tests for equality of means in subgroups:*

|        | F     | Group R | Group F |
|--------|-------|---------|---------|
| GDP    | 0.315 | 0.784   | 0.634   |
| GDPCAP | 0.004 | 0.709   | 0.001   |
| OPEN   | 0.467 | 0.064   | 0.015   |
| FIN    | 0.327 | 0.535   | 0.407   |

**Table 3.4**  *Continued*

|        | F     | Group R | Group F |
|--------|-------|---------|---------|
| DIVGEO | 0.024 | 0.064   | 0.067   |
| DIVCOM | 0.004 | 0.007   | 0.288   |
| TERMS  | 0.054 | 0.122   | 0.105   |

*Note*: Last two columns: *t*-tests for group N and group R and F, respectively.

*Kruskal–Wallis test and Mann–Whitney test for location of distributions*

|        | KW    | Group R | Group F |
|--------|-------|---------|---------|
| GDP    | 0.119 | 0.929   | 0.317   |
| GDPCAP | 0.003 | 0.833   | 0.000   |
| OPEN   | 0.030 | 0.060   | 0.008   |
| FIN    | 0.156 | 0.877   | 0.203   |
| DIVGEO | 0.021 | 0.036   | 0.967   |
| DIVCOM | 0.004 | 0.003   | 0.856   |
| TERMS  | 0.058 | 0.955   | 0.071   |

*Note*: Last two columns: one-sided Mann–Whitney tests for group N and group R and F, respectively.

## 3.5   Logit and Probit Models

In this section we complement the analyses of section 3.4 by estimating logit and probit models for the choice of the countries' exchange rate system.[11] Following the analyses of section 3.4 the logit and probit models are estimated to explain the current exchange rate regimes and the changes in the exchange rate arrangements. The models are estimated both as ordered and non-ordered ones, with two or three categories and with several alternative aggregations of countries. Since the data for the terms of trade variable were available only for 46 countries, the models were estimated with and without the TERMS variable. All estimations were executed by Greene's (1992) LIMDEP.

In the binomial model the dependent variable obtains the value of 0 when the country belongs to groups A–D and the value of 1 when the country belongs to the group E of independently floating economies. Alternatively, groups A-C are considered as one aggregate, and groups D and E as the other one. As Heller (1978) points out, the characterization of the exchange rate regime of Germany is somewhat controversial. On the one hand, Germany belongs to the EMS and thus it cooperates with other EMS countries. Accordingly, the IMF classifies Germany with other EMS countries in group C. On the other hand, Germany is considered to be a leader in the EMS and the EMS can be interpreted as floating against the currencies outside the system. Also, in Germany monetary policy targets are set in terms of the growth rate of monetary aggregates, which is typical of the floaters. Accordingly, we alternatively classify Germany in group C with other EMS countries or in group E with the floaters. The specifications where groups A–C were considered as one aggregate and groups D and E as the other performed slightly better than the models with groups A–D versus group E. The binomial models performed slightly better when Germany was included in group E instead of group C, indicating that Germany is more similar to group E countries than those which do not float freely.

Some estimation results for the binomial models are reported in Table 3.5. Specification (5A) includes all the variables, except the inconvertibility dummy, while in specification (5B) we have omitted the TERMS variable. Although GDP, OPEN, FIN, DIVCOM, and TERMS have the expected signs in specification (5A), only OPEN and DIVCOM are statistically significant. In specification (5B) with 125 countries only DIVCOM is statistically significant and of expected sign. In the binomial models the inconvertibility dummy was not statistically significant.

Besides the binomial models we estimated ordered and non-ordered multinomial logit and probit models with three classes. In these models the dependent variable obtained the value of 0, 1 or 2. Here too we

**Table 3.5** Two category probit models

|  | (5A) | (5B) |
|---|---|---|
| GDP | 0.217 | 0.546 |
|  | (0.623) | (1.380) |
| GDPCAP | −0.413 | −0.683 |
|  | (1.074) | (2.610)*** |
| OPEN | −3.297 | 0.039 |
|  | (2.218)** | (0.127) |
| FIN | 0.313 | −0.098 |
|  | (1.009) | (0.990) |
| DIVGEO | 0.040 | 0.008 |
|  | (1.850)* | (0.914) |
| DIVCOM | −0.040 | −0.020 |
|  | (1.894)* | (2.854)*** |
| TERMS | 3.245 |  |
|  | (0.813) |  |
| INCONV |  | −0.364 |
|  |  | (1.255) |
| Log-likelihood | −21.203 | −82.759 |
| $\chi^2$ | 15.680** | 19.724*** |
| Observations | 46 | 125 |

*Note*: Constant terms are not reported. Absolute *t*-statistics are displayed in parentheses under the coefficient estimates.
*: test-statistic is significant at the 10% level; ** (***): significant at the 5% (1%) level. Scale of coefficients: GDP $10^{-6}$, GDPCAP $10^{-4}$. The dependent variable obtains the value of 0 for group A–C countries and the value of 1 for group D and E economies. Germany is classified in group C.

estimated the models with several alternative aggregations of countries. As in the binomial models we alternated the position of Germany.

In the ordered multinomial models the best specification was that where the dependent variable obtained the value of 0 for group A and B countries, 1 for group C and D countries, and 2 for group E economies. In Table 3.6 in specification (6A) we display the model for the small sample of 46 countries without the inconvertibility dummy. Specification (6B) is the model for the large sample of 125 countries with the inconvertibility dummy. In both models only DIVCOM is of expected sign and statistically significant. In the large sample also the inconvertibility dummy is significant.

The ordered multinomial models support the view that Germany resembles more the independently floating economies than those which restrict fluctuations in exchange rates. Although the performance of the ordered models is not very satisfactory, it is important to notice that the estimated threshold was always statistically significant, indicating that the countries in the groups have some common features.

The IMF's classification of exchange rate arrangements implicitly implies that the flexibility of an exchange rate system increases when we

**Table 3.6**  Three category probit models

|  | (6A) | (6B) |
|---|---|---|
| GDP | 0.610 | 0.502 |
|  | (0.439) | (0.839) |
| GDPCAP | −0.014 | −0.210 |
|  | (0.043) | (1.000) |
| OPEN | −2.132 | 0.035 |
|  | (1.541) | (0.114) |
| FIN | 0.337 | −0.041 |
|  | (1.275) | (0.510) |
| DIVGEO | 0.050 | 0.003 |
|  | (2.155)** | (0.410) |
| DIVCOM | −0.052 | −0.011 |
|  | (1.803)* | (1.804)* |
| TERMS | 5.270 |  |
|  | (1.220) |  |
| INCONV |  | −0.584 |
|  |  | (2.288)** |
| THRESHOLD | 1.500 | 0.889 |
|  | (3.957)*** | (6.424)*** |
| Log-likelihood | −33.137 | −116.38 |
| $\chi^2$ | 27.960*** | 21.836*** |
| Observations | 46 | 125 |

*Note*: The dependent variable obtains the value of 0 for group A and B countries, 1 for group C and D economies, and 2 for group E nations. Germany is classified in group C. The variable THRESHOLD is the threshold between the second and third class; the threshold between the first and second class is normalized to be zero.

move from group A towards group E. We agree that this is true to some extent but as the analyses in section 3.4 indicate we also have some reasons to suspect this view. This is true, in particular, when we consider group C. Consequently, we also estimated three class nonordered models. In these models the dependent variable obtains the value of 0 for group A and B countries, the value of 1 for group C countries, and the value of 2 for group D and E countries. Since TERM and INCONV were not significant in the nonordered models, we report in Table 3.7 the results with the large sample of 125 countries without INCONV. Not surprisingly the non-ordered three class models performed better than the two class models or the three class ordered models. We observe that large countries belong to group C or they tend to adopt rather flexible exchange rate arrangements, while small nations tend to restrict fluctuations in exchange rates. Consistent with the results in section 3.4, the countries in group C are the most developed ones; developing economies tend to peg either to a single currency or a basket of currencies or, even more likely, they tend to adopt a flexible exchange rate regime. The openness of the goods producing sector is highest in group C. FIN and DIVGEO are statistically insignificant. High commodity diversification of international trade is typical for the aggregate of groups D and E.

We also estimated logit and probit models to explain the change of exchange rate regime in terms of these same country characteristics (*cf.* part B of Table 3.1 and Table 3.4). The models were estimated as two (groups R and N aggregated or group R omitted) or three category specifications and as ordered or non-ordered ones. These estimations (not reported here) confirm the results in section 3.5: it is developing

**Table 3.7**  Three category non-ordered logit models

| Estimates for group | C | D and E |
|---|---|---|
| GDP | 8.098 | 10.663 |
|  | (2.048) | (2.682)*** |
| GDPCAP | 1.019 | −1.796 |
|  | (1.854)* | (2.737)*** |
| OPEN | 1.333 | 0.909 |
|  | (1.731)* | (1.428) |
| FIN | 0.162 | −0.066 |
|  | (1.343) | (0.424) |
| DIVGEO | −0.038 | 0.018 |
|  | (1.148) | (1.170) |
| DIVCOM | −0.002 | −0.029 |
|  | (0.136) | (2.373)** |
| Log-likelihood | −93.808 | |
| $\cdot^2$ | 48.189*** | |
| Observations | 125 | |

*Note*: Germany is classified in group C. The parameters for group A and B countries are normalized to be equal to zero.

countries which have moved towards more flexible exchange rate arrangements; the countries with high diversification of exports have moved towards more rigid exchange rate practices. There is also weak evidence that countries with low volatility of terms of trade have adopted more rigid exchange rate systems.

## 3.6 Discussion

In this paper we have studied how different country characteristics are associated with the choice of countries' exchange rate arrangements. When we studied the current country positions, we found some support for the view that small economies tend to restrict exchange rate fluctuations rather than let their currencies float freely.[12] The same holds for economies with low commodity diversification of foreign trade.[13] Thus small countries with low diversification of foreign trade are the most likely candidates to peg their exchange rates and use the exchange rate as an intermediate target of monetary policy. Other country characteristics, like the level of economic development, openness of the real or financial sector, geographical diversification of trade, and fluctuations in the terms of trade, have in practice hardly any power in explaining the choice of a country's exchange rate system.[14]

When we studied the changes in country positions, we found that it is developing countries which have moved towards more flexible exchange rate arrangements during the last 10 years. Meanwhile economies with well diversified exports have adopted more rigid exchange rate practices. These tendencies are opposite to the 'conventional view' but support the views expressed by Kenen (1969) and Giersch (1973).

In the light of our evidence and 'conventional wisdom', the emerging monetary cooperation among the EC countries is somewhat peculiar. On the one hand, the EMS countries are quite large and rich, they are well integrated financially, and their trade is well diversified. According to 'conventional wisdom' economies of this type tend be floaters rather than restrict fluctuations in exchange rates.[15] It is also important to notice that although many countries, in particular developing countries, are moving towards more flexible exchange rate arrangements, the rich EC economies are driving hard towards monetary unification. On the other hand, the EMS countries are very open in terms of the real sector, and terms of trade fluctuations have been very low in the EMS economies. Traditionally economies of this type are considered to restrict fluctuations in exchange rates.[16]

Overall the country characteristics do not help very much to explain the countries' choice of exchange rate regime. It might be that the choices are based on some other factors, economical or political, rather than those analysed here. The results in Melvin (1985) indicate that current or very recent economic conditions may matter: the greater the recent foreign price shocks the more likely a float, and the greater the recent domestic money shocks the more likely a peg. Microeconomic implications, like the transaction costs or risks due to fluctuations in exchange rates, may motivate the monetary unification in the EC. Also the arguments by Feldstein (1992) should be taken seriously; it is possible that the choices are based more on political pressure or fads than on economic grounds.[17]

The evidence in our study can also be interpreted to support indirectly the view of new classical macroeconomics. Since the country characteristics studied here do not help very much to explain of the choice of exchange rate regime and since in some cases the observed choices are opposite to the predictions of conventional theory, one may infer that this provides indirect evidence for the view that (in the long run) the exchange rate regime does not have any real effects.[18] The evidence may also suggest that the way in which exchange rate policy is conducted given a chosen regime and the role or independence of the central bank are more important and relevant issues than the exchange rate regime as such.

Is there any sense in the analyses we have performed in the study? When we studied the predictions of our models, i.e. we compared the models' predictions with the prevailing exchange rate practices on 31 December 1991, we observed the following pressures. First, Italy, Spain, the United Kingdom, and Bangladesh should have floating exchange rates. Second, Israel, New Zealand, and Switzerland should adopt more rigid practices than their current ones. This is also true for many developing countries which float. Third, according to our models Finland is the only country which should join group C which consists mainly of the EMS countries. We will leave the reader with these predictions on the future.

## Appendix

### *Countries in the Sample*

Group A (country pegs to a single currency): Antigua and Barbuda, Argentina, Bahamas, Barbados, Belize, Djibouti, Dominica, Ethiopia, Grenada, Liberia, Nicaragua, Oman, Panama, St Lucia, St Vincent and the Grenadines, Sudan, Suriname, Syria, Trinidad and Tobago, Yemen (all of these countries peg to the US dollar); Benin, Burkina Faso,

Cameroon, Central African Republic, Chad, Comoros, Congo, Côte d'Ivoire, Equatorial Guinea, Gabon, Mali, Niger, Senegal, Togo (all of these countries peg to the French franc); Bhutan, Lesotho, Swaziland, Yugoslavia. Total of 38 countries.

Group B (country pegs to a currency composite): Burundi, Iran, Libya, Myanmar, Rwanda, Seychelles (all of these countries peg to the SDR); Algeria, Austria, Bangladesh, Botswana, Cape Verde, Cyprus, Czechoslovakia, Fiji, Finland, Hungary, Iceland, Jordan, Kenya, Kuwait, Malawi, Malaysia, Malta, Mauritius, Morocco, Nepal, Norway, Papua New Guinea, Solomon Islands, Sweden, Tanzania, Thailand, Tonga, Uganda, Vanuatu, Western Samoa, Zimbabwe (all of these countries peg to a currency composite other than the SDR). Total of 37 countries.

Group C (limited flexibility in terms of a single currency or a group of currencies): Bahrain, Qatar, Saudi Arabia, United Arab Emirates (these countries are classified under the title of limited flexibility in terms of a single currency); Belgium (Luxembourg is aggregated with Belgium), Denmark, France, Germany, Republic of Ireland, Italy, Netherlands, Spain, United Kingdom (these countries belong to the EMS). Total of 13 countries.

Group D (currency is adjusted according to a set of indicators or other managed floating): Chile, Colombia, Madagascar, Zambia (these countries adjust their exchange rates according to a set of indicators); People's Republic of China, Costa Rica, Ecuador, Egypt, Greece, Honduras, India, Indonesia, Israel, Korea, Mauritania, Mexico, Pakistan, Poland, Portugal, Romania, Singapore, Somalia, Sri Lanka, Tunisia, Turkey (these countries are classified under the title of other managed floating). Total of 25 countries.

Group E (independently floating): Afghanistan, Australia, Bolivia, Brazil, Canada, Dominican Republic, El Salvador, Gambia, Ghana, Guatemala, Guyana, Haiti, Jamaica, Japan, Lebanon, New Zealand, Nigeria, Paraguay, Peru, Philippines, Sierra Leone, Republic of South Africa, Switzerland, United States, Uruguay, Venezuela, Zaire. Total of 27 countries.

The exchange rate arrangements are according to the situation on 31 December 1991. In the estimations Germany is classified either in class C or in class E.

When compared the position on 31 March 1982 to the one on 31 March 1992, the following countries have moved to a more rigid exchange rate regime (Group R): Argentina, Greece, Iceland, Israel, Morocco, Spain, Thailand, United Kingdom, Western Samoa, Yugoslavia. Total of 10 countries.

The following countries have moved to a more flexible exchange rate system (Group F): Afghanistan, Australia, Bolivia, Brazil, Burundi, Chile, People's Republic of China, Dominican Republic, Ecuador, Egypt, El Salvador, Gambia, Ghana, Guatemala, Guinea, Guinea-Bissau, Guyana, Haiti, Honduras, Indonesia, Jamaica, Laos, Libya, Madagascar, Maldives, Mauritius, Nepal, New Zealand, Nigeria, Paraguay, Peru, Philippines, Romania, Rwanda, Sao Tome, Sierra Leone, Singapore, Somalia, Sudan, Tunisia, Uganda, Uruguay, Venezuela, Vietnam, Zaire, Zambia. Total of 46 countries.

Since data were not available for all of group F countries, these economies are not included in the analysis of sections 3.3–3.5 of the study. For the countries included in the sample, see groups A–E above.

### Definition of Variables and Data Sources

The size of a country is measured by GDP in US dollars. The average of the annual observations covering the period 1987–90 is used to even out the contribution of cyclical fluctuations and possible excessive movements in exchange rates. The exchange rate is the average of each year. Source of the raw data: *International Financial Statistics* (IFS). Variable: GDP.

Degree of economic development is measured by GDP per capita in US dollars. The average of the annual observations covering the period of 1987–90 is used. Source of the raw data: IFS. Variable: GDPCAP.

Openness of the goods producing sector of the economy is measured by the ratio of foreign trade (imports plus exports) to GDP. The average of the annual observations covering the period of 1987–90 is used. Source of the raw data: IFS. Variable: OPEN.

Degree of international financial integration is measured by the ratio of foreign assets of the banking system to the money supply. The average of the annual observations covering the period 1987–90 is used. Source of the raw data: IFS, line 21 (foreign assets of the banking system) and line 34 (money supply). Variable: FIN.

Geographic concentration of foreign trade is measured by the percentage of the three largest export destinations in 1987–8. Source: *The Economist Book of Vital World Statistics* (1990). No data were available for Antigua and Barbuda, Bhutan, St Lucia, Swaziland, or Botswana. Variable: DIVGEO.

Commodity concentration of foreign trade is measured by the Hirschmann index of exports for 1988. The index is normalized to take values ranging from 0 to 100 (maximum concentration). Sources: *Handbook of International Trade and Development Statistics* (1990), Table 4.5, is the main source; for some countries *Direction of Trade*

*Statistics* (1991) is used. No data were available for Antigua and Barbuda, Bhutan, Djibouti, Swaziland, Botswana, Czechoslovakia, Tanzania, People's Republic of China, Poland, Romania, Afghanistan, or Lebanon. Variable: DIVCOM.

Fluctuations in the terms of trade is measured by the coefficient of variation of terms of trade over the period of 1980–90. Quarterly data are used when available. Source of the raw data: IFS. Data were available for Liberia, Trinidad and Tobago, Burkina Faso, Central African Republic, Côte d'Ivoire, Senegal, Togo, Austria, Bangladesh, Cyprus, Finland, Iceland, Jordan, Kenya, Malawi, Malaysia, Malta, Mauritius, Norway, Sweden, Thailand, Zimbabwe, Belgium, Denmark, France, Germany, Republic of Ireland, Italy, Netherlands, Spain, United Kingdom, Greece, India, Israel, Korea, Pakistan, Sri Lanka, Turkey, Brazil, Canada, El Salvador, Japan, New Zealand, Philippines, Switzerland, United States. Variable: TERMS.

Dummy variable to indicate the inconvertibility of a currency obtains the value of 1 for the countries with inconvertible currency and the value of 0 otherwise. Source: *Exchange Arrangements and Exchange Restrictions*. Variable: INCONV.

# Notes

We received helpful comments from participants at the CEPR/Bank of Finland Conference on Exchange Rate Policies in the Nordic Countries, 21–22 September 1992, Helsinki, Finland, and at seminars at the Central Bank Policy Department/Bank of Finland, University of Helsinki, and Finnish Postgraduate Programme in Economics. Special thanks go to Bernard Delbecque and Alan Sutherland, our discussants at the CEPR/Bank of Finland Conference, Alberto Giovannini, Thorvaldur Gylfason, Antti Suvanto, and Charles Wyplosz for insightful views. Carolina Sierimo provided excellent reseach assistance. We gratefully acknowledge financial support from the Bank of Finland. The views expressed here are our own and do not necessarily coincide with those of the Bank of Finland or CEPR.

1. Stockman (1983, 1987) provide an excellent discussion on the equilibrium approach to exchange rate determination.
2. As in Dornbusch (1976).
3. De Grauwe (1992) provides a nice introduction to all of these approaches. Agenor (1991) gives a good review of the credibility aspect.
4. Notice that the information in Table 3.1 concerns all the countries classified by the IMF. According to Avhegli et al. (1991) the same pattern also holds for the group of developing countries.
5. Dreyer (1978) uses a data set of 88 developing countries, Bosco (1987) a set of 92, and Savvides (1990) a set of 39. Heller (1978) analyses a data set of 86 developing and industrialized countries, Holden et al. (1979) a set of 75, and Melvin (1985) a set of 64. Edison and Melvin (1990) provide a survey on the previous literature.
6. An alternative measure of the degree of international financial integration might be the difference between domestic and foreign interest rates. This measure might, however, be quite sensitive to speculative periods. Moreover, it is not available for as many countries as the measure used here.

7. Difficulties in collecting taxes might be a powerful incentive to pursue high inflation, which often can be sustained only in a floating exchange rate regime.
8. Group C is dominated by the EMS countries. The empirical analyses were also done so that group C consists only of the EMS economies. The results do not differ from those reported here for the larger group C.
9. Historical fluctuations in the effective exchange rate of a country would be an alternative measure of the flexibility of an exchange rate regime. The official IMF classification may depend to a certain extent on wishful thinking: some countries classify themselves as having more rigid regimes than they do have in practice.
10. The analyses were also done so that we omitted the ten countries which announce a freely floating exchange rate (group E) and at the same time claim an inconvertible currency. The results do not differ from those including all countries.
11. On logit and probit models see, for instance, Maddala (1983) and Greene (1992).
12. The results in Heller (1978), Melvin (1985), and Bosco (1987) also support this view.
13. Holden et al. (1979) obtain the same results. In Bosco (1987) and Savvides (1990) the commodity diversification of trade is not statistically significant; in Dreyer (1978) it is statistically significant but opposite to the hypothesis presented here.
14. In the previous empirical studies the contribution of these country characteristics is mixed. Only the view that countries with an open real sector tend to restrict fluctuations in exchange rates is supported quite consistently; Savvides (1990) is the only one to reject this view.
15. However, these observations are consistent with the views of Kenen (1969) and Giersch (1973).
16. The results concerning the EMS countries might be somewhat biased due to simultaneity. Monetary integration may have affected the openness, diversification of trade and fluctuations in the terms of trade of these economies. In this study we do not have any opportunity to tackle the possible simultaneity problem.
17. Recall also that because of simultaneity we do not have inflation differentials as an explanatory variable. Control of inflation has been a major factor in European monetary integration.
18. Stockman (1983) studies also empirically the relationship between the variability of real exchange rates and the exchange rate system. His results provide some evidence against the neutrality hypothesis: flexible exchange rate systems are associated with greater variability of real exchange rates.

# References

Agenor, P.-R. (1991), 'Credibility and exchange rate management in developing countries', International Monetary Fund, Research Department, Working Paper No. 91/87.

Avhegli, B. B., Khan, M. S. and Montiel, P. J. (1991), 'Exchange rate policy in developing countries: Some analytical issues', International Monetary Fund, Occasional Paper No. 78.

Bosco, L. (1987), 'Determinants of the exchange rate regimes in LDCs: Some empirical evidence', *Economic Notes*, **16** (1), 119–43.

De Grauwe, P. (1992), *The Economics of Monetary Integration*, Oxford University Press, Oxford.

Dornbusch, R. (1976), 'Expectations and exchange rate dynamics', *Journal of Political Economy*, **84** (6), 1161–76.

Dreyer, J. S. (1978), 'Determinants of exchange-rate regimes for currencies of developing countries: Some preliminary results', *World Development*, **6** (2), 437–45.

Edison, H. J. and Melvin, M. (1990), 'The determinants and implications of the choice of an exchange rate system', in William S. Haraf and Thomas D. Willett (eds), *Monetary Policy for a Volatile Global Economy*, The AEI Press, pp. 1–44.

Feldstein, M. (1992), 'The case against EMU', *The Economist*, 13–19 June, pp. 19–22.

Giersch, H. (1973), 'On the desirable degree of flexibility of exchange rates', *Weltwirtschaftliches Archiv*, **109** (2), 191–213.

Greene, W. H. (1992), LIMDEP, Version 6.0. Econometric Software, Inc.

Heller, H. R. (1978), 'Determinants of exchange rate practices', *Journal of Money, Credit, and Banking*, **10** (3), 308–21.

Holden, P., Holden, M. and Suss, E. C. (1979), 'The determinants of exchange rate flexibility: An empirical investigation', *Review of Economics and Statistics*, **61** (3), 327–33.

Kenen, P. B. (1969), 'The theory of optimum currency areas: An eclectic view', in R. Mundell and A. Swoboda (eds), *Monetary Problems of the International Economy*, University of Chicago Press, Chicago, pp. 41–60.

Maddala, G. S. (1983), *Limited-Dependent and Qualitative Variables in Econometrics*, Cambridge University Press, Cambridge.

McKinnon, R. I. (1979), *Money in International Exchange: The Convertible Currency System*, Oxford University Press, Oxford.

Melvin, M. (1985), 'The choice of an exchange rate system and macroeconomic stability', *Journal of Money, Credit, and Banking*, **17** (4), 467–78.

Pikkarainen, P. (1991a), 'Behavior of the open economy firm: The basket peg regime', University of Helsinki, Department of Economics, Discussion Paper No. 307.

Pikkarainen, P. (1991b), 'International portfolio diversification: The basket-peg regime', *Journal of International Money and Finance*, **10** (3), 432–42.

Savvides, A. (1990), 'Real exchange rate variability and the choice of exchange rate regime by developing countries', *Journal of International Money and Finance*, **9** (4), 440–54.

Stockman, A. C. (1983), 'Real exchange rates under alternative nominal exchange rate systems', *Journal of International Money and Finance*, **2** (2), 147–66.

Stockman, A. C. (1987), 'The equilibrium approach to exchange rates', *Economic Review, Federal Reserve Bank of Richmond*, **73** (2), 12–30.

## Data Sources

*Direction of Trade Statistics* (1991), International Monetary Fund.

*Exchange Arrangements and Exchange Restrictions*, Annual Report (various issues), International Monetary Fund.

*Handbook of International Trade and Development Statistics* (1990), United Nations Conference on Trade and Development.

*International Financial Statistics* (various issues), International Monetary Fund.

*The Economist Book of Vital World Statistics* (1990), The Economist.

# Discussion

## Bernard Delbecque

*Université Catholique de Louvain and International Monetary Fund*

I found this an interesting paper. Nevertheless, in my view, two aspects of the analysis need to be qualified. One concerns the discussion about the expected effects of country characteristics on the choice of an exchange rate system. The other pertains to the interpretation to give to the empirical findings of the paper.

## Conventional Wisdom

The authors argue that, according to 'conventional wisdom', large and rich countries with well diversified trade and integrated financial markets should be floaters, whereas countries with open real sector and low volatility of terms of trade would be better off with a more rigid exchange rate arrangement. I have some reservation concerning this point. Indeed, I believe that there is no 'conventional wisdom' in this area of economic theory. The point is that country characteristics influence the choice of an exchange rate system in several ways, and consequently, it is difficult to feature an unambiguous relationship between a country's structural characteristics and its optimal exchange rate regime. This can be illustrated by discussing how trade diversification and openness influence the choice of a country's exchange rate regime.

The authors appropriately indicate that export diversification reduces the necessity to change the exchange rate frequently, as was suggested by Kenen (1969). However, they argue that, according to 'conventional wisdom', countries with well diversified exports should opt to be floaters, as export diversification will allow them to experience greater stability in foreign exchange earnings. It is unclear why 'conventional wisdom' gives no support to Kenen's view.

A similar line of reasoning applies for the openness of the country. The authors argue that the more open the economy, the stronger the case for fixing the exchange rate because the more vulnerable it is to changes in the economic developments in its foreign trading partners. Prima facie, this argument appears to be of importance. However, the literature has also recognized that openness increases the effectiveness of an exchange rate adjustment in stabilizing output in the face of external shocks, such as movements in the foreign price level. According to this view, open economies should find exchange rate flexibility more attractive than closed economies. Thus, openness per se does not unambiguously determine the choice of exchange rate regimes.

## Empirical Cross-Country Evidence

Against this background, it is not surprising that the paper provides weak empirical support for the 'conventional wisdom', as it shows that (i) country characteristics have hardly any power in explaining the choice between fixed and flexible rates; (ii) small and poor developing countries exporting only few commodities have moved towards more flexible exchange rate arrangements since the mid-1970s; and (iii) large and rich EMS countries with well diversified trade and integrated financial markets have opted for monetary union.

The authors interpret this as evidence that, in the long run, the exchange rate regime does not have any real effects. I think that this conclusion goes beyond the scope of the study. Instead, I would just conclude that the empirical evidence shows that country characteristics do not matter. On this basis, we can engage into a discussion on the factors that should be viewed as relevant to the choice of an appropriate exchange rate regime. In my view, those factors are to be found, first, in country prevailing macroeconomic 'circumstances'—as opposed to structural characteristics—, second, in recent developments in economic theory, and lastly, in changes in the global economic environment.

The importance of macroeconomic circumstances can be illustrated by focusing on developing countries. It is quite clear that since the mid-1970s, many of those countries have shifted away from pegging towards more flexible exchange rate management because of severe macroeconomic problems (high inflation and current account deficit). They found that greater exchange rate flexibility would enable them to maintain international competitiveness and ensure sustainability of their balance of payments.

Among the factors that economic research has recently highlighted as being important in the choice of a currency system, one can mention (i) the nature and origin of the exogenous shocks to the country, (ii) the degree of real wage flexibility, and (iii) reputational considerations. One important point in this literature is that a commitment to fix the exchange rate for an extended period can help provide a strong anchor for price stability. In the aftermath of this research, a number of countries, including the United Kingdom and Spain, opted for participation in the exchange rate mechanism of the EMS.

Finally, since the collapse of the narrow-band EMS, it has become quite clear that something important has changed in Europe. Governments have discovered that their commitment to defend fixed parities could be reduced to nothing by a firm consensus in the financial markets. This fundamental change in the global economic environment will make it more difficult for governments to favor fixed rates, even if the case for exchange rate stability can be defended in narrow economic terms.

In view of all this, it is not surprising to find little empirical support for the country-characteristics approach. Clearly, the choice of an exchange rate regime bears on other broader considerations. In that respect, I agree with the authors that mini-skirts can be followed by maxis. Why? Because any exchange rate arrangement that appear good at one thing or one time (e.g. exerting discipline on governments when inflation is high) is likely to be bad in different circumstances (e.g. protecting monetary policy against financial markets speculation). Against this background, I would suggest that more work be done to study how prevailing macroeconomic 'circumstances' and recent changes in the global economic environment affect exchange rate management. Hopefully, this would help rewriting a much-needed economic rule-book for the conduct of exchange rate policy.

## Reference

Kenen, P. B. (1969), 'The theory of optimum currency areas: An eclectic view', in R. Mundell and A. Swoboda (eds), *Monetary Problems of the International Economy*, University of Chicago Press, Chicago, pp. 41–60.

# Discussion

## Alan Sutherland
*University of York and CEPR*

The main conclusion of this paper is that there are few statistically significant factors which explain the choice of exchange rate regime. The only two factors which the authors identify as being significant are the size of the country and the diversification of its exports. In fact I do not find the authors' negative results too surprising. Before explaining my reasons for reaching this conclusion it will be useful to give a brief outline of some of the theoretical issues which arise in the discussion of choice of exchange rate regime.

The first criterion which is typically considered in the theoretical debate on exchange rate regimes is the ability of a particular regime to insulate against shocks. The well known result is that flexible exchange rates are good at dealing with shocks to real goods demand while fixed rates are good at dealing with shocks to money demand. So if a country is subject to demand shocks more than monetary shocks it should float—and vice versa.

The second approach to the choice of regime is closely related. It is the 'optimal currency area' approach. This says that if two countries

1.  are subject to the same type of shocks (i.e. the shocks are symmetric),
2.  have relatively free factor mobility and flexible factor prices, and
3.  have a high degree of mutual trade,

then a fixed exchange rate (and a common currency) is likely to be optimal.

This approach is essentially about finding countries for which demand shocks are relatively unimportant—either because the shocks are symmetric or because they are easily absorbed by the real economy without exchange rate adjustments.

The third theoretical issue involved in the choice of regime is the question of inflation. The desire to reduce inflation is seen as a reason for a high inflation country choosing to join a fixed rate system. The reasoning being that increased credibility and/or a recession caused by loss of competitiveness will reduce inflation to the level of the centre country.

That is my brief outline of the theory and I think the criteria listed by the authors can be fitted into this framework in one place or another. For instance, the diversification of exports affects the degree to which a country is subject to demand shocks—as does the degree of openness and the volatility of the terms of trade.

There are three basic reasons why I am not surprised by the authors' results. First, for a number of the theoretical criteria for choosing a regime the theory is not conclusive on which regime is supported. For instance, some economists would argue that the more open an economy is the more susceptible it is to demand shocks and therefore it is more suited to flexible exchange rates. But others would argue that very open economies are very vulnerable to shocks which come direct from the foreign exchange market and therefore open economies are better with fixed exchange rates.

Another example of ambiguity is the question of real wage flexibility. The optimum currency area approach suggests countries with flexible labour markets should fix their exchange rate. But it can also be argued (as the authors suggest) that fixing can be seen as a good way of changing real wage behaviour. This sort of theoretical ambiguity is also evident in the authors' own description of the theory on the question of export diversification.

If the theory is ambiguous in this way it is not surprising that governments adopt a variety of responses. It is therefore not surprising that the observed choices of governments do not show a strong correlation to any particular theory.

The second reason why I am not surprised by the authors' results is that I think they have left out some important explanatory factors. The most important of which is inflation.

If one considers the United Kingdom's entry into the ERM, it is clear from government statements that the decision to adopt a fixed rate was dominated by the desire to control inflation. Government ministers repeatedly asserted that the ERM parity was the centre-piece of the Government's anti-inflation policy. I am sure the same attitude to the ERM is (or was) shared by a number of other ERM members.

It must be the case, therefore, that the desire to control inflation is one of the main factors determining the actual choice of regime by a number of the European countries in the authors' sample. This must be a factor which overrides the other factors that the authors consider.

I realize that the authors do discuss inflation as a possible criterion and I take their point that it is difficult to determine, in an appropriate quantitative way, just how it fits in. However, I do think that it would have been possible to make some qualitative points in their conclusions.

The third reason for not being surprised by the authors' results concerns the global environment in which countries make their choices. In the Gold Standard and Bretton Woods periods it was possible to talk about there being a straight choice between fixing and floating. There was a single global system of fixed exchange rates which countries could join or not join as they chose. Nowadays there is a much wider range of choices. This is not just in terms of the degree of flexibility, as the authors consider, it is also in terms of which system to join.

As an example of this, the United Kingdom can choose to be a member of the ERM, or it could be a member of some informal dollar standard, or it could float. The United Kingdom and other EC countries therefore have a wider choice of regimes than non-EC countries. This is likely to affect their decision about floating or fixing relative to similar countries which do not have the option of joining the ERM. I suspect that the ERM option may be encouraging EC countries to fix while similar non-EC countries choose to float because nothing as good as the ERM is available to them. Thus, a fragmented global system is producing a fragmented response from governments.

# 4

# Monetary Policy in Denmark in the Last 10 Years

## Peter Erling Nielsen
*Institute of Economics, University of Copenhagen*

## 4.1    Introduction: A Brief Overview of Policies and Developments[1]

The title of this paper—chosen by the organizers—is extremely apt, as Danish economic policy was changed fundamentally in the second half of September 1982 by the then incoming government. The heritage was an economy in a difficult phase: high inflation, growing unemployment, and an economic growth that was fuelled by government spending and deficits. The balance of payments had drifted into heavy deficits, as competitiveness had been eroded by two-digit increases in wages and prices. The currency had been devalued repeatedly even though Denmark joined the ERM in the EMS in 1979. The nominal and real interest rates were among the highest in the OECD.

The fiscal stance was changed (see Figure 4.1) as spending was cut and taxes increased, an incomes policy was introduced (the escalator clause was abandoned by an act of law) and the government made a strong commitment *never* to devalue again.

It was hardly believed that monetary policy—that had been assigned to external stabilization since the late 1960s—in itself could do much to stabilize the economy and bring down interest rates. But the decision to maintain the exchange rate vis-à-vis the ECU in the March 1983 realignment within the EMS and the partial liberalization of the capital controls some weeks later bolstered confidence. Interest rates fell dramatically (see Figure 4.2).

The outcome of this bout of adjustments surprised most observers (and the government itself). Growth picked up in 1984, now driven by private spending, unemployment decreased, and inflation rose again from 1986.

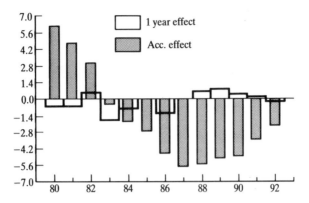

**Figure 4.1**   Effects of fiscal policy. The 1 year bars show the effects—measured by the change in real GNP—of the contemporary fiscal policy, i.e. the effects of the 1983 fiscal policy changes on the 1983 GNP. The accumulated effects bars demonstrate the effects on real GNP by all fiscal changes since 1970 up to the present year, i.e. the impact on 1983 GNP by all fiscal measures from 1970 to 1983. It is obvious that the size and distribution of the effects depend critically on the econometrical model employed. No 1993 data have been released yet. *Source*: Ministry of Finance, Fiscal Report 1992

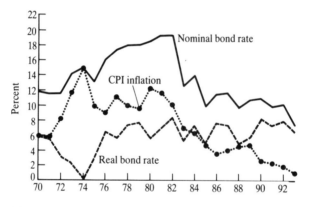

**Figure 4.2**   Nominal and real interest rates. Nominal interest rates have come down but the real interest rate has hardly changed

The external deficit widened each year from 1984 until 1987 (Figure 4.3). It is beyond the scope of this presentation fully to discuss the fact that the policy mix of the day could be that expansionary.[2] A possible line of explanation could be, however, that falling interest rates (higher share and bond prices) and a general feeling of optimism led to higher prices

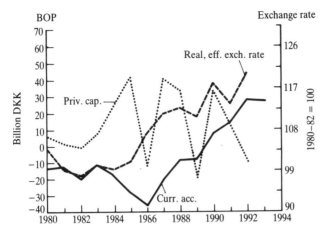

**Figure 4.3** BOP current account and private capital inflows. Real, effective exchange rate from J P Morgan: World Finance Markets. As can be seen, the change of the balance of payments current account from 1986 to 1992 was of a magnitude of about Danish kroner (DKK) billion 70. Private capital inflows have been—with the critical year of 1986 as an exception—of an adequate size

of capital goods and houses (Figure 4.4) which, again, pulled up private consumption.

The economic expansion was eventually killed off, firstly by traditional fiscal measures and rising real interest rates and secondly by the 1986 tax

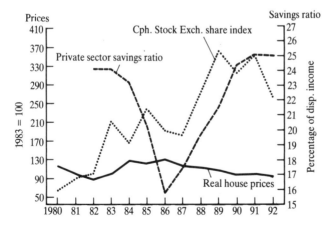

**Figure 4.4** House prices, share prices and private savings. No consistent savings ratio data available prior to 1982

reform[3] that increased after tax interest rates for all households. The reaction, as measured by the private savings ratio (Figure 4.4), has been quite dramatic—the highly indebted household sector appear to be reducing their loans to the financial sector. Growth stopped, unemployment rose, inflation came down and competitiveness was restored by cuts in employers' social contributions (not reflected in the real, effective exchange rate shown in Figure 4.3). The BOP current account went into surplus.

Two supplementary factors behind this story of a reasonable successful development should be mentioned. In the late 1980s the heavy investments in oil and gas production and distribution started to pay off as production rose quickly, and the unification of Germany appears to have changed the structure of German imports in a way that suits Danish firms well; Danish market shares have increased.

The title of the paper is also well chosen in the sense that the general economic policy has been modified since the change of government in January 1993. The incoming majority social democratic led cabinet is working to increase government and private consumption to boost growth (Figure 4.5) and fight unemployment. Export is growing slowly due to low foreign demand and real appreciations of the Danish kroner (DKK). Many kinds of incentive-orientated reforms are still on the political agenda but the administration appear to believe that unemployment has risen well above any conceivable value of the NAIRU. The Fiscal Bill for (calendar) 1993 included some fiscal stimuli but a radical change of fiscal policy is expected for 1994.

The importance of observing the Maastricht criteria for government debt and deficit is given less weight as a consequence of the breakdown of the EMS—because of the similar development in other European countries.

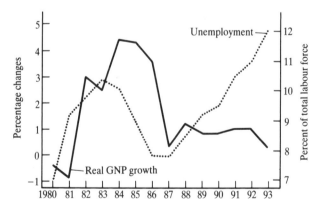

**Figure 4.5**  Growth and unemployment

## 4.2    Problems in the Late 1970s

In principle, Danish authorities have always believed in fixed exchange rates and free capital movements. But the fact is that the DKK was devalued repeatedly (within the Snake and the EMS) up to 1982, and currency regulations were only liberal when it came to short-term business transactions and long-term *borrowing* abroad. Even though, monetary policy had been external orientated since a rather painful currency crisis in the Spring of 1969. If private capital flows/the exchange rate are the goal variables, interest rates are the obvious choice as indicators. It appears, however, that the actual nature of the regime was not completely realized until the beginning of the 1980s when the need to bring down the interest rates was felt to be imperative and the incoming government decided to liberalize as much as possible.[4]

In the 1970s the large and important bond market—in which the mortgage credit institutions fund themselves when financing housing, agriculture and industry and where the government have been active since the public sector developed a borrowing requirement in the mid-1970s—was functioning freely as the Nationalbank gave up manipulating long-term interest rates in 1969. But the banking sector was constrained by a *credit ceiling arrangement*, the purpose of which was to suppress consumer spending and to promote business borrowing abroad without pushing bank rates 'too' high.

In the end, few believed that the system was, in fact, dichotomizing the financial markets. The interest rates rose to record levels (Figure 4.2) as a result of an ever-present fear that the DKK was soon to be devalued (again) and the credit ceiling arrangement and the interest rate controls were suspended. Instead, business borrowing abroad became subsidized.

From 1975 government finances were in deficit and the borrowing requirements (and the debt) rose dramatically until 1984, when the debt/GNP ratio levelled out at about 55%. According to an informal rule, 90–110% of each year's deficit was covered by sales of government bonds and bills. This added to the pressures to bring down nominal and real interest rates—or rather, to decrease the interest rate differential vis-à-vis the Deutschmark (DM) (Figure 4.6). The objective of monetary policy was from that movement clearly to stabilize the capital flows only. No 'degrees of freedom' were available for domestic purposes. When that was realized, the road was paved for the reorientation of the entire economic policy.

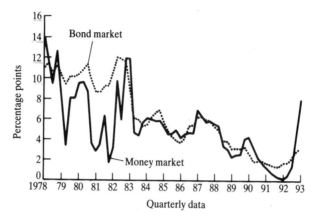

**Figure 4.6**   Interest rate differentials (DKK vis-à-vis DM)

## 4.3   1982–93

As can be seen from Figures 4.2 and 4.6, much had to be, and was in fact, done. It appears that the overall strategy has succeeded to a reasonable degree, even though the DM differentials have not been eliminated completely yet (an important point to be discussed below).

The details of monetary management may be grouped into three areas.

### 4.2.1   *Exchange Rate and Capital Controls Policies*

As mentioned the official Danish attitude has always been that the Kingdom was best served by participating in a fixed exchange rate system—and given the size and the openness of the economy that is hardly worthwhile debating. So given the membership of the EEC, it was an obvious choice first to join the Snake and later to become a founding member of the EMS. The controversial question, however, is the degree of hardness within the system. There has, to the best of my knowledge, never been official declaration[5] or clarification about Danish exchange rate policy but since late 1982 the policy appears to have been (see Table 4.1) to stick to the ECU value of the DKK when more complex realignments within the EMS were taking place and to follow the DM during the one-sided adjustments. Lately—and certainly during the turmoil of 1992—one may speak of a genuine DM peg.

As is obvious, movements within the EMS band are also of import-ance—but clearly, the exchange rate has been stabilized, see Figure 4.7

Table 4.1  Major realignments in the EMS since 1982

| | DM | French franc | Dutch gilder | Belgian franc | Italian lira | Irish punt | Spanish peseta | United Kingdom pound | Spanish peseta | Danish krone |
|---|---|---|---|---|---|---|---|---|---|---|
| 22 Feb 1982 | — | — | — | -8·5 | — | — | □ | □ | □ | -3·0 |
| 14 Jun 1982 | +4·25 | -5·75 | +4·25 | — | -2·75 | — | □ | □ | □ | — |
| 21 Mar 1983 | +5·5 | -2·5 | +3·5 | +1·5 | -2·5 | -3·5 | □ | □ | □ | +2·5 |
| 22 Jul 1985 | +2·0 | +2·0 | +2·0 | +2·0 | -6·0 | +2·0 | □ | □ | □ | +2·0 |
| 7 Apr 1986 | +3·0 | -3·0 | +3·0 | +1·0 | — | — | □ | □ | □ | +1·0 |
| 4 Aug 1986 | — | — | — | — | — | -8·0 | □ | □ | □ | — |
| 12 Jan 1987 | +3·0 | — | +3·0 | +2·0 | -6·8 | — | □ | □ | □ | — |
| 14 Sep 1992 | — | — | — | — | ■ | — | — | — | — | — |
| 17 Sep 1992 | — | — | — | — | □ | — | -5·0 | ■ | — | — |
| 23 Nov 1992 | — | — | — | — | □ | — | -6·0 | □ | -6·0 | — |
| 1 Feb 1993 | — | — | — | — | — | -10·0 | — | □ | — | — |
| 1 Aug 1993 | | | | | Final breakdown | | | | | |

— No change  
□ Not participating  
■ Leaving

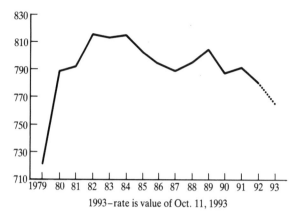

**Figure 4.7**   DKK vis-à-vis ECU (yearly average)

(some details concerning movements within the band are to be discussed below).

Gabriela Mundaca raised, in her comments during the conference, the profound—and somewhat difficult—question which exchange rate system would best serve Danish exporters. She indicated that a DM peg may be too demanding as Danish exports to Germany only amounts to about 25% of total exports. Pegging to the DM can be a tough policy and may have cost some output and employment, but the benefits—low inflation and a low interest rate differential—makes these sacrifices (made in the 1980s) worthwhile. The Danish Phillips curve is believed to be almost vertical at least in the medium term, and the DM peg is seen as a simple and well defined bench-mark.

### 4.2.2   *Direct control of banks' assets and liabilities*

As mentioned, a ceiling on bank lending was introduced in the early 1970s. Banks were allowed at certain intervals incremental growth—the rate being common to all—in their loan portfolios. The effectiveness of that instrument—given its design and the availability of other sources of credit—was the object of much debate. Was one putting an effective brake on lending and/or were credit flows distorted with higher profits and less competition in the banking sector as the only lasting result?[6]

As is obvious[7] credit ceilings would have to be supplemented by some kind of interest rate control to secure genuine credit *rationing*. So that was introduced in Denmark as in many other countries with similar systems.

Growing discontent with the resulting lack of competition and the many—often sophisticated—ways of evasion in combination with a low demand for loans led to the above-mentioned suspension of the credit ceiling arrangement in 1980. When demand picked up in 1983, a tougher version was revived. Now the object of control was the actual amount of credits, and not, as in the previous version, granted credits.[8] In order to introduce some degree of competition, banks enjoying a growth in deposits above average were allowed to expand their lending faster than the policy-determined macrotarget while banks with slowly growing liabilities had to stay below the target value.[9] The Nationalbank punished banks—by making their borrowing with the Bank more expensive—that went above the threshold value. But it was soon realized that one had created an engine that produced extraordinary high growth in deposits and M2 (see Figure 4.8), as all units endeavoured to stay above the average. Short-term interest rates were being kept artificially high as well.

The June 1985 (Table 4.2) change of capital controls gave the final blow to all kinds of credit rationing as demand for loans—even in DKK— could now be satisfied from abroad. The Nationalbank, however, still wanted some emergency brake on growth in banks' assets and liabilities, so a new instrument with the impressive sounding title of 'The Market Orientated Surveillance System' was introduced. What it all amounted to was, in fact, a marginal reserve requirement arrangement, based upon growth in deposits. When a certain threshold value was reached, banks would deposit with the Nationalbank a fraction of their excess deposits. Interest was paid on accumulated required reserves with a rate equal to the money market rate,[10] but this level could be, and was, reduced when money growth was considered unacceptable.

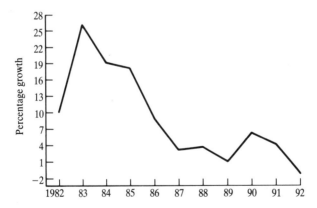

**Figure 4.8**   Annual growth, M2

**Table 4.2** Major changes in the capital controls since 1982

| | |
|---|---|
| Starting point, 1982 | Free trading credits (in and out). Foreigners may buy private Danish bonds and shares. Danes not allowed to buy foreign shares and bonds (some exceptions) Eligible firms may take limited loans abroad. Many restrictions on direct investments (in/out), but special licences often granted. |
| May 1983 | Danes may buy foreign bonds, but not short-term papers (commercial papers, treasury bills, etc.) Foreigners may buy Danish government bonds. Eligible firms may loan abroad without limits. |
| January 1984 | Danes may buy foreign shares. |
| June 1985 | Higher limits for direct investments without licence. Firms may borrow abroad freely. |
| October 1988 | The remaining restrictions lifted: all Danes—households and businesses—may take loans and make deposits in foreign currency; no restrictions on transactions in bills and papers. |
| January 1992 | No restrictions on banks' net positions in foreign currency—never seen as part of the currency regulations, as non-DKK positions have always been free. |

The purpose of this arrangement remained unclear, at least to me, as a required reserves scheme can, in principle, hardly be more 'market orientated' than a credit ceiling, and a mild version would hardly put a brake on anything, certainly not on huge capital outflows during a currency crisis. The least worst line of explanation of why it was introduced at all, appears to be that one wanted to remind banks of the importance of not buying too many bonds when deposits grew fast instead of reducing borrowing with the Nationalbank.[11]

The Market Orientated Surveillance Scheme faded away when money growth slowed in the late 1980s (Figures 4.8 and 4.9). The scheme was suspended in 1988, and finally abolished in 1991.

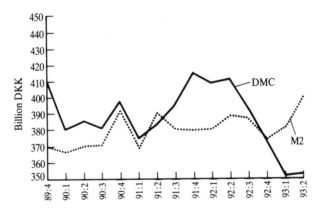

**Figure 4.9** Domestic money creation and M2

The Nationalbank takes a continued interest in the size and structure of bank portfolios—and in the way in which domestic factors contribute to the developments in credit and money—as it has commenced publishing times series of the domestic money creation (DMC).[12]

The interest shown for a concept as DMC can hardly be seen as a prelude to any future direct management of banks' assets and liabilities, but rather as an attempt to construct an indicator of total Danish credit expansion to be used by the EMI and a future European Central Bank, should Denmark eventually join the EMU. It can be seen from Figure 4.9 that M2 and DMC may diverge dramatically. The two concepts are telling different stories. If *credit* is the relevant topic, the DMC is the appropriate indicator: it hardly matters whether banks grant credit or buy (non-government) bonds. But if *deposits* is the preferred gauge of monetary conditions, M2, of course, is the most interesting variable. An eventual divergence between M2 and DMC underlines the importance of a large and effective market for private bonds.

### 4.2.3    *Open Market Operations*

The Nationalbank realized in the aftermath of a currency crisis in 1969 that bond market interest rates could, and should, not be seen as possible targets any more. The attempts of suppressing interest rates were given up and that, as a consequence, ruled out discretionary open market operations (OMO). On the other hand, large sales of government bonds and bills have been taking place—in accordance with the previously mentioned informal rule of not monetizing government debt and maturing debt.

How money is being influenced is clearly seen from this well known accounting identity:

$$GSD = \Delta GGD - MAT + CUR + OMO + \Delta H$$

where GSD is government sector deficit, $\Delta$GGD is changes in government gross debt, MAT is maturing debt, CUR is central bank purchases of foreign currency, OMO is conventional open market operations and $\Delta$H is changes in government monetary liabilities (= changes in high powered money).

Government sector borrowing requirement (GSBR) is GSD + MAT and $\Delta$H can be split into $\Delta$R (changes in private bank net position with the central bank) and O (all other factors, such as changes in coins and notes and central bank profits).

$$GSBR - \Delta GGD - CUR - OMO - O = \Delta R$$

As can be seen from Table 4.3, OMO has played no major role in Danish monetary policy with one interesting exemption. In the summer of 1986 the Nationalbank engaged itself in an aggressive attempt to stop a slide in bond prices. It was all in vain, and again, the Bank withdrew from the market. The purchases in 1991 have a quite different background, soon to be discussed.

It can of course be argued that GSBR-$\Delta$GGD should be added to OMO to give a more complete picture of central bank transactions in the bond market, as the Nationalbank is in charge of the day-to-day business of Danish debt management policy.[13]

Government bonds are sold on tap which means that the Nationalbank is fixing prices and leaving the quantities to be determined by the market. This, of course, invites the interpretation that OMO-like considerations may sneak into day-to-day decisions: if interest rates are rising and bank liquidity is tight, the Bank could be expected not to lower bond prices or vice versa. The impression is, however, that the Nationalbank is operating according to fairly rigid plans.

Treasury bills (TB, zero coupon papers with time to maturities of 3, 6 and 9 months) are sold by auction on the third latest banking day in each month. While these outright sales certainly count as parts of the $\Delta$GGD, they do not play the fine-tuning role well known from other financial systems.[14] Rather, the stocks of TBs serve as the fulcrum for repurchase–purchase transactions (RPs) which are very important in the management of bank liquidity.

**Table 4.3** Counterparts to changes in bank net position with the Nationalbank

| Billion DKK | GSBR | $\Delta$GGD | CUR | OMO | O | Net position | |
|---|---|---|---|---|---|---|---|
| | | | | | | $\Delta$R | R |
| 1982 | 80·2 | −66·8 | −18·2 | 1·7 | −2·1 | −5·2 | −6·3 |
| 1983 | 100·9 | −101·1 | 2·0 | 1·4 | −2·3 | 0·9 | −5·4 |
| 1984 | 98·1 | −103·9 | 8·5 | −1·5 | −5·5 | −4·3 | −9·7 |
| 1985 | 104·5 | −103·2 | 11·9 | −0·3 | −2·2 | 10·7 | 1·0 |
| 1986 | 54·3 | −57·9 | −48·5 | 12·1 | 4·3 | −35·6 | −34·6 |
| 1987 | 67·0 | −60·4 | 16·0 | −0·1 | −5·6 | 16·9 | −17·7 |
| 1988 | 95·1 | −94·7 | 18·8 | −0·1 | 3·1 | 22·2 | 4·6 |
| 1989 | 112·2 | −108·7 | −23·0 | −0·3 | −2·9 | −22·6 | −18·0 |
| 1990 | 105·0 | −101·8 | 16·0 | 2·0 | −4·4 | 16·7 | −1·3 |
| 1991 | 106·3 | −114·4 | 7·5 | 12·0 | 4·2 | 15·7 | 14·4 |
| 1992 | 126·3 | −124·8 | −20·7 | −11·8 | 2·0 | −29·1 | −14·7 |
| 1993[end Sept.] | 110·0 | −112·6 | −45·4 | 17·6 | −0·5 | −42·7 | −57·4 |

## 4.4  Managing Money Market Interest Rates

### 4.4.1  *Can Capital Flows be Estimated?*

It should by now be clear that money market interest rates are of the utmost importance in the design of monetary policy. They are the obvious choice as operating targets, as they are assumed to transmit monetary impulses to the goal variable, the private net capital flows. To demonstrate the importance of money market interest rates, it would be tempting to demonstrate empirically that there is a reasonable amount of interest rate elasticity in an estimated capital flow relation. On the other hand, it is well known that this is a somewhat frustrating area of research, certainly when it comes small countries with currency and monetary policy regimes similar to the Danish one.[15]

The conventional approach is to estimate functions like:

$$\frac{\overline{\Sigma cap}}{Py} = \alpha + \beta_1 rdif + \beta_2 \dot{e} + \beta_3 \left(\frac{G\&S}{Py}\right) + \beta_4 \left(\frac{\Sigma cap}{Py}\right)_{-1}$$

where $\frac{\Sigma cap}{Py}$ (*Sprivcap* in the regressions) is accumulated private net capital inflows[16] scaled by $Py$, $rdif$ (*srdif* in regressions) is the interest rate differential vis-à-vis the DM, $dkks - dems$ (the data were plotted in Figure 4.6), $\dot{e}$ (*dex* in regressions) is the annualized changes in the DKK/DM ratio[17] and G&S is the BOP goods and services account, scaled by $Py$, that is brought in as an indicator of trade related credits (an improvement of the goods and services account leads to capital outflow). Relative growth in Danish and foreign wealth and/or investment activity was tried—even though acceptable data are difficult to find—without any success.

Using quarterly data, the simple OLS version[18] came out like this:

Equation (4.1) Modelling *Sprivcap* by OLS

The Sample is 1978 ( 3) to 1992 ( 3) less 0 Forecasts

| VARIABLE | COEFFICIENT | STD ERROR | HCSE | *t*-VALUE | PARTIAL $r^2$ |
|---|---|---|---|---|---|
| *Sprivca1* | .89845 | .10052 | .12728 | 8.93761 | .6296 |
| CONSTANT | .73456 | 11.77042 | 10.36481 | .06241 | .0001 |
| trend | .80475 | .77087 | .91257 | 1.04394 | .0227 |
| *srdif* | −.18192 | 1.11086 | .46468 | −.16377 | .0006 |
| *srdif* 1 | .83787 | 1.18004 | .72908 | .71004 | .0106 |
| *srdif* 2 | .30233 | .99707 | .71387 | .30322 | .0020 |
| *dex* | .47425 | .22993 | .18122 | 2.06256 | .0830 |
| *dex* 1 | −.06877 | .23427 | .21440 | −.29354 | .0018 |
| G&S*Py* | .02664 | .06415 | .06643 | .41534 | .0037 |
| G&S*Py* 1 | −.03994 | .06473 | .06035 | −.61709 | .0080 |

$R^2 = .9736981$ Õ $= 15.5703644$ F$( 9, 47) = 193.33 [ .0000]$ DW $= 2.050$
RSS $= 11394.5036565461$     for 10 Variables and 57 Observations
Information Criteria: SC $=$     6.01; HQ $=$     5.79; FPE $=$     284.97
$R^2$ Relative to DIFFERENCE+SEASONALS $= -.43691$

SEASONAL MEANS of DIFFERENCES are
18.35893          2.96812          3.25959          $-9.49332$

Solved     STATIC LONG RUN Equation

*Sprivcap* $=$     7.233     $+$     7.924 *trend* $+$     9.436 *srdif*
SE     (     112.09428)     (     3.30926)     (     18.09121)
$+$   3.993 *dex*          $-.131$ *G&SPy*

(     5.02707)     (     .51861)

The trend variable takes the value of 1, 2, 3. . . . . starting in 1983:I
where the new policy regime was introduced.

Even though the *static long run solution* points to some positive interest
rate elasticity, the regression is clearly not very impressive as neither
*srdif*, nor its lagged value turn out to be significant.

Obviously, the Danish money market rate (and *srdif*) are not
exogenous; what the Nationalbank does is to watch and shadow carefully
foreign (German) interest rates—and from time to time the authorities
try to nudge down *srdif* as much as the markets permit. So, *dkks* and *srdif*
are highly, but not completely, endogenous. This indicates that OLS is
not the appropriate estimation technique.

To compensate for this—and to shed extra light upon interest rate
determination and monetary policy—it has been tried to estimate
equation (1) above by an instrument variable approach by substituting
*srdif* with a new variable *srdif̂*, defined as

$$d\hat{k}ks - dems$$

where *dk̂ks* is estimated as

$$d\hat{k}ks = \alpha + \beta dkks_{-1} + \gamma dems + \delta capy$$

*capy* is the BOP current account scaled by *Py*.

EQ( 2) Modelling *dkks*          by OLS
The Sample is 1978( 3) to 1992( 3) less 0 Forecasts

| VARIABLE | COEFFICIENT | STD ERROR | HCSE | t-VALUE | PARTIAL $r^2$ |
|---|---|---|---|---|---|
| *dkks* 1 | .53471 | .10501 | .14043 | 5.09205 | .3371 |
| CONSTANT | 1.70338 | 1.13750 | 1.46733 | 1.49747 | .0421 |
| *dems* | .06341 | .46353 | .64264 | .13680 | .0004 |
| *dems* 1 | .99311 | .77428 | .99647 | 1.28262 | .0312 |
| *dems* 2 | $-.61919$ | .46371 | .53045 | $-1.33529$ | .0338 |
| *capy* | $-.12763$ | .04710 | .05405 | $-2.70995$ | .1259 |

$R^2 = .6412939$ Õ $= 2.0060052$ F$( 5, 51) = 18.24 [ .0000]$ DW $= 2.176$
RSS $= 205.2269085227$     for 6 Variables and 57 Observations

Information Criteria: SC = 1.71;   HQ = 1.58;  FPE = 4.45
R$^2$ Relative to DIFFERENCE+SEASONALS = .34380

    Solved   STATIC LONG RUN Equation
    *dkks*  =  3.661  +  .940 *dems*  −.274 *capy*

SE  ( 2.12171)  ( .26747)  ( .09360)

Again, an equation in need of improvements.[19] The static long run solution certainly indicates that Danish interest rates are determined south of the border even though improvements in the current account may reduce the level somewhat. The fact that most of the contribution of *dems* is related to *dems*$_{-1}$ may be reflecting[20] that the Nationalbank on some occasions has reduced the interest rate differential too much only to experience unsatisfactory capital flows over the following months. Further adjustments of the interest rates were needed to put things right. It is not unrealistic that the effect should be running from *dems*$_{-1}$ via *srdif* to *dkks*.

Finally, *dk̂ks* or rather *srd̂if* (*srdifh* in the regression) is tried in a regression similar to EQ(1):

EQ( 3) Modelling *Sprivcap* by OLS
The Sample is 1979( 1) to 1992( 3) less 0 Forecasts

| VARIABLE | COEFFICIENT | STD ERROR | HCSE | *t*-VALUE | PARTIAL $r^2$ |
|---|---|---|---|---|---|
| *Sprivca*1 | .86057 | .09112 | .08595 | 9.44427 | .6647 |
| CONSTANT | −34.68776 | 15.74324 | 11.95920 | −2.20334 | .0974 |
| trend | 1.10504 | .62256 | .51922 | 1.77499 | .0654 |
| *srdifh* | 2.89534 | 1.59514 | 1.38314 | 1.81510 | .0682 |
| *srdifh* 1 | −1.21628 | 1.67265 | 1.04969 | −.72716 | .0116 |
| *srdifh* 2 | 2.63601 | 1.53230 | 1.27739 | 1.72030 | .0617 |
| *dex* | .49010 | .21804 | .14126 | 2.24777 | .1009 |
| *dex* 1 | −.02600 | .22339 | .16638 | −.11641 | .0003 |
| G&S*Py* | .03049 | .06243 | .06788 | .48841 | .0053 |
| G&S*Py* 1 | −.02721 | .06390 | .05874 | −.42580 | .0040 |

R$^2$ = .9755880 Ō = 14.7147286 F( 9, 45) = 199.82 [ .0000]  DW = 2.106
  RSS = 9743.5456853861  for 10 Variables and 55 Observations
Information Criteria: SC = 5.91;  HQ = 5.68;  FPE = 255.89
R$^2$ Relative to DIFFERENCE+SEASONALS = −.33519

      SEASONAL MEANS of DIFFERENCES are
    3.25959  −9.49332  19.61888  1.59448

Solved  STATIC LONG RUN Equation
    *Sprivcap* =  −249.  +  7.925 trend  +  30.947 *srdifh*
SE  ( 180.16577)  ( 2.19652)  ( 26.71059)
+  3.328 *dex*  .024 G&S*Py*
( 2.91088)  ( .46183)

This makes more sense. But, of course, conclusions have to be made with great care—but at least, it does not appear to be ruled out that one can identify the net capital flow equation that reflects the reality of the Nationalbank.

In her comments on this paper, Susan Collins raised the interesting and important question of possible structural shifts in equation (3) above— it certainly should be expected that the gradual lifting of the currency controls, the liberalization of the domestic monetary policy and the improving macroeconomic performance would have influenced the coefficient of *srdifh*. So it has, indeed. To demonstrate this, equation (3) has been re-estimated by a recursive least square procedure and the $\beta$-coefficient of *srdifh* has been plotted in Figure 4.10; only estimates from 1983–4 onwards are available due to initialization.

As can be seen, $\beta$ has been moving up almost continuously. The obvious interpretation is that the credibility of the exchange rate regime has increased with the gradual improvement in the current account and the growing lapse of time since the last Danish devaluation within the EMS. There has, however, been one jump and that appears in the critical first quarter of 1985 where foreign borrowing was made available to all firms (Table 4.2).

### 4.4.2   *The Choice of Technique*

The core of Danish monetary policy is the management of the short-term interest rate. The Nationalbank has been involved in a continuous process of refinement of its techniques ever since it was decided to make the overnight money market rate the target variable.

To control the money market rates one has to manipulate banks'

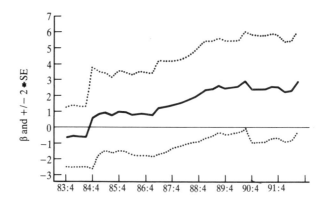

**Figure 4.10**   $\beta$-coefficient for *srdifh* $\pm$ 2 standard error

demand for liquidity (reserves)—the Bank often refers to the fixing of interest rates as 'the liquidity management system'.

The starting point is very short run versions of Table 4.3. GSBR, CUR and O are exogenous variables, while ΔGGD (and, in principle, OMO) is an instrument (although the fact that government bonds are sold on tap indicates that short run demand for bonds must be forecast). Given the Nationalbank's ability to forecast GSBR, CUR and O, the Bank is capable of steering banks' net position with some degree of precision. Obviously, individual banks need not be affected in identical ways, but an efficient interbank market levels out liquidity and determines one money market (or interbank) interest rate.[21] That, at least, was the situation until recently.

The first version of the system was introduced in 1975 and was in active use until the early 1980s. The banks were locked in a debt position vis-à-vis the Bank—by sales of government bonds—and the interest rate was determined by changing and shifting the supply curve for liquidity (borrowed reserves).

Each bank was given access to an amount of loans (a predetermined fraction of its net wealth) over a 3-month period. The supply of loans was made an increasing function of the quantity of borrowing, (Figure 4.11). After some years, a deposit facility opened[22] to put a floor below the interest rate should banks (mainly due to large, unexpected values of CUR) eventually end up in a positive net position.

The interbank market aggregated individual demands to a macro-demand for borrowed reserves.

The arrangement had its drawbacks. As equilibrium was often established by step 2 or 3 of the supply curve, banks enjoyed a consumers' surplus of some size. More important, perhaps, was the fact that the

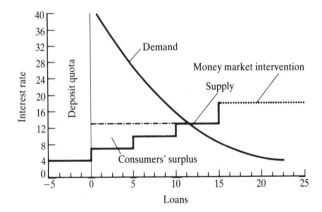

**Figure 4.11**   Demand and supply for central bank loans, 1975–82

system could not cope with severe currency (outflow) crisis, certainly not, had borrowing rights for a new 3-month period been granted recently. It proved too difficult to put up interest rates quickly. The response to this was cuts in the official borrowing quotas followed by supplementary Central Bank intervention directly in the interbank market.

But that was not without problems either. Knowing that the Nationalbank would often (or always) be in the market made it profitable for banks with ample capacity for borrowing to draw fully their cheap quotas (steps 1 and 2) and subsequently 'invest' them in the interbank market, only to know that they would be rescued afterwards by the Bank when they themselves needed money.

From 1985 to 1987 the Nationalbank tried a credit position based system—no loans granted, only deposits accepted—made possible by huge capital inflows in the first half of 1985. The bank issued (to the banking sector only) central bank certificates of deposits (CDs) but accepted ordinary deposits (bearing a market determined interest rate) as well. The system did only work for a brief period as the build up of CDs and deposits turned out to be too small given the large outflows during late 1985 and early 1986. Or to put it more brutally: the Nationalbank hesitated in increasing the interest rate and accepted for a while these outflows. Direct interbank market intervention had to be relied on once more.

In the end the Nationalbank was not content with this. Danish interbank loans of the day were of the simple, unsecured type which meant that bank failures would inflict losses upon the lending part. And the Nationalbank lost a large amount of money in 1987 in its interbank market transactions.

The 1988–92 system was relatively simple. It was realized that a liquidity management should preferably be symmetrical, being able to cope with positive as well as negative positions, as the Danish currency markets are extremely large compared with the size of economy;[23] swings in CUR may change banks' liquidity fundamentally and swiftly. So, banks were allowed to make unlimited deposits with the bank. They were also granted the right to—on a monthly basis[24]—to borrow from the bank. Individual bank quotas were determined as fractions of bank net wealth. All borrowing had to be secured by financial assets (mainly bonds). The principles of the system is demonstrated in Figure 4.12.

The spreads between borrowing and lending rates have been taking the values of either 50 or 100 basis points. A small spread implied a continuous development in the interest rate when the net position passed though the zero point. But a larger spread promotes interbank activity and efficiency.

Figure 4.12 may be compared to Figure 4.13[25] which shows, based on

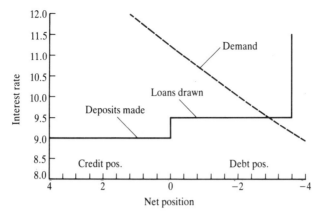

**Figure 4.12** Borrowing from and deposits with the central bank, March 1988 – March 1992

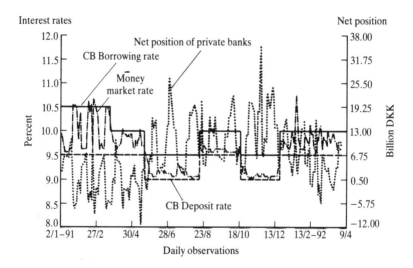

**Figure 4.13** Net position and the money market rate

daily observations, the functioning of the system from 2 January, 1991 to 31 March, 1992 (when it was terminated).

In the summer of 1990 capital inflows were running high and the demand curve of Figure 4.11 shifted to the left. The Nationalbank appeared to have expected these inflows, caused by foreign demand for Danish bonds, to have been of a temporary nature and decided not to cut the system's two interest rates by more than 50 basis points. To smoothen the effects of the capital flows on domestic liquidity the day-to-day management was supplemented by heavy intervention in the forward currency markets. The purpose of these transactions were not to influence the forward rates but only to postpone the impact on the domestic liquidity.

Returning to the details of the ordinary liquidity management system, one should have expected only to observe extreme values of the money market rate variable: the borrowing rate have acted as the upper bound for the money market rate while the deposit rate should have been very close to the lower bound.[26] But the evidence was somewhat disturbing. When market participants forecast a small positive value of the net position, risk adverse bank may have preferred to borrow at a rate in the middle of the band about noon, to be safe, rather than to wait till the afternoon when the market may or may not close at an interbank rate near the bottom. That was perhaps understandable, but the market performed less and less well. The rate has been above the upper bound even when the banking system had unused borrowing capacity,[27] and borrowing often took place while other market participants were making deposits. All this is understandable, but added to a general feeling that the system did not perform well. It can even be shown[28] that the Nationalbank's grasp of the money market rate appears to have been loosening since 1989.

It is not difficult to point out explanations. Identifying and managing credit risks in the interbank market have become increasingly important given the strains felt by the financial sector.

Banks have set up elaborate systems to determine the limits of their positions with other participants in the market. Another factor is the increased awareness of transaction costs. Fees and spreads do not appear to cover fixed costs when small loans are arranged.

More important, however, is the complete change of the Danish banking structure that took place in 1990.[29] The 'big six' became the 'big two'; and these 'mega-banks' are now in charge of about 60% of all bank assets and liabilities. These two banks—normally enjoying a surplus of deposits over loans—appear to find it difficult to fund minor competitors who make no secret of their desire to 'steal' some of the big banks' customers who, after the mergers, may be searching for a new second bank. Also, a conservative feeling that is not right to fund lending in the interbank market is being aired by one of the mega-banks.

A final consideration is that the Nationalbank must have realized that the liquidity management system was not compatible with the one that might be expected to be introduced by a future European Central Bank. In most other countries[30] the interbank markets are being securitized and the management systems are often based on repurchase transactions.

So given this and the fact that Danish banks had commenced securities lending and borrowing—often with TBs as the underlying assets[31]—the Nationalbank from 1 April 1992 once again changed its procedures.

Preparations had been made in 1991 when the Bank increased sales of TBs—this is what was referred to earlier, when debt management policy and monetary policy were said to have been integrated to a higher degree—at the quarterly auctions. In December the new system was rehearsed when the Bank temporarily increased bank liquidity by a repurchase transaction in TBs, reversed in January. This is why OMO takes the value of +12 billion DKK in 1991 in Table 4.3. A similar transaction took place in September 1993 when the Bank bought back TBs with a time to maturity too short to make the bills eligible for repurchase operations.

But TBs are not the only financial assets applied in the present set-up. The Bank also issues CDs[32]—that happens on the last banking day in each week. One has, on certain occasions, also been selling on other days. The time to maturity of the CDs is 14 days. Banks are still allowed to make ordinary deposits with the Nationalbank—a temporary arrangement to ease the transition for smaller banks to the new and more advanced techniques—but only in limited amounts. The authorities clearly want to promote interbank activities on a secured base which means that banks are supposed to build-up portfolios of TBs and CDs to cope with changes in their liquidity positions.

We now face a three-layered system. Again, considering Table 4.3, one realizes that liquidity is tuned roughly by sales of government bonds and in the quarterly TB auctions. Here, banks have to make purchases according to their *long-term* portfolio strategies and to enable themselves to level out swings in their liquidity.

In the *medium term* (that is on a weekly basis) banks must decide how many CDs they need to buy (let expire) and/or by how much their accounts with the Nationalbank should increase (decrease). These decisions are based upon liquidity forecasts and on banks previous acquisitions of TBs and CDs.

Now, consider the *short term*. Banks can engage into RP transactions in TBs with the Nationalbank. RPs are basically secured credits with a time to maturity of 14 days. But given a technologically determined settlement period of 2 days,[33] RPs can not be used in genuine day-to-day smoothing. Overnight transactions (illustrated in Figure 4.14) are carried out by repurchase transactions in CDs, but only when the Bank considers it relevant to quote a buying price (published as an interest rate). When the interest rate is falling—the demand curve has shifted to the left of the zero-point in Figure 4.14—the Bank may quote a selling price even if the day considered does not coincide

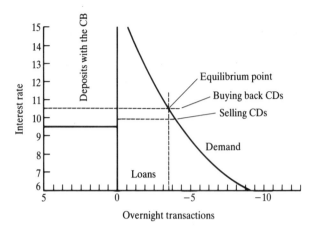

**Figure 4.14**  The new system 'overnight equilibrium'

with the second latest banking day. This is how the fine tuning works.

In Figure 4.14 it is assumed that the relevant part of the demand for liquidity curve is to the right of the zero-point (banks need to borrow) which means that the repurchase (or buying back) CD rate determines the equilibrium rate and amount of loans.

In June and July 1992, after the first Danish referendum on the Maastrict Treaty, one experienced some strain, as the RPs in TBs were running at a very high level and the sum of CDs and deposits with the Nationalbank was decreasing. As can be seen from Figure 4.15, the amount of the amount of outstanding TBs began to fall in July which

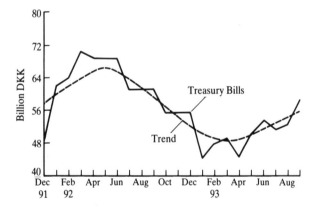

**Figure 4.15**  Outstanding amounts of treasury bills

brought the systems capacity for liquidity smoothing—and the opportunity for banks to conduct interbank transactions on a secured basis—
into some doubt. The severe currency crisis in September and November
made things worse. In late September capital outflows depleted domestic
liquidity to such a degree that banks' net position (deposits + CDs − RPs
in TBs) turned negative,[34] see Figure 4.16—and the capacity for further
borrowing appeared to have become very limited.

Now, depletion of domestic liquidity is also depletion of the currency
reserves, so the Nationalbank was given the choice between putting
interest rates higher to maintain foreign and domestic liquidity or holding
interest rates slightly lower and accepting some outflow while intervening
in the old fashioned way in the interbank market. In a few, critical days
the authorities opted for genuine crisis management by not allowing RPs
in TBs—not an important decision, as only little further borrowing would
have been possible—and by limiting repurchase transactions in CDs.

Confidence in DKK was restored—for a time at least—in early
October 1992, the foreign reserves were quickly rebuilt (the inflow was
even larger than the previous outflow) and the liquidity management
system was resumed.

In November, after the devaluation of the Swedish kronor and the
Norwegian kroner some crisis phenomena reappeared, and the interest
rate had to be raised again. But after the December EEC Summit in
Edinburgh the markets again calmed down for a while.

The new system has been tested under very extreme circumstances as

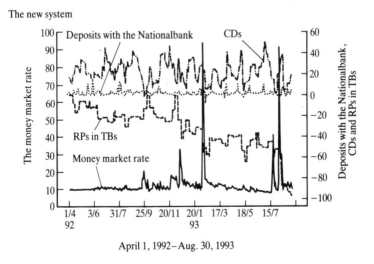

April 1, 1992–Aug. 30, 1993

**Figure 4.16**   Bank liquidity and the money market rate

the DKK has been under almost continuous pressure from June 1992 to (the time of writing in) October 1993.

The most dramatic episodes of crises were experienced in February and July 1993 when interest rates in the overnight money market reached 90 pct. Some elements of quantitative management were introduced on days of severe crisis—mainly limits in the supply of loans from the Bank to the banking system. The money markets were often disrupted,[35] interest rates became extremely volatile and spreads were grotesque. By and large, the system survived, however, in the sense that demands for liquidity were met even though interest rates (and spreads vis-à-vis the DM) had to be kept high.

It can be seen from Figure 4.18 that banks' demand for liquidity eventually outstripped the outstanding amounts of TBs and CDs, so the Nationalbank was forced to make all government bills and bonds eligible for repurchase operations.

It is obvious, however, that the Danish system does not represent the only possible design. In Figure 4.14 we saw that the Nationalbank is determining the money market rate by a vertical supply curve. This means that quantities (domestic liquidity, currency reserves, etc.) are likely to fluctuate relatively a lot. In the corresponding Swedish set up,[36] for a comparison, see Figure 4.17, the supply of borrowed reserves is upward sloping (the supply curve is shaped as a staircase with 20 steps). This system has some resemblance to the Danish 1975–82 version, even though the Riksbank is manipulating demand in a more sophisticated way than the Nationalbank did then.

The advantage of the Swedish system is that interbank rates increase automatically, should difficulties arise as the demand curve will shift,

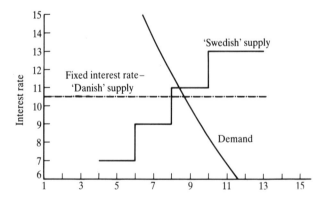

**Figure 4.17**   The Danish and Swedish models compared

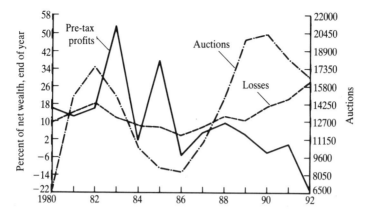

**Figure 4.18** Banks' pre-tax profits and expected losses: auctions by court order

while discretionary policy is needed in the Danish context. On the other hand, if fluctuations are of a more innocent and stochastic nature, the Swedish markets may experience unnecessary movements in the money market interest rates (which may be transmitted unto other interest rates). There appears to be a trade off between (the consequences of) disturbances in interest rates and relevant quantity variables.[37]

But, after all, the present Danish system is working without many of the weaknesses of its predecessors and it fits well into a common European grid. The Nationalbank's daily procedures appear to be rather close to, but are not identical with, what the Bundesbank is doing.[38]

## 4.5 The Interest Rate Differential

### 4.5.1 *Consequences of a High Real Rate of Interest*

The final question to be addressed is the one related to the size of the interest rate differential (see Figure 4.6 and also the discussion in section 4.4).

It is clearly painful to experience very high real interest rates. With the only exceptions of a few years in the 1920s, money has never been as dear as now, and that is also true when tax deductions are taken into account. Even though high real interest rates may well be an important factor behind the high and rising savings ratios, the present phase is clearly difficult. Just to give some indication of what is going on, we may take a quick glance at banks' pre-tax profits and expected losses (due to bad debt and—in some years—falling asset prices).

A major factor behind this rather frightening development is the many bankruptcies of property (house) owners[39] (also plotted in Figure 4.18) that have almost disrupted the lending activities of the mortgage credit institutions and some banks.

This rather frightening development—the 1993 figures will indicate some improvement but that is only the consequence of increases in bond and share prices—has been the object of much concern and debate. On the other hand, the Danish situation is comfortable compared to the one in the other Nordic countries where bank profitability has become catastrophic and vast amounts of government money has had to be injected into the banks as fresh share capital.[40]

The background for the difficulties within the Danish banking sector is apparently quite clear. As can be seen from Figures 4.2 and 4.5, the rate of inflation has come down from 12 to under 2%, real growth has declined and unemployment has soared. That, in itself, is enough to increase bank losses. Add to this the very high real interest rate and the mentioned tax reform—and notice that many loans are carrying a fixed interest rate higher than the present rate. It then becomes obvious that the problems are compounding for many business and households.

It can be asked whether the liberalization of the monetary policy— mainly the lifting of the credit ceiling in 1985—has played any role in this. To the best of my judgment, the answer must be negative. As was seen in Figure 4.8, M2 has been decelerating from 1984 onwards—and so has bank lending. There was clearly no post-liberalization boom in bank credits as was the case in Norway when restrictions were lifted in that country, also in the mid 1980s. Rather, it can be argued that Danish banks were slow to adjust to the new, low inflation environment. Most consumer credits, and many business sector loans as well, used to be based on the ever increasing nominal values of the collateral presented, and not on thorough examinations of profitability, financial strength and growth of income.

As inflation came down and nominal house prices began to fall, much of the collateral was wiped out as firms and households had to realize that their net wealth had turned negative, and in fragile circumstances, only minor economic blows are needed to inflict losses upon financial institutions.[41]

What we see in Denmark and in other countries experiencing transition from high and stable inflation rates to (almost) price stability are high adjustment costs. As the credit controls were never very strict and as solvency in Danish banks has been, and still is, high compared to the levels in most other countries, the losses can presumably be absorbed.

The difficulties for the mortgage credit institutions, not accounted for here, have been worse, but again, problems are being coped with.

But obviously, a real interest rate at a level above 7% (pre-tax) is clearly painful.

### 4.5.2    Understanding the Interest Rate Differential

Now, the real interest rate is clearly a function of the foreign (German) nominal rate, the differential and the domestic inflation. The latter has had to be suppressed to restore competitiveness and the confidence in the fixed exchange rate policy; German rates are clearly exogenous—but what about the differential (*rdif*)?

It has often been suggested to decompose rdif into three variables[42]

$$rdif_t = cp_t + rp_t + dex_t$$

$cp_t$ is the country premium, $rp_t$ is the exchange risk premium and $dex_t$ is the expected change in the exchange rate in period $t$.

It is hardly worthwhile to discuss *cp* as the default risk of the Kingdom must be minimal. When it comes to money market rates, the relative ratings of Danish banks—given even the poor earnings—have hardly become worse.[43]

It is perhaps difficult to estimate *rp* directly as such a variable is affected by many unpredictable factors: stochastic changes in international payments, the timing of portfolio decisions and changes and timing of the fixing of official interest rates.

But if we consider the decision-making in a financial unit engaged in, say interest rate arbitrage it is of course important to know whether DKK is moving in step with DM. A Danish firm borrowing short tem in the German market, or a German bank purchasing Danish TBs have a keen interest in knowing whether an increase in the DM position within the EMS band is likely to be followed by a similar—or an opposite—movement in the Danish currency. If DKK is shadowing DM completely, a smaller value of *rdif* is needed to establish an equilibrium in the currency markets than in the case where DKK is following an independent course.

As can be seen in Figure 4.22, *rdif* began to increase in late 1991—can we detect a simultaneous change in the currency markets? To get some idea of this a simple correlation matrix has been calculated using daily observations (end of 1990 to end of June 1992) of the changes in positions of DM and DKK in the EMS band. The level values of these variables (to end of September 1992) are plotted in Figure 4.19. The sample has been split into three subsamples: in the first one we see a decreasing value

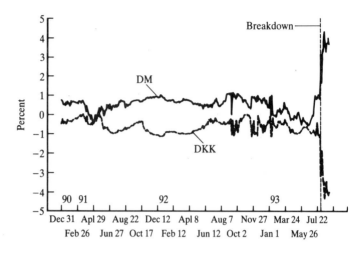

**Figure 4.19** Positions of DM and DKK in the EMS: daily observations from end 1990 to end August 1993

of *rdif* while the second and third sub-samples are characterised by an increasing value of *rdif* (Table 4.4).

As can be seen, a fairly fundamental change has occurred. In the first subsample, the standard deviation of ΔDKK was smaller than the standard deviation of ΔDM, and the correlation was positive. From a German point of view the DKK was a stable currency often moving (in the short run at least) in the same direction as the DM.

In the second subsample the standard deviation of the DKK has become larger and the correlation negative, and from November 1991 onwards one saw a higher (and increasing) interest rate differential (see Figure 4.23 below). The growing instability of the DKK was probably due to increasing concern about the outcome of the Danish Maastricht referendum and, more importantly, the growing uncertainty of the future of the EMS and the EMU should France reject as well.

The third subsample is covering a period marked by continuous pressure in the currency markets and further increases in the value of *rdif*. Again ΔDM and ΔDKK are negatively correlated.

We finally consider the expected changes of the exchange rate, *dex* (actual changes were used in the regressions in section 4.4).

To get some idea of what has been going on, we take a look at the positions of DM and DKK in the EMS; daily observations from end 1990 to end August 1993 are plotted in Figure 4.19.

**Table 4.4** Means and standard deviations of variables, and correlation matrix of the three subsamples

*First subsample (31 Dec. 1990 to 17 Oct. 1991)*
Means of variables

| DKK | DM | ΔDKK | ΔDM | |
|---|---|---|---|---|
| −0.4857 | 0.4275 | 0.0001 | 0.0001 | |

Standard deviations of variables

| DKK | DM | ΔDKK | ΔDM | |
|---|---|---|---|---|
| 0.2933 | 0.2880 | 0.0708 | 0.0858 | |

Correlation matrix

| | DKK | DM | ΔDKK | ΔDM |
|---|---|---|---|---|
| DKK | 1.0000 | | | |
| DM | 0.0654 | 1.0000 | | |
| ΔDKK | 0.1210 | 0.1378 | 1.0000 | |
| ΔDM | 0.0187 | 0.1507 | 0.5328 | 1.0000 |

*Second subsample (18 Oct. 1991 to 30 June 1992)*
Means of variables

| DKK | DM | ΔDKK | ΔDM | |
|---|---|---|---|---|
| −0.8303 | 0.7188 | 0.0006 | −0.0018 | |

Standard deviations of variables

| DKK | DM | ΔDKK | ΔDM | |
|---|---|---|---|---|
| 0.2221 | 0.1589 | 0.0468 | 0.0400 | |

Correlation matrix

| | DKK | DM | ΔDKK | ΔDM |
|---|---|---|---|---|
| DKK | 1.0000 | | | |
| DM | −0.6317 | 1.0000 | | |
| ΔDKK | 0.1315 | −0.1645 | 1.0000 | |
| ΔDM | −0.0440 | 0.1646 | −0.3879 | 1.0000 |

*Third subsample (1 July 1992 to 30 Aug. 1993)*
Means of variables

| DKK | DM | ΔDKK | ΔDM | |
|---|---|---|---|---|
| −0.7782 | 0.6254 | −0.01333 | 0.01204 | |

Standard deviations of variables

| DKK | DM | ΔDKK | ΔDM | |
|---|---|---|---|---|
| 0.8122 | 0.8834 | 0.2396 | 0.2252 | |

Correlation matrix

| | DKK | DM | ΔDKK | ΔDM |
|---|---|---|---|---|
| DKK | 1.0000 | | | |
| DM | −0.7507 | 1.0000 | | |
| ΔDKK | 0.2512 | −0.1374 | 1.0000 | |
| ΔDM | −0.1680 | 0.2228 | −0.3813 | 1.0000 |

It can readily be seen that the Nationalbank used to peg—right up to the final breakdown of the EMS on 1 August 1993—the DKK not too far from the lower bound, thereby reducing the maximum, EMS-compatible Danish depreciation (*dexmax*).

Adding[44] the annualized value of dexmax to the German interest rates yields us the highest possible Danish interest rates within the present set of exchange rates and rules of the EMS. An actual value above such a maximum would indicate lack of credibility in the Danish exchange rate policy.

Obviously, very short run interest (i.e. money market rates) will never be bounded at all, but short to medium term differentials appear to be small enough to vindicate credibility. Long run interest rates are still too high to be compatible with the EMS bounds (they ought to be almost identical to their German counterparts).

One way of putting this is that the good relative[45] performance of the Danish economy over the past 3–5 years may have persuaded market participants that the DKK exchange rate was credible in the short run— that at least appeared to be the case before the first Danish Maastricht referendum (see Figure 4.20). After the turmoil in the currency markets and after the breakdown of the EMS more uncertainty persists (see Figure 4.21). It should even be emphasized that in early 1992 as well as in mid-1993 the long-term interest rates indicate more doubts about the

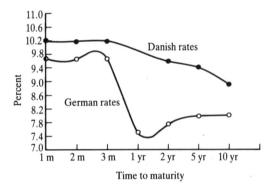

**Figure 4.20** Selected German and Danish interest rates: pre-Maastricht referendum unrest (end March 1992)

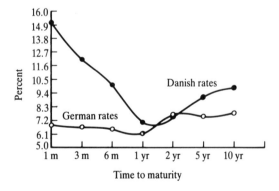

**Figure 4.21** Selected German and Danish interest rates: post-EMS breakdown (August 1993)

robustness of the Danish economy—these rates may have been telling a truer story all the time.

So to diminish the interest rate differential and thereby to reduce Danish interest rates it appears to be imperative to maintain a prudent stance of the economic policy in order to maintain and strengthen credibility. The task of bringing, and holding, down interest rate differentials may have become more difficult since it was decided to make fiscal policy more expansionary. And the breakdown of the EMS, followed by a small, but significant drop in the DKK, can well prove to become an expensive experience.

One may ask the simple, if somewhat hypothetical, question of whether it is possible to improve economic performance to such a degree that the interest rate differential would turn negative. Even if we realize that German interest rates are determined from domestic considerations and are dictating the level of all rates within the EMS, could it be that these interest rates were not always the lowest?

Take the case of Dutch gilder, and recall that the Dutch economy has performed at least equally as well as the German economy over the past 10–20 years. The Dutch are enjoying a very strong position with enormous current account surpluses, huge net foreign assets, low inflation, etc. Never the less, it can clearly be seen from Figures 4.22 and 4.23 that Dutch and German interest rates are more or less identical.

So economic performance is important in establishing credibility but given the absolute German resistance to, and need of, devaluations and the policies of smaller countries to tie their exchange rates to the DM

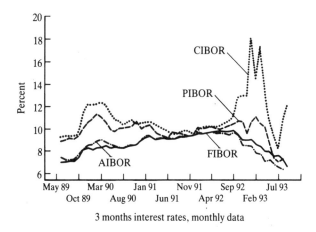

3 months interest rates, monthly data

**Figure 4.22** FIBOR, AIBOR, PIBOR and CIBOR: from May 1989 to August 1993

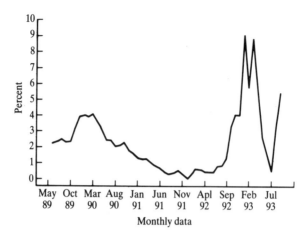

**Figure 4.23**  Difference between CIBOR and FIBOR: from May 1989 to August 1993

(and the policies of France, Belgium, the Netherlands and Denmark may still be characterized in that way) a systematically negative interest rate differential appears to be ruled out.

## 4.6  Summing Up

Danish monetary policy has not contributed directly to the improvement of the macroeconomic performance over the past 10 years, but it has played its role—to stabilize exchange rates and capital flows—in an effective way.

The core of the monetary policy is the management of short-term interest rates. The system has been undergoing continuous reform and the present set-up appears to be working.

The real interest is clearly too high and one cannot do much about this. The only option available is a further strengthening of the exchange rate credibility.

The international environment—mainly the EMS—has clearly been of the greatest importance by providing bench-marks and relevant exchange and interest rates pegs. Denmark has probably gained more than most other countries by its membership, so the rejection in 1992 of the Maastricht Treaty may appear odd, and the decision certainly added to the difficulties of conducting Danish monetary policy.

It is, of course, impossible to point out those elements of the Maastricht

Treaty which led to the Danish rejection. But in October 1992, seven out of eight parties in the Danish parliament reached a so-called *National Compromise* clarifying the conditions for the vital Danish ratification of the Treaty. At the December EEC summit in Edinburgh, these demands were met.

Denmark will not apply for membership of the WEU, nor take part in any European defence cooperation outside the Nato, will not introduce the European citizenship (but will accept that EC citizens resident in Denmark take part in elections for local councils and the European Parliament) and will not accept the symbolic, but certainly the practical, parts of the increased judicial cooperation. In addition to this it has been clarified that all member countries have the right to introduce environmental legislation and rules stricter than the common European standards.

It is understandable when other countries find these details of little relevance; the overwhelming problem, however, was to make all this legally binding without making a new round of ratifications in ten national parliaments necessary. Finally, the circle was squared, and most heads of states and governments were satisfied.

In the context of this paper the most interest element happens to be that Denmark 'gained the right' not to take part in Phase Three of the formation of the EMU—the currency union and the adoption of a common currency. This was in the Maastricht Treaty already, but again, some kind of recognition was supposed to be necessary. This did not indicate that Denmark wanted to leave the EMS, it had been underlined that when other countries eventually moved on to Phase Three, Denmark would participate in the currency cooperation (meaning that DKK should be pegged to the ECU). If this had been the crucial question, one may conclude that the Danish general public viewed the macroeconomic development over the last 10 years quite differently than the interpretation in this paper.

When I have been arguing that it was only by taking external constraints seriously that credibility was built up; and that, again was a necessary condition for improved macroeconomic performance. The implicit reasoning behind the National Compromise appears to be that the results have been reached by national political decisions and that the fixed exchange rates should be seen as no more than a convenient arrangement.

All this is now being tested after the breakdown of the EMS and the likely postponement of the EMU. It is slowly being accepted that a formally higher degree of independence requires at least as tough a monetary policy as before. A new tightening of the fiscal stance is not on the agenda yet, but as can be seen from the cases of Belgian and Swedish currency markets react swiftly when fiscal and budgetary policies are judged to be getting out of control.

Fortunately, the question of returning to an EMS-like arrangement may be discussed at some not too distant stage. Public attitudes towards Danish participation in Phase Three may even change as we learn how difficult it may be for a small, open economy to be on its own.

## Notes

1. Improvements suggested by my two discussants, Susan Collins and Gabriela Mundaca and by Alberto Giovannini are gratefully acknowledged. The final responsibility is, however, mine alone. Data used in this paper is extracted from accessible sources: *The Statistical Bureau of Denmark, Danmarks Nationalbank, OECD Economic Outlook* and *IMF International Financial Statistics*—unless indicated in the text. Some data series shown in the graphs have been extended to include 1993-forecasts which have been obtained from *The Ministry of Economics: Economic Survey*, August 1993, *The Council of Economic Advisors: The Danish Economy*, June 1993 and *OECD: Economic Outlook*, July 1993.
2. See Giavazzi and Pagaro (1990).
3. All household capital income is now taxed—and tax deductions for interest payments made—by a uniform rate of 51%—down from an average rate at about 68%. The corporate tax rate has been cut gradually from 50 to 34%. From 1987 a temporary surcharge was levied on household net interest payments (mortgage interest were not included).
4. Whether the (minority) government believed that liberalizations and commitments would support their policy through increased confidence or, rather, they searched actively for undisputable external constraints to make parliamentary life easier, was perhaps unclear.
5. Apart from the prime minister's often repeated promise that 'there shall be no devaluations in my time'. In a seminar taking place in 1984 the royal governor of the Nationalbank, Erik Hoffmeyer, explained this apparent lack of official policy by saying that 'only deeds and not words are of any interest here'.
6. Blomgren-Hansen (1977) argued persuasively that introducing a credit ceiling in a system with a huge and effective bond market leads to strange results. The constraints on bank behaviour led to less lending, but more bond purchases by banks and *less* foreign borrowing by the non-bank business sector. Some household borrowing may have been put off. It should be emphasized that access to bond financing via the mortgage credit institutions were rationed in the sense that only purposes of lending were accepted (mainly investments and certainly not consumption). Banks' purchases of bonds have never been restrained.
7. See Goodhart (1989), ch. VII.
8. The difference was important as overdraft loans is the traditional type of credit in Danish banks.
9. In 1984 this informal rule was turned into a formula: $l_i=l_{target}+0.5(d_i-d_{aver})$, where $l_i$ and $l_{target}$ were the growth of lending in bank $i$ and the macrobenchmark growth, respectively. $d_i$ and $d_{aver}$ were the growth in deposits in bank $i$ and the macroaverage growth, respectively.
10. Danish solvency rules and ratios were at that time related to deposits which meant that required reserves—even when compensated by the market rate—inflicted some, however minimal, costs on banks.
11. The rising bond prices in 1983 and 1985 had boosted banks profits (*cf*, Figure 4.16), and the Nationalbank may have feared that banks would go for more by increasing their bond portfolios (and the duration of these) and thereby inflicting too much interest risk upon themselves.

12. The Danish M2 is defined as the sum of private non-bank holdings of coins, notes and deposits with banks in DKK and foreign currencies; pension related savings accounts are deducted. The definition is new (the definition of the banking sector has changed as well), so M2-data prior to 1982 are apparently not yet available. DMC is defined as the sum of domestic loans in DKK and holding of DKK-bonds; again, pension savings have been deducted.

13. Government bonds are issued in the name of the Kingdom by the Ministry of Finance in accordance with Debt Acts passed by the Parliament. In 1991 the Debt Management Office was transferred from the Ministry to the Nationalbank. The consequence of this appears to be that the Nationalbank has gained a greater say in the design of debt instruments and that conventional monetary policy and debt management policy has been integrated to a higher degree; see next section.

14. See Kneeshaw and Van den Bergh (1989).

15. See Vredin (1988) who has worked on the Swedish case and Vikøren (1989) who made similar estimations on Norwegian data.

16. Direct investments are excluded.

17. Should $\dot{e}$ have turned out to be important in the explanation of $\dfrac{\Sigma cap}{Py}$ that could have amounted to mean that financial operators had forecast exchange rates and acted accordingly. One obvious difficulty with alternative, mechanical expectational schemes appears to be that they 'predict' repeatedly Danish or German violations of the rules of the ERM.

18. All estimations are carried out by PC-Give ver. 6.0.

19. In her comments to this paper, Gabriela Mundaca suggested that the GMM procedure should be tried. That could certainly be interesting but only in the case we were able to obtain better and stronger instrument variables. That presumably amounts to identifying the reaction function behind German monetary policy.

20. The highly autocorrelated nature of *dems* may provide a more prosaic explanation of the lag structure.

21. The Copenhagen market is based upon the activities of two brokerage firms who earn their fees by connecting—by phone or fax—lenders and borrowers. Major banks are known to have done some direct deals to save spreads.

22. It has always been possible to make interest free deposits with the Nationalbank but from this movement, the Bank began to pay interest.

23. A recent survey conducted by the Nationalbank for the BIS—see Andersen, B. (1992)—indicates that apart from the special cases of Singapore and Hong Kong, the size of the Danish markets are second only to the British when scaled by GNP.

24. In the last couple of years, even shorter periods were used.

25. The net position data were kindly provided by the Nationalbank.

26. It has not happened often that the money market rate has reached the Central Bank deposit rate as lending banks and the brokers demand fees in the area of six basis points. Only in the case of complete liquidity saturation (no banks demanding loans) the lower bound prevails.

27. In those cases, the Nationalbank has often intervened briefly to calm the nerves.

28. See Nielsen (1992).

29. It is beyond the scope of this presentation to discuss in any detail the background of this shake up of the Danish banking sector as it appears to be unrelated to the monetary policy. The possibilities of economics of scale, an expected increase in foreign competition due to the EEC Single Market for Financial Services and new restrictions on the size of the maximum size of loans to one customer were the official explanations. Managerial problems within some of the merging banks is the favourite unofficial reason.

30. See Kneeshaw and Van den Bergh (1989) and also the *Annual Reports* of the BIS.

31. To avoid credit risks and to attract business from non-bank customers at home and abroad.

32. Can only be traded within the banking sector.

33. All transactions in assets quoted on the Stock Exchange—and that includes TBs—

have to pass through the computerized Asset Settlement Centre. TBs clearly ought to be handled more quickly.
34. Data were kindly provided by the Nationalbank.
35. The fact that some of the market participants were (supposed to be) in trouble made things much worse.
36. See Sveriges Riksbank, various issues, Hörngren and Westman-Mårtensson (1991) and Westman-Mårtensson (1992).
37. This discussion has some resemblance with William Poole's classic discussion of the use of monetary policy in a stochastic setting—even, though, he considered a closed economy (Poole, 1979).
38. Compare, for instance, with the panel entitled 'Operating variable in the money market' which appears in each *Monthly Report of the Deutsche Bundesbank*. Referring, again, to the question of stability under strain, it is interesting to note the absence— at least from a formal point of view—of any formal Lombard facility (an upper bound for the money market interest rate) in the Danish liquidity management system. It can be said, however, that the officially not-occurring interbank market interventions on an unsecured basis is the 'last resort' facility of the Nationalbank. That, at least, was the case during the turmoil in the Autumn of 1992.
39. When lenders detect arrears and rescue operations seem fruitless court orders are automatically granted to arrange 'compulsory auctions' where the property is sold.
40. See Norges Bank (1992).
41. The perils of negative equity is also being felt within the British financial system— certainly by the building societies—see Bank of England (1992).
42. See, for instance, Froot and Rogoff (1991).
43. It has been discussed whether the increased spread between the Government bond rate and that of the mortgage credit institutions could have been caused by an international refusal of the MCI bonds. That may well be the case, but some evidence appears to suggest that the major factor is the odd characteristics of these bonds and not any feelings of default risk.
44. This procedure have been discussed and used by Svensson (1990) and Andersen, T. (1992).
45. It is not only of interest to see what will happen to the Danish economy—the post-unification performance of the German economy is equally as important, see Figure 4.20.

# References

Andersen, B. (1992), 'Survey of the Danish foreign exchange markets—April 1992', *Danmarks Nationalbank, Quarterly Review*, November.
Andersen, T. (1992), 'The Monetary Policy in 1991'. *Danmarks Nationalbank, Quarterly Review*, May.
Bank of England (1992), 'Negative equity in the housing market'. *Bank of England, Quarterly Bulletin*, August.
BIS, *Annual Reports*, various issues, Basle.
Blomgren-Hansen, N. (1977), 'Bank credit ceilings as an instrument of money and capital movements control: The experience of Denmark, 1970–74'. *The Scandinavian Journal of Economics*, **77**, 442–56.
Danmarks Nationalbank, *Annual Report, Quarterly Review*, various issues (available in English) and various issues of *Press Releases* and *Monthly Financial Statistics* (in Danish), Copenhagen.
Deutsche Bundesbank, *Monthly Report*, various issues, Frankfurt.
Froot, K. A. and Rogoff, K. (1991), 'The EMS, The EMU, and the transition to a common currency', *NBER Macroeconomics Annual*, NBER, Cambridge, MA.

Giavazzi, F. and Pagaro, M. (1990), 'Can severe fiscal contractions be expansionary? Tales of two small european countries', *NBER Macroeconomics Annual*, NBER, Cambridge, MA.

Goodhart, C. A. E. (1989), 'Money, information and uncertainty', 2nd edn, Macmillan, London.

Hörngren, L. and Westman-Mårtensson, A. (1991), 'Swedish monetary policy: Institutions, targets, and instruments', Sveriges Riksbank, Working Paper no. 2.

Kneeshaw, J. T. and Van den Bergh, P. (1989), 'Changes in central bank money market operating procedures in the 1980s', *BIS Economic Papers*, **23**.

Nielsen, P. E. (1992), 'The Danish money market—Development and reform' (in Danish), *Nationaløkonomisk Tidsskrift*, **130**.

Norges Bank (1992), 'Basic information on the banking crisis in Norway and abroad' (in Norwegian), *Norges Bank, Quarterly Review*.

Poole, W. (1970), 'Optimal choice of monetary policy instruments in a simple stochastic macro model', *Quarterly Journal of Economics*, **84**.

Svensson, L. E. O. (1990), 'The simplest test of target zone credibility', NBER Working Papers, no. 3394.

Sveriges Riksbank, Penning & Valutapolitik (Quarterly Bulletin), various issues, Stockholm.

Vikøren, B. (1989), 'An empirical study of the currency net positions of the business sector' (in Norwegian), *Norges Bank, Arbeidsnotat*, **11**.

Vredin, A. (1988). *Macroeconomic Policies and the Balance of Payments*. Stockholm School of Economics, Stockholm, 1988.

Westman-Mårtensson, A. (1992), 'The interest rate staircase' (in Swedish), *Sveriges Riksbank, Quarterly Bulletin*, **130**.

# Discussion

## Susan M. Collins
*Georgetown University, the Brookings Institution and CEPR*

This paper provides a considerable amount of useful information about Danish monetary policy over the past decade. It describes key elements of the evolution of policy, discusses some of the implications for economic performance and provides an interesting section on Danish monetary policy during the 1992–3 ERM upheavals. In this sense, the paper is very informative, and instructive. Along the way, the paper touches on a large number of issues that are of interest both from the perspective of the Danish economy and from the broader perspective of lessons for the role of macroeconomic policies in open economies.

Although I agreed with much of what the author had to say, I also found some of his claims quite provocative and disagreed with some of his arguments.

I will structure my comments by discussing each of the four points he makes in the conclusion. The first conclusion is that Danish monetary policy has not contributed directly to the improvement of macroeconomic performance, but has been indirectly helpful through its role in stabilizing exchange rates and international capital flows. I agree with this conclusion. However, as discussed below, it seemed to me that some relevant factors were inadequately stressed in the paper's assessment.

By some indicators, Danish economic performance has been strong during 1982–92. Authorities brought down domestic inflation, and have succeeded in keeping it down. After declining in the first years after the stabilization, private saving rates have recovered, providing additional resources to finance investment. The country was able to avoid a currency crisis, during periods of extremely turbulent markets, even after controls on international capital flows were removed. Monetary policy no doubt played some role in these achievements. However, real economic activity has not shown sustained improvement. Unemployment rates are high and appear to be rising, with recent growth rates extremely sluggish. Thus, the author's conclusion is based on a somewhat narrower view of 'the improvement of macroeconomic performance' than I would have chosen.

At the same time, some special features of the Danish experience are likely to have made it easier to follow a monetary policy consistent with pegging the DKK to the DM. These were mentioned in the body of the paper, but in my view deserved additional emphasis, especially if one would like to draw more general lessons from the Danish experience. First, Denmark has had 'good news' in the form of an increase in demand for its exports. This international environment makes it much easier to sustain a pegged exchange rate than the environment facing countries that found recent export demand diminished because of sluggish US growth and/or the collapse of markets in the former Soviet bloc. The Danish central bank did not need to oversee the response to a large negative external shock.

Second, Denmark has had a history of not monetizing budget deficits. Thus, authorities were not attempting to convince the public that the link between deficits and money creation had been severed at the same time that they initiated a stabilization programme. In this sense, they began with a greater degree of 'credibility' than countries with a different history. While it is difficult to quantify, this difference in history may well make it easier for a government to convince the private sector that it will follow through on a stabilization policy, and thereby succeed in altering private sector price and wage setting behaviour more quickly. A related point is that the Danish government combined its announcement of an exchange rate peg with real changes in fiscal policy.

The conclusion's second point is that interest rate management has been at the core of monetary policy. The Nationalbank's approach to this policy has evolved and the present approach appears to be effective. This point is well documented in the paper, which presents an informative history of the evolution from an approach based on direct credit controls in the 1970s to one closer to the repurchase transactions used elsewhere in the EMS.

The paper then presents an empirical analysis of the relationship between domestic interest rates and private capital flows. While the empirical work raises some interesting issues, I found it difficult to interpret. I took the underlying issue to be whether Danish interest rate movements (relative to interest rates abroad) provide useful information about shifts in money demand relative to supply that are not attributable to easily observable variables. In a fixed exchange rate regime with free capital mobility, these shifts lead to private capital flows. (Outflows will undermine the ability of monetary authorities to defend the peg, as in the now standard balance of payments crisis literature.) If relative interest rate movements do provide such information, then it makes sense to adjust monetary policy in response to interest rate develop-ments.

Thus, the author regresses an indicator of private capital flows on domestic interest rates (relative to those in Germany) and other explanatory variables. However, the initial findings using OLS are not very supportive of the hypothesis that interest rate differentials help predict private capital flows—coefficients on current and lagged interest rates were insignificant. The author interprets the poor fit of the OLS equation as evidence that the domestic interest rate (and thus the differential) is endogenous. Using lagged German interest rates and the current account balance as instruments for the Danish interest rate, he re-estimates the equation. These instrumental variables results show some evidence that the fitted interest rate differential variable is positively related to capital flows.

I have some questions about this procedure. First, the contempor-aneous current account balance may well be endogenous as well. The positive and significant coefficient estimate on fitted interest rates in the second stage may simply be picking up the relationship between the external balance and private capital flows that was suggested in the OLS results. It is worth noting here that the current account, and not the German interest rates, have most of the explanatory power in the first stage regression.

Second, it is not clear why lagged German interest rates should be correlated with the part of domestic interest rate changes that the Danish authorities are most concerned about—developments specific to Denmark that could lead to capital outflows, compromising the bank's ability to defend its fixed exchange rate. For example, lagged German interest rates are likely to provide little help in forecasting a change in Danish expectations of a surge in inflation, or the government's commitment to maintaining a peg. Another way to make the point is that the desired instruments should be ones to explain the interest differential between Denmark and Germany, not the level of the Danish interest rate. The fact that the level of German interest rates is correlated with the level of Danish rates does not imply that they are good instruments for the differential.

Third, the equations assume that there was no structural shift in the determinants of private capital flows during the period 1979–92. This assumption is extremely strong for a period that saw the removal of capital controls as well as a major macroeconomic stabilization. Of course, the limited number of observations does make it difficult to test for structural changes. None the less, the issue does warrant some discussion.

The third conclusion of the paper is that the real interest rate is 'clearly' too high, but that there is relatively little that can be done to reduce it in the short run. I agree with the second part of this claim: as the paper argues, Denmark is unlikely to get its nominal interest rates below those in Germany soon. However, it is not as clear to me that real rates are currently 'too' high—even though they are high by historical standards and appear to have contributed to the large number of recent Danish bankruptcies. For example, is the current differential vis-à-vis Germany surprisingly high in light of the large residual stock of government bonds? Interest rates came down sharply in the aftermath of the fiscal consolidation—'should' they have come down even more? Additional discussion of the appropriate bench-mark(s) for evaluating the level of Danish interest rates would have been interesting and useful. On this topic, I found the reported evidence that the correlation between Danish and German interest rates shifted from a small positive number during December 1990–October 1991 to a large negative number during October 1991–June 1992 provocative and an interesting area for further analysis.

The final point in the paper's conclusion is that Denmark has gained more than others from its participation in the EMS. The claim suggests that Denmark would have been less successful in reducing its inflation rate if it had not participated in the exchange rate mechanism. While this may be true, it is very difficult to document conclusively. There are a number of other countries that have also carried out successful inflation reduction programs (including Australia and New Zealand) without such a membership. It is not at all clear that membership has made disinflation 'easier' for countries such as France and Italy. Recent estimates do not suggest that the output costs of disinflation in these countries were lowered as a result of membership.

A different interpretation of the claim about Denmark's (net) gain from membership relative to gains of other members links up with a point made at the beginning of my comments. Giving up exchange rate adjustment as a policy tool is more costly for countries that experience large real shocks (such as changes in world demand for their exports). Perhaps the EMS has implied a greater (net) gain for Denmark because it has been faced with fewer real shocks for which the ability to change exchange rates would have assisted the domestic adjustment. Of course, this interpretation puts the implications of participation in the ERM in a very different light.

# 5

# Disinflationary Stabilization Policy —Denmark in the 1980s

## Torben M. Andersen
*University of Aarhus and CEPR*

## 5.1    From Failure to Success

The economic situation in Denmark in the early 1980s was very bleak. On almost any score the Danish economy faced problems, including high inflation and unemployment, as well as persistent deficits on the current account and for the public sector. The situation was considered disastrous and it was feared that the Danish welfare state was eroding.

Within a decade the situation has been turned upside down, and the Danish case is by many considered to be a success story. Inflation has been substantially reduced and is now the lowest in Europe, after 30 years of systematic trade deficits we now run comfortable trade surpluses and the current account is in surplus, the government finances are under control and the deficit very modest, though the unemployment problem is still as pressing as it was in the early 1980s. Figure 5.1 shows how the 'quadrant of problems' has been substantially reduced during the 1980s.

The policy pursued up to 1982 was guided by a so-called switching strategy according to which the twin problems of unemployment and trade deficits could be solved by switching private into public demand. As a consequence, numerous policy packages included tax increases to curtail private demand and expansions of public demand and in particular employment programmes. These changes did not necessarily take place simultaneously as the policy had a stop–go character with tax increases in times where the current account was considered out of control and public expansion in periods with focus on the unemployment problem. As part of this strategy a loose exchange rate policy was pursued since discrete devaluations were believed to re-do the harms of excessive domestic wage increases. Over the period 1979–82 the Danish government

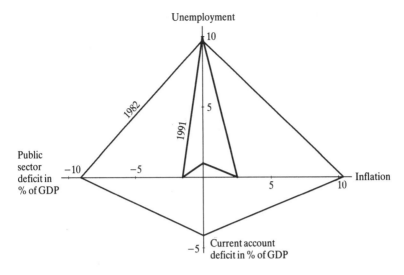

**Figure 5.1** Depiction of how the 'quadrant of problems' has been substantially reduced during the 1980s

thus undertook four discrete devaluations despite its participation in the EMS. Underlying this policy view was an accommodative attitude towards the labour market in the sense that the government accepted a responsibility for the employment level.

In the autumn 1982 there was a shift in government from a social democratic minority government to a liberal–conservative minority government. The new government launched an economic policy based on the idea that the problems underlying the Danish economy could only be solved in a medium-term perspective by an expansion of private sectors capable of facing international competition. The policy consisted of a disinflationary policy grounded in a fixed exchange rate policy and a tight fiscal policy. The policy shift signalled that the government focused on the current account as its most important policy objective leaving the responsibility for the employment level to the labour market.

The new 'production strategy' conceived that the double balance problem could be solved by expanding the private sector in general, and the tradables sector in particular. Increased production of tradables would create employment while at the same time reducing the trade deficit. It aimed at enhancing supply incentives in the tradeable sector, possibly in part by transferring supply capacity from the non-tradables sector. This adjustment process was assumed to be speeded up by a reduction in aggregate demand, especially for non-tradables. This aggressive strategy of export-led growth, denoted the production strategy, was thus intended to address the double balance problem directly.

This policy has not been given up but its contour has been less sharp both due to political changes but also due to the experience in the mid 1980s. Denmark experienced a tremendous upturn in the mid 1980s which further deteriorated the trade balance and which led to huge wage increases in 1987 in excess of the norms of the disinflationary policy. Some initiatives were taken at that time to curtail private demand. Since then the policy view has been a 'wait and see' position without any major policy changes since it is perceived that it takes a long time for structural changes to work themselves through. There is intensive debate on policy changes aiming at overcoming structural problems in the labour market and the taxation system, but no initiatives as yet.

The economic mood during the 1980s has thus moved through the phases of pessimism, optimism to prudence/consolidation. The aim of this paper is to analyse the changes induced by the policy shift in 1982 and the economic development since then. The focus will in particular be on the role of the exchange rate policy as part of this policy.

The paper is organized as follows. Section 5.2 lays out in more detail the ingredients of the policy initiatives since 1982. Section 5.3 provides a discussion of theoretical aspects relating to the Danish stabilization programme. The credibility of the disinflationary policy and the resulting nominal adjustments are addressed in section 5.4, while the real effects of the policy are considered in section 5.5 in a discussion of different hypothesis for the expansionary effects of the disinflationary stabilization programme. Finally, section 5.6 points to some policy lessons from the Danish experience. Section 5.7 is a postscript on the Danish implications of the recent turmoil in exchange rate markets.

## 5.2   The 1982 Policy Programme

Denmark has participated in the European exchange rate cooperations since the 'snake' arrangement was set up in 1972. In the EMS the participating countries fix a parity relative to ECU, and the exchange rate is allowed to fluctuate around this parity by ±2.25%. However, even though a formal fixed exchange rate policy, the Danish government initiated four discrete devaluations in the period 1979–82, and pursued thus a very soft 'fixed' exchange rate policy. This policy was abandoned in late 1982 when the government declared a fixed exchange rate policy which remains in force.

The policy programme did not make precise what was understood by a fixed exchange rate except that Denmark would continue its participation in the EMS. Later developments made clear that it did not mean an objective of keeping an unchanged exchange rate to Deutschmark (DM), ECU or some trade weighted exchange rate basket. Actually Danish kroner depreciated relative to DM, while the effective exchange rate appreciated (Table 5.1). The policy meant that the Danish Government would not take any initiatives to change the parity of Danish kroner in the EMS. Changes in the effective exchange rate were thus not to be avoided—and could not be avoided due to foreign shocks—but would not be caused by active measures by the Danish Government to improve competitiveness. At the core of the exchange rate policy is thus a distinction between an active or passive use of the instrument, rather than a fixed exchange rate in the literal sense of the term.

The disinflationary goal of the policy programme was supported by incomes policies. An important part of these initiatives were the abolition of indexation of wages and salaries in both the private and the public sector. The indexation of unemployment benefits was also suspended until the government in 1986–7 introduced a new system for adjusting benefits. Moreover, the government issued wage norms and intervened in negotiations to control nominal wage increases. Figure 5.2 shows nominal wage increases over the last couple of decades.

Financial markets used to be heavily regulated in particular with respect to the possibilities for private persons to borrow and to make cross-border financial transactions. Financial deregulation meant not only that quantity restrictions on private borrowing and selective interest rate policies were abandoned, but also that restrictions on transactions between foreign and domestic markets were reduced (see chapter 4). The deregulation vis-à-vis foreign capital markets follows the rules of EEC.

**Table 5.1** Changes in the effective exchange rate and wage competitiveness

| Year | Effective Exchange Rate[a] | Wage Competitiveness[b] |
|------|------|------|
| 1982 | −5.0 | −2.4 |
| 1983 | −1.4 | −1.4 |
| 1984 | −3.8 | −4.9 |
| 1985 | +0.9 | 0 |
| 1986 | +5.3 | +4.7 |
| 1987 | +3.7 | +8.2 |
| 1988 | −1.9 | −5.7 |
| 1989 | −2.6 | −4.4 |
| 1990 | +6.9 | +5.8 |
| 1991 | −1.9 | −2.8 |
| 1992 | +0.1 | −0.3 |

*Note*: [a] A minus sign indicates a depreciation of the effective exchange rate calculated by use of double weighted expert shocks. [b] A minus sign indicates a reduction in relative wage costs increase in common currency, i.e. improved competitiveness. *Source*: Det Økonomiske Råd

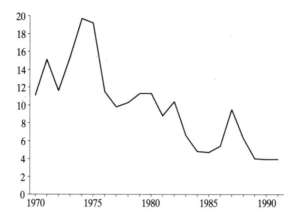

**Figure 5.2**   Nominal wage increases. *Source*: Danmarks Statistik

This meant a loose monetary policy. It should also be pointed out that by increasing capital mobility, the question of defending the exchange rate to a large extent became a match to market forces.

The cornerstone of economic problems in the early 1980s was the increasing public debt since it constrained the use of fiscal policy in pursuing other objectives. It was considered that public debt was growing at a rate which would undermine the welfare state (Figure 5.3). The 1982 policy programme thus included a strict fiscal policy aiming at bringing the growth in public expenditure under control. Changes in budgetary practices and the control of local fiscal authorities were enacted to stop the growth of (real) public expenditures. The upturn contributed also in itself significantly to lowering public debt through automatic stabilizing effects in the budget. To distinguish between discretionary and automatic stabilizing influences, Figure 5.4 shows the effect of discretionary changes in fiscal policy evaluated by means of the ADAM-model used by the central administration in macroeconomic policy evaluation. The figure shows the effect on GDP of discretionary changes in fiscal policy within the year.

It is worth noting that the government stressed when the programme was launched that it would have temporary contractionary effects. To mitigate these, the government undertook selective measures to improve private investments and to increase activity in the construction sector.

An immediate target of the policy reform was the current account and given the persistent deficit of the Danish economy (Figure 5.5), the government tied the credibility of its policy very closely to solving this problem. It was thus a declared objective that the current account should

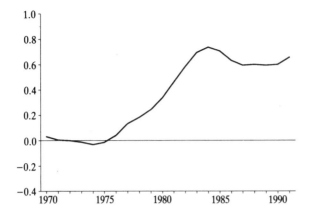

**Figure 5.3**  Public debt in % of GDP. *Source*: Danmarks Statistik

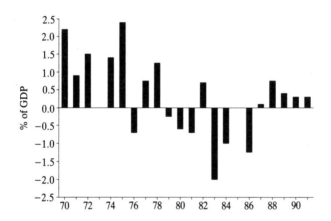

**Figure 5.4**  Effect of discretionary changes in fiscal policy.
*Source*: Budgetdepartmentet (1991)

be balanced already in 1986. Subsequent experience showed a rather
different current account development and the government successively
changed the current account objective and eventually gave up on a formal
target.

A reason for the deteriorating current account in the mid 1980s was a
huge increase in domestic demand which was unexpected in light of the
restrictive stance of the disinflationary policy. Both consumption and
investments were increasing rapidly and the real-growth rate for domestic

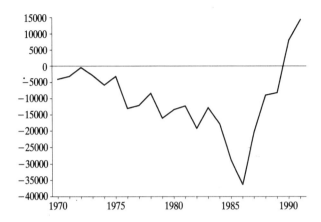

**Figure 5.5** Current account

demand topped in 1985 at 5.7%. The economy was booming and in the 1987 it resulted in large wage increases threatening the disinflationary policy. The government undertook different measures in 1986 to reduce private demand both through increased excise taxes and through a special tax on loan financed consumption which was booming. Since then the economy has been in recession leaving room for an expansion of net exports. The policy stance has been more or less passive since then.

## 5.3    Theoretical Aspects

Switching from an inflationary to a disinflationary regime by means of fixing the exchange rate raises an immediate credibility problem and the risk of causing a recession. Is the announced exchange rate policy credible or could further devaluations be expected? The credibility of the exchange rate depends both on the private sector's perception of the preferences of the policy-maker as well as the medium-term sustainability of the policy.

Let us first deal with the problem policy-makers have in convincing the private sector of its genuine intention to lower inflation and abstain from further discrete devaluations. The announcement of a fixed exchange rate is not necessarily credible since any government has an incentive to pretend that it is not contemplating a devaluation. Consider the following scenario: In the past recurrent devaluations have been undertaken and inflation is accordingly high. A new government takes office and proclaims a non-inflationary policy anchored in a fixed exchange rate.

Is the new government really aiming at a low inflation or is it just trying to talk down inflationary expectations to enhance the gains from a devaluation? The private sector cannot be sure which type it is up against and will accordingly have to judge the reputation of the policy-maker by its actions. The longer no devaluations are undertaken and the more the exchange rate is made consistent by other policy changes, the more likely it is that the policy maker is really pursuing a disinflationary policy. During this period of credibility building there will be a premium in inflationary expectations in the sense that some inflation is expected since the private sector is uncertain about policy objectives but—if the policy-maker is actually aiming at low inflation—no inflation is experienced (the peso problem). Despite rational expectations there are systematic forecast errors due to incomplete information on the intention of the government (Andersen and Risager, 1991).

During this transition period nominal variables like the interest and nominal wages will carry this inflation or devaluation premium as illustrated in Figure 5.6(a) showing actual ($\pi$) and expected inflation ($\pi^e$) in the case where a non-inflationary government replaces an inflationary government at time $t$, but the new policy does not gain credibility until time $s$.[1] The consequences of this premium are increases in the real wage and the real rate of interest during the transition period of credibility problems, which in turn causes a recession (Figures 5.6(b) and (c)).

The recessionary consequences of a disinflationary policy depend not only on expectations concerning inflation but also on the extent of backward-looking elements in wage formation. Such elements may arise from either overlapping contracts or indexation.[2] We shall focus on the latter effect since this is the most important in the Danish labour market.

A simple dynamic wage equation including indexation can be specified as

$$\hat{w}_t = \lambda \pi_{t-1} + (1 - \lambda)\pi^e_t, \quad \lambda \in [0,1] \tag{5.1}$$

**where** $\hat{w}$ is the change in nominal wages and $\lambda$ is the indexation parameter building past inflation into current wages.

Reducing the rate of inflation from some positive level to say 0, would cause a transition period with wage increases exceeding price increases as illustrated in Figure 5.7—assuming the disinflationary policy to be credible $\pi^e = 0$—and this contributes to a worsening and lengthening of the recessionary consequences of a disinflationary policy. Sluggishness induced by indexation is therefore alongside credibility a reason why a disinflationary policy may have contractionary effects. If indexation is removed ($\lambda=0$), eliminating the backward looking element, the adjustment of wages comes to depend only on current anticipations

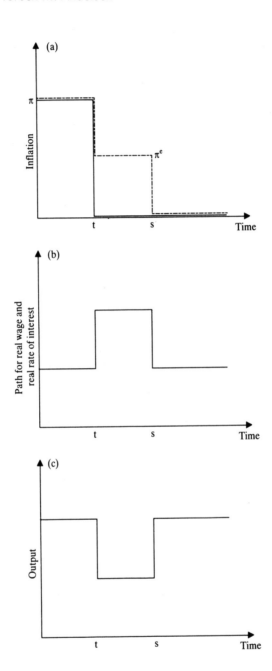

**Figure 5.6**   Effects of credibility problems of a policy change

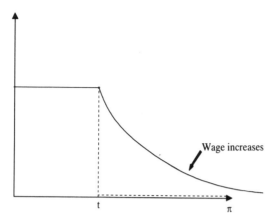

**Figure 5.7**   Wage adjustment to a credible disinflationary policy under indexation

concerning the exchange rate while the overhang from previous high inflation periods is eliminated. As a consequence, the recessionary consequences depend only on the credibility of the new regime making the inflationary history of no importance. The recessionary costs can thus be said to have been reduced at the cost of an intensified credibility problem—without indexation the gains to the government from a surprise devaluation have been increased.

The credibility of a fixed exchange rate policy also depends on its sustainability. Inherent in a disinflationary policy based on a fixed exchange rate is the view that nominal changes would not contribute to significant changes in the real exchange rate but rather to a wage–price-devaluation spiral pushing up the inflation rate. Hence, a necessary part of such a stabilization programme must be other measures aiming at the real exchange rate so as to ensure attainment of medium-term objectives. If not, the government will be forced to abandon the exchange rate or would be tempted to exploit short-term nominal rigidities by undertaking a devaluation to attain its objectives.

The design of fiscal policy is important in that respect and the so-called 'production strategy' was envisaged as a way to address the double problems of internal and external balance. The idea of this strategy can be illustrated by means of Figure 5.8 showing the potential crowding in effect of a reduction in government demand (here for non-tradables). The figure is based on a small and open economy with a tradables and a nontradables sector. Prices of tradables are given, while prices of non-tradables are determined by market clearing, and wages are determined at centralized bargains (see Andersen, 1990).

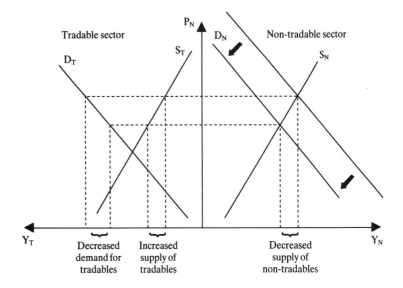

**Figure 5.8**   Effects of reduced demand for non-tradables

Consider the effects of a decrease in government demand for non-tradables. The decreased government demand for non-tradables does not produce a corresponding fall in the level of activity in this sector since private demand is crowded in via price decreases, thereby inducing demanders to substitute tradables for non-tradables. This effect is reinforced by the fact that lower prices also moderate nominal wages.

There is an indirect crowding-in effect on the supply of tradables arising from the wage moderation induced by lower prices of nontradables. Consequently, the level of activity in the tradable sector increases (Figure 5.8). The reduction of the non-tradable sector should thus be seen relative to an expansion of the tradable sector! The positive effects of decreased private demand for tradables on the trade balance is thus reinforced by an increase in the supply of tradables. This crowding-in effect is due to the wage–price formation process and not the traditional crowding in induced by lower interest rates. Actually, this type of crowding out is ruled out in the present setting by the implied small open economy assumption with respect to financial markets. Overall the effect of this policy is an improvement in the trade balance, while the employment effect is ambiguous.

If the government is perceived to follow a policy which counteracts any tendency for unemployment to rise by, for example, increased public employment, there will be a potential wage crowding out effect in a setting with centralized wage bargains. Such a policy effectively reduces the perceived sensitivity of employment to wages, and wages rise. By the end of the day, such a policy may create wage increases without reducing unemployment (Calmfors, 1982). It is an implication that a credible non-accommodation policy may induce a crowding-in effect in the form of wage moderation to the extent that the labour market perceives the employment costs of wage increases to have risen.

## 5.4 Credibility and Nominal Adjustment

The announcement of a disinflationary policy based on fixing the nominal exchange rate raises a credibility problem. The immediate effect is that nominal interest rates and wages include inflationary premiums since the private sector has to take precautions against the possibility that the fixed exchange rate policy is abandoned (Figure 5.6). We shall in this section discuss the nominal adjustment to the policy change to evaluate the credibility of the disinflationary policy programme.

### 5.4.1 *Interest Rates*

One way to evaluate the credibility which the market attaches to the exchange rate is to consider financial market data. Without any restrictions on cross-border financial transactions the interest rate differential is determined by the possibility of exchange rate changes (expectations and risk premia). In Figure 5.9. the long-term interest rate spread between Denmark and Germany is shown.

It is seen that the policy programme in 1982 implied a substantial drop in the interest rate spread indicating that some credibility was attached to the announced exchange rate despite the historical experience with several discrete devaluations (see Andersen and Risager, 1985, 1988, for an analysis of this period). The figure conceals the sharp reduction in both short- and long-term interest rates by 8 percentage points (p.p.) between October 1982 and May 1983. In this period there were two substantial discrete jumps in interest rates, with the long-term interest rate dropping by 1.6 p.p. the first trading day after the parliament approved the policy programme in October 1982, and by 1.2 p.p. in February 1983, the day after a labour market agreement in accordance with the disinflationary policy was settled. There remains, however, a non-trivial spread for most of the 1980s. It is interesting to note that the spread increases during the period 1986–7 where the policy programme runs into trouble with growing current account deficits and excessive

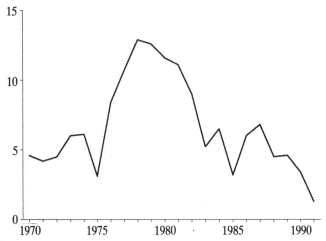

**Figure 5.9** Long-term interest rate spread: Denmark–Germany.
*Source*: Andersen and Sørensen (1992)

wage increases (see below). Later in the consolidation period when these problems are under control the spread decreases, and it is currently of the order of 1%.[3]

Judging credibility directly by considering the interest rate spread does not, however, take into account the specific arrangement of the EMS allowing some variation in the exchange rate around the parity and thus some interest rate spread. Considering this explicitly leads to a more sharp and still simple test of the credibility of the exchange rate band (Svensson, 1990). The highest possible devaluation arises when the exchange rate moves to the upper band, while the highest possible revaluation takes place when the exchange rate moves to the lower band. Hence, if the exchange rate band is credible the domestic interest rate cannot exceed the foreign interest rate plus the highest possible devaluation, and oppositely it cannot fall below the foreign interest rate minus the highest possible revaluation. Figure 5.10. shows the interest rate band implied by a credible exchange rate band for both short-term and long-term papers. On the basis of the short-term rate the exchange rate band is credible for most of the period, while the opposite is the case for long-term papers, where it is only recently that the rate of interest approaches the band implied by a credible exchange rate.

The fact that the exchange rate is not still fully credible may be attributed to either the possibility the market attaches to Denmark not entering the EMU or if it does, there might be an ultimate realignment at the start of EMU.

The fact that the exchange rate (band) is not fully credible has an

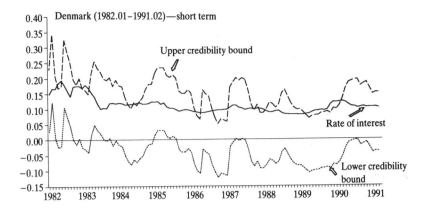

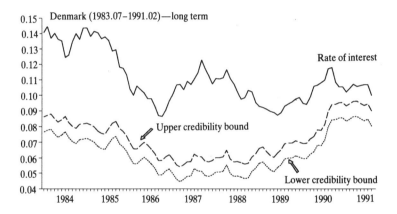

**Figure 5.10** Credibility bands for short- and long-term interest rates.

immediate cost in terms of a higher real rate of interest. Figure 5.11 shows the development in the real rate of interest, and it is seen that it has been at a high level also during the disinflationary period. The after tax real rate of interest has, however, been increasing. Actually we find the somewhat paradoxical result that recently when the exchange rate seems to have been the most credible the real rate of interest has been raising again. This reflects both the little room a small open economy with a fixed exchange rate has to pursue an independent monetary policy and the disadvantage of being a forerunner in the combat against inflation.

In the current situation with a (almost) credible exchange rate the interest rate is determined by the interest rate in the EMS-area. The nominal rate of interest is thus adapted to the average rate of inflation in

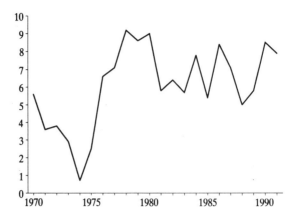

**Figure 5.11**   Real rate of interest. *Source*: Andersen and Sørensen (1992). *Note*: long-term interest rate less actual inflation

this area which exceeds the Danish rate of inflation. As a consequence, a country with a lower inflation than average faces an unintentional restrictive monetary policy. This situation is unlikely to be tenable in the long run and points to the need for coordination of economic policy in a monetary union.

### 5.4.2   *Wages*

Crucial to the success of a disinflationary policy is the extent to which nominal wage increases can be reduced. Since inertia in labour markets are usually perceived to be larger than in financial markets the response of wages is usually the cornerstone of the success of disinflationary policies.

As noted the Danish policy package included a substantial incomes policy involving suspension of indexation of wages and unemployment benefits and interference in labour market negotiations.

The development in actual wage inflation as well as the targets for nominal wage increases over the period is given in Table 5.2.

Table 5.2 gives an indication of how effective these policies have been in terms of reaching the wage–inflation targets. Roughly, policies were on target for 1983–4 and slightly off for 1984–5. But the highly ambitious targets for the following 2 years have obviously not been reached in the private sector. However, if we compare the average wage increase for 1983–5 with the recent past, wage inflation is only about half the size

**Table 5.2** Actual and target wage inflation

| | 1980–81 | 1981–82 | 1982–83 | 1983–84 | 1984–85 | 1985–86 | 1986–87 | 1987–88 | 1988–89 | 1989–90 | 1990–91 |
|---|---|---|---|---|---|---|---|---|---|---|---|
| Actual wage inflation | 8.6 | 9.8 | 8.4 | 4.5 | 4.9 | 5.5 | 7.7 | 8.1 | 6.4 | 4.0 | 3.9 |
| Target wage inflation | — | — | — | 4.0 | 4.0 | 2.0 | 1.5 | — | — | — | — |

*Note*: Average hourly wage increase in manufacturing is from first quarter to first quarter next year. Target wage growth refers to 1 March to 1 March next year.
*Source*: Statistiske Efterretninger

experienced previously. The income policies played a significant role in disinflating the economy, whereas the inflation revival in the late 1980s is attributed to the (time inconsistency) problem of maintaining a tight incomes policy prior to an election as well as to insufficient control of aggregate demand.

## 5.5    Real Adjustment

The disinflationary policy worked successfully in the short run bringing down nominal interest rates and wage increases avoiding any recessionary effects. On the contrary, the Danish economy soon experienced a remarkable upturn in the private sector over the period 1982–6 implying that 'the growth of output, employment and investment has been stronger than elsewhere in Europe' (OECD, 1986). This upturn should, however, been evaluated against a deep recession with negative growth rates in the years preceding the policy change.

The stabilization programme was based on ideas of crowding-in, although the expansionary effects turned out to be much larger than expected. There was a notable number of striking features about the development during this period in particular the tremendous increase in domestic demand and the fact that despite high official unemployment rates, lack of labour constrained the expansion of output. As a consequence, the current account developed into record deficits and the medium-term objectives of the policy programme were violated. The consequences of this situation have already been mentioned in the form of wage increases in excess of the low inflation target, which signalled a shift in the business cycle to a still ongoing recession. Part of this change can be attributed to policy changes aimed at strengthening savings incentives, particularly by reducing the implicit tax-subsidy to loan-financed consumption. The aim of this section is to discuss some reasons for the expansionary effects of the disinflationary policy.

### 5.5.1    *Windfall Gains*

As noted, the government did expect some initial contractionary effects of its programme, but the development turned out to be much better than forecasted. This might have been important in reinforcing the mood of optimism the government tried to create and thus in itself contribute to the expansion. It is especially noteworthy that the current account improved substantially already in 1983, although it later deteriorated significantly as already noted. This initial improvement in economic performance must primarily be attributed to two factors, namely, an upturn in international activity and falling energy prices as well as improvements in competitiveness caused by previous devaluations and the EMS-realignment in March 1983 in combination with the incomes policy, *cf.* the improvements in competitiveness in 1982 and 1983 (Table 5.1). In short, some expansion was to be expected the new policy programme notwithstanding.

### 5.5.2   Non-accommodation

An essential part of the policy programme was the non-accommodative stance leaving the responsibility for employment to the labour market. Previous governments had shown a great willingness to accommodate excessive wage increases, and this change was an important part of the production strategy basing a solution of internal and external balance problems on an expansion of the private sector. Focusing on the current account rather than unemployment as the direct target of the policy signalled a shift to a less accommodative policy.

It turned out that the behaviour in the labour market actually changed, and the development of real wages was significantly moderated. In a study of wage formation in Denmark by Andersen and Risager (1990), indication is found that the non-accommodative policy can explain a fall in real product wages up to 5–6%. This, in turn, means an increase in employment of the order of 4–5% potentially can be assigned to changed behaviour in the labour market. The total increase in manufacturing employment from 1982 to 1986 is about 10%. This study also confirms that the real-wage responds to the terms of trade such that wages in the long run tend to increase proportionately to improvements in terms of trade leaving profitability of firms unchanged. It is thus an implication that an increase in domestic demand induced by say fiscal policy would lead to wage increases which in the long run would leave the activity unaffected. The wage crowding-in effect of a fiscal contraction works thus fully in the long run (Andersen and Risager, 1990; Andersen, 1990). This shows why the initial fiscal policy shift may not have been as contractionary in a medium-term perspective as well as explains why the domestic demand boom was releasing a wage pressure inconsistent with the overall policy targets.

Figure 5.12 shows that it actually was possible to make the private sector the engine of economic progress since the share of public employment was falling at the same time as employment was growing. This expansion of production in the private sector in itself fuelled the upturn since it induced a large increase in investments. After a prolonged

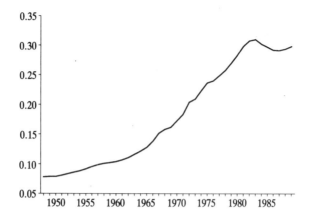

**Figure 5.12** The share of public employed in total employment. *Source*: Danmarks Statistik

recession production capacity was depleted and investments were necessary to expand production.

The needed increase in investments (1984, 12.5%, 1985, 14.1%) was underestimated at the outset of the stabilization programme, and it naturally meant that the current account would temporarily deteriorate and thus violate the medium-term objectives of the programme. Although these current account deficits caused by increased investments did not constitute a problem, they came to do so due to the stress the government had put on solving the current account problem within a fairly short span of time.

Another important supply constraint which turned out to be crucial to the problems faced during the second half of the 1980s was the labour market. It turned out that the labour market constrained the expansion of production to meet the increases in demand. There were shortages of different types of workers, that is, the qualifications demand by firms were not those possessed by the unemployed. To put it differently, even though the rate of unemployment was high it was not much above the non-inflationary level of unemployment. Recent estimates by the OECD (1990) and the Government (Budgetdepartmentet, 1991) evaluates the non-inflationary rate of unemployment to be around 8%. As a consequence, production did not expand as much as could be expected given the increase in demand. This meant both a further deterioration in the current account and the wage increases in 1987 inconsistent with the low inflation target and thus the fixed exchange rate policy.

### 5.5.3    *Financial Markets and Wealth Effects*

The sharp drop in nominal interest rates implied huge increases in asset prices and thus wealth. This increase led to increases in private demand which contributed to the expansionary effects of the disinflationary policy. This can be seen as the reverse mechanism of the well known contractionary effect of a devaluation due to reductions in wealth (Marston, 1985). If wealth was accumulated anticipating high inflation, there is an increase in perceived real-wealth when low inflation becomes credible or to put it differently, the real rate of return of fixed interest rate bounds (the dominant type in Denmark) increased substantially. Empirical evaluations for Denmark (Christensen, 1987) suggest that increases in wealth associated with a 1 p.p. fall in nominal interest rates cause the level of consumption to increase by 8%. This means that more than half of the increase in private consumption over the period 1982–6 can be attributed to the increase in wealth.

It should be noted that this wealth effect arose even though the real rate of interest after taxes increased. It could thus be discussed whether private wealth properly measured actually rose in the period. It is, however, the case that an important component of wealth increased, namely, the value of the housing stock and the net assets of the private sector. The increase in these wealth components is, however, related to the economic development and in particular the fall in interest rates. This effect is thus crucially dependent on the gain in credibility of the programme as analysed above and this points to some self-reinforcing mechanisms in the adjustment. It should also be noted that the wealth-term found relevant in empirical analysis is inconsistent with Ricardian Equivalence since the public debt is included in private wealth.

Besides this direct effect there were also important indirect effects from the fall in nominal interest rates and the liberalization of financial markets.[4] This arises both from relaxing the liquidity constraint in consumption by making acccess to consumer credits easier as well as the fact that over this period financial institutions vividly competed in an effort to gain market shares. The housing market plays an important role for the functioning of financial markets in Denmark. The basic financing of houses in Denmark takes place through 'realkreditinstitutioner' issuing fixed interest rate bonds based on the value of houses. Loans used to be granted as a given percentage (80%) of the nominal market value of the house. Often the remaining funds can be raised through mortgages or bank loans. The housing bonds function as an efficient way of intermediating between the demand and supply of funds. This system has worked very smoothly and the riskiness of such loan arrangements used to be very marginal since high inflation rates ensured that nominal house prices were increasing. Hence, the loans based on past house prices would only in very special case be in a risky position, even if the house owner was in financial problems. During the mid-1980s competition between financial institutions were intensified and with rising house prices due to the expansion the basis for expanding credit was automatically created, this process was reinforced by liberalization of the rules of these institutions.

This development took place against a background of falling inflation. In retrospect it is rather clear that the market underestimated the risk involved in financing houses in a low inflation economy and subsequent substantial losses have had important repercussions within the financial sector. Without inflation to continuously push up nominal house prices there is a risk not only that real but also nominal house prices will fall. This was what happened when the recession started and losses were inevitable. There is no doubt that the market had to go through a learning process in adjusting to the role of the housing market under low inflation. During the mid-1980s behaviour was still grounded in the perception that loans with houses as collateral were riskless and thus the granting of loans proceeded more or less automatically. It cannot be ruled out that house-buyers tended to underestimate the real rate of interest by focusing on the nominal financing costs which were substantially lower than in the past.

An idea of the size of this credit boom is given by Figure 5.13 showing total credits granted to the private sector by financial institutions as a

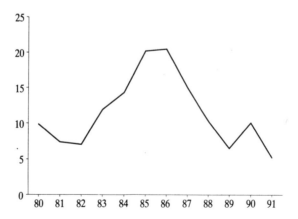

**Figure 5.13**   Credits to private sector in % of GDP. *Note*: Credits granted by domestic and foreign supplies of credit to the private sector and municipalities. *Source*: Annual report, Danmarks Nationalbank, various issues.

percentage of GDP. The figure shows the dramatic expansion of credits during the period 1982–6. The figure does not allow us to separate between whether increasing credit is based on loan financed consumption grounded in wealth increases or due to excess credits caused by intensified competition, liberalized rules and misperceptions of risks. Despite this caveat there is no doubt that loan financed demand was a crucial factor in the expansion of domestic demand during this period.

### 5.5.4 *Fiscal Consolidation and Expansion*

It has been argued that a fiscal consolidation could cause an expansion because it signals future tax cuts. Hence, reductions in public spending which are considered permanent would signal lower taxes—even though taxes temporarily might increase as part of the stabilization programme —and this would induce households to increase demand. This idea has been advanced by, e.g., Vastrup (1988) and Giavazzi and Pagano (1990). Giavazzi and Pagano (1990) argue, based on an econometric study, that this channel helps explain the consumption boom in Denmark.[5]

Giavazzi and Pagano (1990) estimate a consumption function relating consumption of non-durables to its own lagged value, lagged after-tax labour earnings, current and lagged wealth and current and lagged disposable income. The latter is supposed to capture eventual liquidity constraints, but was not found significant. It is noted that the wealth series used include public debt. Based on this consumption function, they consider how much of the changes in consumption can be explained by the changes in wealth and labour earnings. Considering the out-of-sample dynamic forecast errors, they conclude that there is a consumption puzzle since the model underpredicts consumption in the years 1985–7 of the order of 2 p.p. By relating these residuals to unanticipated changes in permanent government consumption, they conclude that fiscal restraint has contributed to the consumption boom and thus have been expansionary. This effect runs counter to the usual Keynesian prediction of contractionary effects of fiscal consolidation and has been termed the 'German view' on fiscal consolidation.

It is noteworthy that the underprediction of consumption does not arise until 1985 despite the introduction of the policy programme in 1982–3 as well as that the model overpredicts consumption in 1987 when consumption actually fell after a further fiscal tightening. Using measures of discretionary policy changes (Figure 5.4) rather than total government outlays which has a built-in counter-cyclical component does not leave any clear-cut relationship between residuals and changes in fiscal policies. Moreover, the reported consumption function is open to discussion and potentially misspecified. In a study of savings behaviour in the Nordic countries, Lehmussaari (1990) finds that consumption is somewhat delayed relative to the economic changes since the model first overpredicts and then underpredicts the actual consumption development (Christensen, 1987). This does not seem to support the existence of a consumption puzzle caused by fiscal consolidation.

In order to go further in the evaluation of this hypothesis, we need to consider whether the policy programme gave reasons for expectations that the tax burden would be lowered in the future and whether consumption is sensitive to such future changes.

First, even if government consumption was lowered, it is not clear whether this is temporary or lead to lower taxes in the future. The historical experience did not in any way suggest that it would be possible to permanently lower public consumption and no promises were made that tax cuts would appear in the future. Moreover, a substantial improvement of the budget was attained by taxing pension funds (realrenteafgiften) hence, if the future tax burden was expected to be lower so was future income.

Moreover, even if there were expectations about future tax cuts which could induce some perceived wealth increases, it is not clear that it would have expansionary consequences since there would be countervailing intertemporal substitution effects. These will not arise with lump-sum taxes but changes in actually used tax instruments would release such effects. If future tax cuts are in the form of lower income taxes, there would be an incentive to substitute work today for work tomorrow and this will have a contractionary effect. This effect is unlikely to be strong in the Danish case. If the taxes on consumption goods (vat or excise taxes) are lowered, it would induce substitution of consumption from today to tomorrow. Both of these effects would lower the expansionary effect. This effect is fairly strong as can be seen from the experiment with a temporary reduction of the vat rate in 1973–4. Hence, for the 'German view' to be correct, requires as a minimum that the reduction of public consumption is perceived as permanent and results in a reduction of income taxes. In short, the evidence does not seem consistent with the 'German view' of the effects of fiscal consolidation.

## 5.6 Concluding Remarks

The aim of the disinflationary stabilization programme was to enhance competitiveness and expand the private sector. The cornerstone of this policy was the adoption of a fixed exchange rate policy. The strategy followed can be termed a 'no more' philosophy in the sense that further devaluations would signal a willingness to accommodate wage increases. Numerous attempts with devaluations have only fuelled inflation leaving no real effects. The alternative would have been what can be termed a 'once-and-for-all' strategy as followed by Sweden at exactly the same time signalling that a last large devaluation was undertaken to restore competitiveness, and exchange rate changes would not be used to this end in the future.

The pros and cons of the two strategies can be summarized as follows. The 'once-and-for-all' policy ensures an immediate change in the right direction but encounters credibility problems in the medium term because it fuels inflation, implying that policy-makers might be forced to devalue again. The 'no more' policy causes heavy strain in the short term when the credibility of the low inflation policy is established, implying potential output losses, but eventually it is very effective in curbing inflationary expectations.

The developments in Denmark and Sweden in the recent past bring these differences out very clearly, and in retrospect the 'no-more' strategy has worked surprising well. The Danish experiment shows thus that it is possible to implement a disinflationary policy fairly smoothly avoiding any recessionary consequences. The incomes policy initiatives were extremely important in that respect. One could say that it has worked as a signal of the low inflation target, and given that it was backed with other policy changes, it has been effective. The fact that the government has maintained its fixed exchange rate policy despite later problems primarily the large wage increases in 1987 has implied that low inflation has become a permanent feature of the Danish economy.

The stabilization programme had an expansionary effect which primarily must be attributed to the non-accommodative stance of the policies and the consumption boom caused by wealth increases and expanding consumer credits. Later the programme faced problems and was to some extent killed by its own success in the sense that the following expansion undermined the basis for the policy. These problems arose due to an underestimation of the increases in demand released by a credible low inflation policy and capital market liberalizations, while at the same time the supply capacity (both in respect to capital and labour) was vastly overestimated. This brings out the importance of using fiscal policy instruments to support the relative price changes aimed at by the fixed exchange rate policy.

## 5.7    Postscript: Exchange Market Pressure 1992–3

The turmoil in exchange rate markets starting in the autumn 1992 also affected the Danish kroner, and it was under pressure requiring substantial interventions and increases in short-term interest rates. After the de facto breakdown of the exchange rate mechanism of the EMS in August 1993, it has been questioned why Danish kroner came under pressure. Prior to these events the credibility of the Danish exchange rate policy was at the top and the interest rate spread to Germany had been eliminated. Inflation was among the lowest in Europe, and the current account kept improving. In light of these fundamentals, the pressure on the Danish kroner seems unjustified especially at a point in time when the Danish position on the Maastricht Treaty had been clarified.

The context of this argument is the likelihood of an aggressive Danish devaluation in order to solve domestic economic–adjustment problems. The actual situation gave no grounds to expect any such devaluation as also reflected in the very narrow interest rate differential to Germany. However, the crucial point is that this was of no great importance after the foreign exchange crisis had broken out, and currencies of great significance to Denmark's foreign trade came under pressure and were devalued. The issue in that situation was rather whether Denmark might be forced to devalue as a defensive measure. The fact that such a situation could arise is closely related to the definition of the fixed exchange rate policy in practice.

A fixed exchange rate policy defined within the ERM, and thereby the ECU, implies a systematic difference between on the one hand the basket of currencies and their weighting on which the krone's stability is based, and on the other the basket used in relation to foreign trade. However, maintaining a fixed exchange rate within the ERM has meant that in connection with the foreign exchange crisis the effective krone rate in real terms appreciated by approximately 6%. Such a deterioration in competitiveness, to the detriment of foreign trade and particularly employment, will unavoidably give rise to speculation regarding whether a defensive exchange rate adjustment is required. In other words, the credibility of the fixed exchange rate policy was again put to a test, since it was uncertain whether political willingness existed to bear the consequences of such a substantial and sudden change in competitiveness. This problem was accentuated by unemployment already being on the rise.

In Denmark's case two factors in particular may have contributed to the fact that a defensive devaluation could not be ruled out. First, the alternative means of adjusting to the deterioration in competitiveness would be a further dampening of wage increases. As this rate is already very low, and is extremely difficult to bring below zero, the effectiveness of this adjustment mechanism in the actual situation must be questioned.

Second, there is the issue of willingness to bear the short-term costs of defending the exchange rate represented by interest rate increases. With a high real interest rate level from the outset such a policy will reinforce the contractive effects of the monetary policy and thus contribute to a further slowdown in the economy and aggravation of the unemployment problem. The fact that the central bank in the spring 1993 after the turmoil in January and February quickly reduced short-term rates of interest signalled to the market that the rate of interest was considered excessive.

The foreign exchange unrest therefore strengthened the incentive to devalue. Although the unrest was not rooted directly in the domestic economic fundamentals, the crisis and the devaluation of other currencies created a new situation in which the krone rate's credibility was put to the test in the context of a sudden deterioration in competitiveness. This does not exclude the influence on developments of more 'irrational speculative' considerations. However, the decisive factor is that due to the way the fixed exchange rate policy is defined in practice, unrest affecting individual currencies can be expected to spread to other currencies, since any devaluations will have a real economic impact in the form of changes in competitiveness.

Subsequent exchange rate changes have brought the effective exchange rate back to the level it had prior to the turmoil, that is, the appreciation of Danish kroner during this period has been undone. In this period, policy-makers have spent much effort in repeating its commitment to a strong currency option.

## Notes

Comments and suggestions from Alberto Giovannini, Kari Puumanen and Charles Wyplosz as well as workshop participants are gratefully acknowledged. The paper was written in 1992 and does not include the more recent shift to an expansionary fiscal policy.
1. The figures build on the analysis of credibility problems in a small open economy in Andersen and Risager (1991).
2. Ball (1990) shows that with staggered price setting, a disinflationary policy need not cause a recession. The result depends on the path chosen for reducing money supply growth. Hence, in the present case of an exchange rate stabilization, staggering in itself would not induce expansionary effects.
3. Weber (1991) claims that Denmark since 1982 seems to have followed a soft currency option, but this is not justified by the data.
4. This development was experienced by all the Nordic countries (see Koskela and Virén, 1992).
5. Note that they wrongly state that the stabilization programme was initiated by a huge discrete devaluation.

## References

Andersen, T. M. (1990), 'Stabilization policies towards internal and external balance in the Nordic countries', *Scandinavian Journal of Economics*, **92**, 177–202.

Andersen, T. M. and Risager, O. (1985), 'Expectations and credibility of economic policy: a term structure of interest rate test for Denmark', paper presented at the Sandbjerg Workshop.

Andersen, T. M. and Risager, O. (1988), 'Stabilization policies, credibility, and interest rate determination in a small open economy', *European Economic Review*, **32**, 669–79.

Andersen, T. M. and Risager, O. (1990), 'Wage formation in Denmark', in L. Calmfors (ed.), *Wage Formation and Macroeconomic Policies in the Nordic Countries*, Oxford University Press, Oxford.

Andersen, T. M. and Risager, O. (1991), 'The role of credibility for the effects of a change in the exchange-rate policy', *Oxford Economic Papers*, **43**, 85–98.

Andersen, T. M. and Sørensen, J. R. (1992), 'Interest rate determination in the Nordic countries', Working Paper.

Ball, L. (1990), 'Credible disinflation with staggered price setting', NBER Working Paper 3555.

Budgetdepartmentet, Finansredegørelsen, various issues.

Calmfors, L. (1982), 'Employment policies, wage formation and trade union behaviour in a small open economy', *Scandinavian Journal of Economics*, **84**, 45–73.

Christensen, A. M. (1987), 'Indkomst, formue og privatforbrug' [Income, Wealth and Private Consumption], Working Paper, Danish Central Bank.

Danmarks Nationalbank, 'Beretning og Regnskab' [Annual Reports], various issues.

Det Økonomiske Råd, 'Dansk Økonomi' [The Danish Economy], various issues.

Giavazzi, F. and Pagano, M. (1990), 'Can severe fiscal contractions be expansionary? Tales of two small European countries', *NBER Macroeconomics Annual*, The MIT Press, Cambridge, MA.

Koskela, E. and Virén, M. (1992), 'Inflation, capital markets and household saving in the Nordic countries, 1992', *Scandinavian Journal of Economics*, **94**, 215–28.

Lehmussaari, O.-P. (1990), 'Deregulation and consumption: saving dynamics in the Nordic countries', *IMF Staff Papers*, **37**(1), 71–93.

Marston, R.C. (1985), 'Stabilization policy in open economies', in R. W. Jones and P. B. Kenen (eds), *Handbook of International Economics* (vol. II), North-Holland, Amsterdam.

OECD, Economic Surveys—Denmark, various issues.

Svensson, L. E. O. (1990), 'The simple test of target zone credibility', *IMP Staff Papers*, **38**(3), 655–65.

Vastrup, C. (1989), 'Economic policy and adjustment in Denmark', in M. Monti (ed.), *Fiscal Policy, Economic Adjustment, and Financial Markets*, International Monetary Fund, Washington, DC.

Weber, A. (1991), 'Credibility, reputation and the European monetary system', *Economic Policy*, **12**, 57–102.

# Discussion

## Kari Puumanen
*Bank of Finland/Suomen Pankki*

In the European context the Danish economy since 1982 is perhaps the clearest case of a successful disinflation using the fixed exchange rate as the intermediate target. Compared with other smaller countries such as Austria and Belgium which also have a good record in achieving price and exchange rate stability, the change in the Danish performance is more profound. No wonder, then, that Denmark became a standard reference in the European policy debate in defence of the Maastricht philosophy, which only adds to the frustration caused by the Danish vote.

Torben Andersen's paper offers an interesting analysis of many of the basic issues in the economics of Denmark. It rightly points out that, to stabilize a devaluation-prone stop–go economy with a structurally weak external balance, a monetary policy commitment to the fixed exchange rate has to be supported by other means, such as medium-term consolidation of fiscal policy, competitiveness-orientated incomes policies and tax policies aimed at reducing debt-financed spending. Given the recent failures of several countries to maintain the fixed exchange rate anchor for their monetary policy, this requirement of consistency in the overall economic policy approach seems to be the main message to be gained from the Danish experience.

In analysing the contribution of fiscal policy to the Danish stabilization process, Andersen emphasises the potential crowding-in of net exports caused by fiscal contraction, resulting in a relative price change in favour of the tradeables sector. This crowding-in effect differs from the current efforts in Sweden and Finland to reduce the adjustment burden of excessively high interest rates by tightening fiscal policy. The paper also discusses the 'German view' (or Ricardian equivalence argument) that a reduction in government consumption leads to a rise in private consumption by increasing perceived household wealth.

Casual observation of the Danish experience lends support to the view that offsetting increases in both the real external balance and private spending have helped to reduce the deflationary consequences of fiscal consolidation. It is not, however, clear from the paper whether the argument is that the role of these crowding-in channels has been significant in Denmark or that the operation of these offsetting forces has, in fact, been so powerful as to make the Danish disinflation a 'free lunch'. Here a second casual glance at the Danish data—reduced GDP growth during the 1980s, a surprisingly sharp drop in the trend of manufacturing productivity and a NAIRU of 8–9% (on OECD estimates), hinting at significant labour hoarding—clearly speaks against the 'free lunch' hypothesis.

It may of course be that the deterioration in the Danish growth performance is due to adverse exogenous country-specific factors or to developments common to most European economics rather than to the Danish stabilization programme. To determine the magnitude of the disinflation adjustment cost, the analysis of the paper should be enlarged so that it can also cope with the changes that occurred in the economic environment of Denmark during the 1980s, thus making it possible to identify the policy effects of other factors.

The arguments concerning the relevance of the crowding-in effects through relative price and Ricardian wealth effects as opposed to the standard Phillips-curve argument and the Keynesian fiscal-monetary policy mix channel (or, in modern terms, the credibility effect of tighter fiscal policy on the interest rate parity) would also be on firmer ground if some reference were made to empirical data. For example, data on profits and relative wage developments in the traded and non-traded goods sectors and estimates of interest elasticity of domestic demand might be helpful.

One of the cruel facts of life is that a 'hard currency' policy cannot achieve credibility before it has been tested by the markets, but such an opportunity does not arise until things get sufficiently out of hand. It follows that the disinflation process to a hard currency status cannot be uniform.

The Danish experience is also illuminating in this respect. After a promising start the stabilisation programme could not prevent the economy from overheating in 1985–6. But by sticking to a non-accommodative policy stance, a rapid improvement in both external balance and price stability was achieved in subsequent years. It seems that it was in this critical period that the battle of Denmark was fought and won and the vicious circle turned into a virtuous circle. The episode therefore warrants special emphasis in the analysis.

Here again, the economic environment is relevant. The boom in Denmark started earlier than in other countries so that the cost of stabilization was probably significantly reduced by rising export demand. In this respect, Denmark had some luck compared to its Nordic neighbours, Sweden and Finland in particular, where the 'Big Bang' took place only on the threshold of the present recession.

# Discussion

## Charles Wyplosz
*INSEAD, Fontainebleau and CEPR*

Up until the mid-1980s Denmark used to be my favourite counter-example that nations fulfil their intertemporal budget constraint. Almost never in the post-war period did Denmark exhibit a current surplus. Despite belonging to one of the most highly indebted countries in the world (see Table 1) Danish institutional borrowers enjoyed favourable ratings on international markets. Today, the country has suffered relatively little from the worldwide recession, boasts a robust external surplus and has one of the lowest inflation rates in the world. Its only dark point is the seemingly unavoidable European-style double-digit rate of unemployment. The paper provides a very useful and lucid description interpretation of this amazing turnaround. In my comments I make an attempt at rejecting this view but conclude that something unusually favourable did occur in Denmark in the mid-1980s.

**Table 1**  Selected ratios of external debt to GDP (1987)

| Denmark | Argentina | Brazil | Mexico |
|---|---|---|---|
| 44% | 66% | 40% | 49% |

*Source*: Sinn (1990)

## The Danish Strategy and Outcome

When the new policy was launched in 1982, Denmark suffered from all macroeconomic evils: high inflation, large external deficits and, surprisingly for a Scandinavian country, high unemployment. The strategy was simple: tighten monetary policy and use the exchange rate as an anchor to build up credibility, use all instruments to shift output from the non-traded to the traded sector and let the labour market take care of itself. By 1987, the outcome was surprising: the economy had been booming, inflation was rising again and the current account deficit had deepened. It is after 1987 that the expected results have come in with declining inflation and a spectacular improvement of the current account. The delay seems remarkably long. Either the policies had the proper but much delayed effect or the policies have not been implemented as quickly as announced.

## A Soft Implementation

In an open economy, it is very difficult to judge the stance of monetary policy. The best indicator is the exchange rate and, in the case of Denmark, it does not point to a very tight policy over the period 1982–7. A serious attempt to use the exchange rate as an anchor would have involved sticking to the DM. Table 2 presents the EMS realignments which have involved either the Danish kroner or the DM, or both. It is clear that until the last EMS realignment before the crisis of 1992 Denmark never followed Germany. Similarly, looking at the fiscal policy indicators provided in the paper, one sees that policy was tight before 1982, relaxed in the election year, tightened thereafter and relaxed in 1987–8, just when the programme was bearing fruit.

**Table 2**  EMS realignments (% vis-à-vis ECU)

|  | 9.79 | 11.79 | 10.81 | 2.82 | 6.82 | 3.83 | 4.86 | 1.87 |
|---|---|---|---|---|---|---|---|---|
| DKK | −2.9 | −4.8 | 0.0 | −3.0 | 0.0 | 2.5 | 1.0 | 0.0 |
| DM | 2.0 | 0.0 | 5.5 | 0.0 | 4.25 | 5.5 | 3.0 | 3.0 |

The boom after (limited) tightening has been ascribed by Giavazzi and Pagano (1990) to the confidence-building effect of the policy switch. Yet, the long-term interest rate differential shown in the paper shows that most of the confidence gain occurred before 1982, most notably after 1979 after the creation of the EMS. After 1982, this indicator of confidence is in fact quite volatile. Thus, the boom after 1982 is less paradoxical than it is made to be: lax monetary policy and confidence build-up after 1979 outweighed a tight fiscal policy.

## The Traded Good Sector Miracle

What remains true is that after 1987 Denmark has maintained a fixed exchange rate vis-à-vis the DM and yet its current account has improved dramatically. The normal effect of adopting the exchange rate as an anchor is to let the real exchange rate appreciate until the traded good sector exerts a moderating influence on inflation.

Andersen offers his interpretation of this miracle: credit should be given to a policy of fiscal retrenchment consciously designed to boost the traded good sector. The channel works as follows. A cut in government spending hurts primarily the non-traded good sector, which leads to a reduction in the relative price of non-traded goods. The pressure is transmitted to wages which then fall relatively to traded good prices. Thus the real producer wage in the traded good sector declines which produces the desired effect and allows the current account to improve. The conclusion is that adding fiscal contraction to tight monetary policy— the exchange rate anchor is equivalent to tight money—has beneficial effects on the traded good sector.

Indeed, the data show that private sector demand has increased by more than the retrenchment in public spending, better than Ricardian equivalence! This is where Giavazzi and Pagano have documented a negative multiplier effect. Their interpretation, that expectations boost demand because future tax liabilities decline, is actually rejected by Andersen. His explanation is that Denmark has benefited from a wealth effect provoked by a fall in the interest rate. But what has declined after 1982 is the nominal, not the real interest rate. For his interpretation to hold, we would need to believe in a strong non-neutrality.

There is another interpretation, though. It notes that in Denmark, as elsewhere in Europe, the mid-1980s have been marked by a substantial deregulation of financial markets. Everywhere the same effects have been observed. To take advantage of heightened competition, house-holds have undertaken a one-shot adjustment in their borrowing. Temporarily the saving rate has dramatically declined, leading to a consumption boom. This pattern is spectacularly confirmed by Figure 5.13.

## Conclusion: The Danish Fairy-Tale

The paper makes a highly convincing case that fixing the exchange rate helps fighting inflation if only because it provides a clear anchor to monetary policy. Does it reduce the cost of disinflation? The proposed Danish fairy tale is that we can have both boom and disinflation. Figure 1 presents the rate of unemployment and the subsequent year's rate of inflation.[1] The largest part of the disinflation (1981–3) certainly did not come for free. After 1987, again we observe the standard unemployment-inflation tradeoff (1986–7 reflects the counter-oil shock of 1986).

The fairy tale occurs between 1983 and 1986, years of sharply declining unemployment and constant inflation. The boom cannot be ascribed entirely to a relaxed monetary policy because, despite several devalu-ations vis-à-vis the DM the current account actually worsened. If it is due to financial deregulation, why was it not accompanied by rising inflation as in the United Kingdom, for example? This left either of two miracles to be explained. The first one is that tight fiscal policy has boosted output. The second one is that wage moderation has prevented the Bristish-style

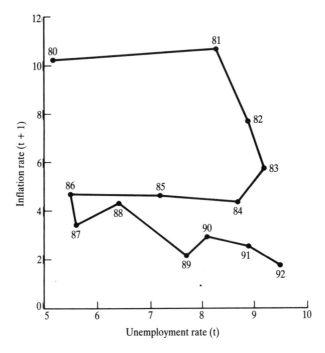

**Figure 1**  Unemployment and lagged inflation, 1980–92.
*Source*: European Economy, March 1993

burst of inflation. Andersen adopts both interpretations when he describes the shift from nontraded to traded good output via a decline in real producer wages in the traded good sector. He may well be right.

## Note

1.  Having contemporaneous inflation does not alter the general shape of the graph nor the conclusions drawn here.

## Reference

Sinn, S. (1990), *Net External Asset Positions of 145 Countries*, Kieler Studien No 234, J.C.B. Mohr, Tübingen.

# 6

## The Struggle to Turn the Swedish Krona into a Hard Currency

**Lars Hörngren and Hans Lindberg**
*Sveriges Riksbank*

### 6.1    Introduction

What is a 'hard currency'? The phrase is frequently used but rarely defined, presumably because it belongs to journalistic rather than academic jargon. To make sense of the title of this paper we must therefore begin by clarifying our terms. The term 'hard currency' is often used to characterize (favourably) nominal exchange rates. 'Hard' is then defined by the absence of depreciations or devaluations.[1] This is obviously a relative measure, the nominal exchange rate being the relative price between two national currencies. Moreover, the exchange rate is at most an intermediate policy target. To be valuable, a hard currency policy must deliver more than a non-depreciating exchange rate. In terms of an ultimate target variable, we define a hard currency—in an absolute sense—as characterized by a stable real value in terms of the consumption basket. Under this definition, a hard currency policy is thus synonymous to a policy aimed at price stability.

Under some assumptions, relative and absolute hardness can be more or less equivalent. The simplest case is to assume that absolute purchasing power parity (PPP) holds as an equilibrium condition in the long run. Then the nominal exchange rate (units of domestic currency per unit of foreign currency) must equal the ratio between the domestic and the foreign price levels. Consequently, if the currency of a (small) country is permanently pegged to a foreign currency with a stable real value, it will also behave as a hard currency in the long run.

The hardness of a currency is tested if there is a shock to the domestic price level, leading to a real appreciation. Then the question arises how PPP will be re-established. Under a hard currency policy, an adjustment

133

period during which the domestic rate of inflation is lower than that in the reference currency is necessary. However, if the economy is characterized by nominal rigidities, disinflation is a trying process, both economically and politically. Pressures may arise for a devaluation, accommodating the increase in the price level. Under less than perfect credibility, this will result in high interest rate differentials and intermittent 'currency crises' when the determination of the policy-makers is put to test.

If we look at Sweden in this perspective, we see a country on a fixed exchange rate that during the second half of the 1980s experienced a real appreciation as a result of an average inflation rate above that in the reference currencies. Sweden did not pass the test of absolute hardness described above, despite the fixed exchange rate. The nominal adjustment was too slow to prevent the economy from going into the worst depression experienced in the post-war period. In the process, inflation dropped to levels consistent with a hard currency policy, but during the turmoil on the European currency markets in September 1992 the krona came under heavy pressure. The fixed exchange rate was assiduously defended with high interest rates and the turmoil subsided. However, tensions soon re-emerged. This time, in November 1992, the capital outflows proved to be uncontrollable, not least because the interest rate levels required to stop the speculation against the krona would have been too much of a burden on an already weak economy. The fixed exchange rate was therefore abandoned. The krona has subsequently dropped significantly in value, i.e. it has not met the relative hard currency criterion. However, the struggle to turn the krona into a hard currency in the absolute sense continues. The Riksbank—the Swedish central bank—has announced an inflation target of 2% from 1995 onwards. Policy-makers are thus determined to maintain the low rate of inflation achieved in recent years through a policy expressed in terms of the ultimate objective of price stability.

The purpose of this paper is to review and analyse the Swedish experience from trying to win a reputation for being a hard currency country, with a special focus on monetary and exchange rate policy. We will not deal in any detail with the motives for choosing a hard currency strategy. At a general level, we interpret this as an acceptance of the vertical Phillips curve as the best description of the long-term relation between inflation and unemployment, making policy-makers choose price stability as the long run target for monetary policy. The fixed exchange rate, in turn, was a means to affect expectations about the policy that will be pursued if the domestic price level should rise, conceivably improving the short run trade-off between inflation and unemployment. If credible, the fixed exchange rate will also reduce the likelihood of price increases caused by expectations of inflationary or accommodative policies in the future.[2]

We will take the devaluation in October 1982 as the starting point for the hard currency policy. This is consistent with the policy statements made at the time and the strong measures taken to defend the fixed exchange rate when its credibility was questioned. This is not to deny that the krona during much of the 1980s failed to live up to the absolute requirements of a hard currency. Neither do we want to absolve the policy-makers from a major part of the responsibility for these deviations from the straight and narrow path. However, we think that it is relevant to interpret the developments in Sweden not as the result of changing policy targets, but as an ongoing struggle to maintain and enhance the credibility of the krona as a hard currency. If we were to put theoretical labels on the policy-makers' behaviour, we would say that they accepted the vertical Phillips curve in the early 1980s, but only gradually recognized the importance of making credible commitments to support the policy statements. As it turned out, this realization came too late, at least in the sense that the Swedish economy was allowed to slip badly off track before major adjustments were made.

It is the process through which this change of perspective has taken place that we will try to chart in this paper. It is organized as follows. In section 6.2, we outline Swedish exchange rate policy in the 'soft' period between the collapse of the Bretton Woods system and the 1982 devaluation. Section 6.3 covers the policies in the past 10 years, characterized by the struggle to establish the credibility of the hard currency policy. In section 6.4, we try to put the Swedish development into a broader perspective by identifying some important characteristics in the Riksbank's behaviour and by linking these observations to recent work on positive analysis of central bank behaviour. Section 6.5 offers concluding comments.

## 6.2 Swedish Exchange Rate Policy 1973–82: A Brief Review

As a background to the current situation, we will in this section briefly describe Swedish exchange rate policy in the period that led up the 1982 devaluation, by assumption, the starting point for the hard currency policy.

After the final breakdown of the Bretton Woods system, the krona was linked to the European currency snake. This system—the precursor to the EMS—implied a Deutschmark (DM) peg and could be interpreted as a hard currency option. However, it soon emerged that policy targets in Sweden and Germany were not congruent. Unemployment is traditionally a target given considerable weight in Swedish economic policy (Figure 6.1). In order to maintain high employment, the first oil price shock was met with a fiscal expansion, the so-called bridging policy period 1974–6. This accommodation of the inflationary impulse, in combination with substantial increases in pay-roll taxes, made Swedish wage costs rise by 42% during 1975 and 1976. In Germany, in contrast, price stability was given priority, leading to tighter policies. Consequently, as Figure 6.2 shows, Swedish and German inflation rates diverged, leading to a real appreciation of the krona (Figure 6.3). To close this gap, the krona parity exchange rate in the Snake was devalued twice, in October 1976 and April 1977, altogether by 9%. Finally, in August 1977, the krona was taken out of the Snake system. At the same time, it was devalued by 10% relative to the new bench-mark, a trade-weighted currency basket.[3] The official motivations on all three occasions emphasized Sweden's competitiveness, i.e. the purpose was to offset the effects of past price and wage inflation. The devaluations in 1976 and 1977 were sufficient to restore competitiveness to the pre-1975 level, which improved the growth rate in real GDP substantially (Figure 6.4). In the years immediately after the switch to the currency basket, inflation was kept roughly in step with the basket weighted international rate of inflation (Figure 6.2).

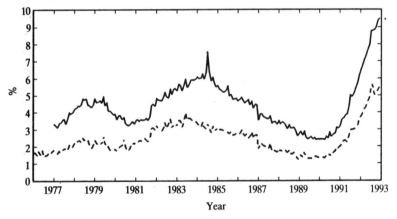

——— Unemployment incl. labour market measures
- - - Unemployment

**Figure 6.1** Unemployment. Monthly unemployment from January 1975 to December 1992 and unemployment including labour market measures from January 1976 to December 1992. *Source*: Statistics Sweden

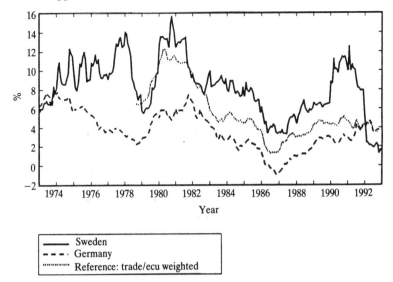

**Figure 6.2** Inflation (year-on-year). For Sweden and Germany from January 1973 to December 1992. A 'reference' inflation rate, defined as the weighted inflation rate of the trade-weighted currency basket and from May 1991 onwards ECU weighted, is also plotted for the period September 1978 to October 1992. *Source*: International Financial Statistics (IFS), OECD, Sveriges Riksbank.

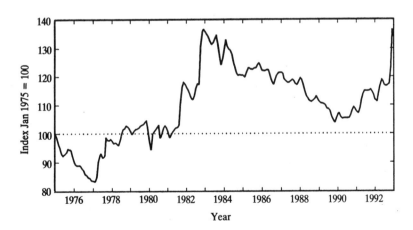

**Figure 6.3** Real effective exchange rate. Monthly figures from January 1975 to December 1992, based on a measure of relative unit labour cost. *Source*: IFS

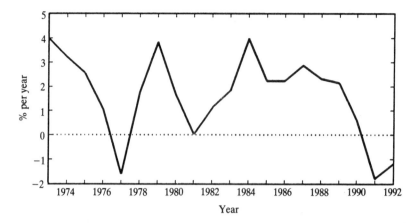

**Figure 6.4** Growth rate real GDP. From 1973 to 1992. *Source*: National Institute of Economic Research and Statistics Sweden

The replacement of the DM with the currency basket is open to several interpretations. On the one hand, policy-makers can be said to have acknowledged that it was impossible and/or undesirable to keep the Swedish inflation rate in step with that in Germany. Devaluations were inconsistent with a hard currency policy. Perhaps more importantly, however, the decision to peg the krona to a basket including currencies of countries that could be expected to have higher average inflation rates than Germany indicated a 'softening' of policy. By shifting to the basket, Sweden made it easier to maintain an unchanged peg, at the same time making room for somewhat higher domestic inflation. This is not to say that the basket was a 'soft option' in an absolute sense, but it set a target equal to an average of international inflation rates rather than that of Germany alone.

It may be argued that from the point of view of how to construct a currency basket that is to protect the domestic economy from international disturbances and stabilize competitiveness, a trade-weighted basket was superior to the DM. In particular, the basket had the advantage of reducing the impact of swings in the US dollar/DM rate. If the DM weakened relative to the US dollar and the basket index was kept constant, the krona would depreciate relative to the US dollar, but also appreciate relative to the mark. In this way, swings in international exchange rates were averaged over several krona exchange rates. A trade-weighted currency basket can thus be seen as a device that smooths the impact of external (nominal) disturbances on the effective real exchange rate.

This illustrates that the peg chosen under a hard currency policy—based primarily on its expected inflation performance—need not coincide with the one preferred given ambitions to stabilize international competitiveness. In principle, the choice between a hard currency peg and a trade-weighted basket should therefore be made on the basis of the perceived structure of nominal disturbances. For example, if inflationary wage increases are common, a pure hard currency strategy, with strong emphasis on the fixity of the peg, may be needed to break these patterns, even if this makes the economy more susceptible to international disturbances.[4]

It is unlikely that the Swedish decision to leave the Snake was motivated by increased concern for short-term exchange rate disturbances.[5] It must be interpreted as an adjustment to the difficulties of keeping inflation in step with the German rate. By accepting higher inflation, policy-makers may have hoped to exploit a Phillips curve trade-off, consistent with Sweden putting greater weight on the employment target than Germany and more in line with the average weight assigned to it by Sweden's trading partners.

In September 1981, the krona was devalued by 10% relative to the basket. This time the official motivation was not based on the standard competitiveness arguments. Instead reference was made to the need to strengthen the tradables sector, i.e. the aim was to rectify perceived structural imbalances. This tradables/non-tradables vision of the economy was even more clearly spelled out in connection with the 16% devaluation in October 1982. The logic underlying this decision can be described as follows. The new government that had just come into power had decided that a fiscal tightening was necessary to reduce the persistent budget deficits (Figure 6.5).

In these circumstances, a devaluation may help to speed up the adjustment of the economy to lower public sector spending, affecting primarily the non-tradables sector, by stimulating demand in the tradables sector. The rise in the relative price between tradables and non-tradables—and the corresponding fall in the real wage rate measured in terms of tradables—is expected to make the tradables sector expand and absorb the labour resources made available by the contraction of the non-tradables sector.

It is interesting to note, not least in the current context, that the original plan was to combine the 1982 devaluation with a return to a DM peg, consistent with the hard currency interpretation of this decision. However, this proposal fell through at the very last moment, primarily due to misunderstandings between the Swedish government and the German Bundesbank.[6] If carried out, this could have strengthened the impression that Sweden intended to embark on a hard currency policy,

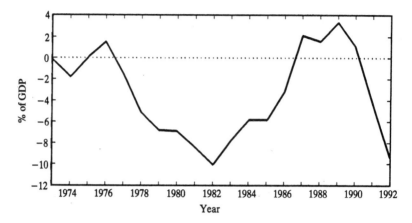

**Figure 6.5**   Central government budget. From 1973 to 1992. Expressed as percent of GDP. *Source:* Statistics Sweden and Ministry of Finance

the DM probably being seen as a 'harder' reference point than the currency basket.

Whether the Swedish economy would have behaved differently during the 1980s under a DM peg is unknown, of course. On the basis of the blueprint, it is still possible to interpret the 1982 devaluation as part of an attempt to break with the patterns and policies that had characterized the Swedish economy in the 1970s, not least in terms of price and wage performance. A big once-and-for-all exchange rate adjustment—not related to an overvaluation of the krona—was to lay the grounds for balanced growth with stable prices and full employment. The declaration that the exchange rate from then on was to be kept fixed was supposed to induce the necessary discipline in price and wage setting behaviour.

Whether this strategy should be seen as sensible from an ex ante point of view is not clear. That it was risky to try to start a hard currency policy by exposing the economy to such an inflationary shock is, however, beyond doubt. The strategy rested on the ability to contain the inflationary impulses from attempts to compensate for the loss in real wages already incurred and to prevent expectations of additional devaluations in the future from pushing up wage and price increases. Rather than attempting a general evaluation of the devaluation strategy—we would have little to add to the one made by Henrekson (1991)—we will study Swedish monetary and exchange rate policy over the past 10 years. We will focus on the adjustments of policies and institutions made to maintain—and from time to time reinstall—the credibility of the fixed exchange rate commitment and the hard currency strategy.

## 6.3 The Struggle to Make a Unilateral Exchange Rate Peg Credible

The possibility to replace the currency basket with a DM peg or some other 'harder' reference point did not come back on the agenda after the 1982 devaluation. It is conceivable that Sweden in the early 1980s could have been accepted as an associate member of the EMS. The EMS at this time, however, was not an obvious hard currency arrangement, although some countries, notably Germany and the Netherlands, pursued hard currency strategies. It is thus not self-evident that Sweden simply by joining the EMS would have gained much in terms of credibility. In any case, the task that Swedish policy-makers set for themselves was to manage a unilaterally fixed exchange rate according to the principles of a hard currency.

### 6.3.1 *The Initial Institutional Setting*

As a background, it is important to recall that in 1982 Swedish financial markets were highly regulated. The Riksbank set both prices and quantities in major segment of the credit market and foreign exchange controls were in force. One effect of the regulations was to secure cheap financing for the government and the housing sector. The government also borrowed heavily in foreign currency. By financing the current account deficits, the government assumed exchange rate risk that otherwise—given that the exchange controls prevented foreigners from holding krona assets—would have been shifted to the domestic private sector. Other things equal, this had the effect of keeping krona interest rates down, which also was intended to encourage investments in the industries given access to domestic credit.

An erosion of the regulatory system was under way, however, and the Riksbank had begun to use its overnight lending rate to banks—'the penalty rate'—to influence short-term capital flows.[7] Banks had unlimited access to central bank credit at a constant interest rate, implying a horizontal supply curve for borrowed reserves. Losses of foreign exchange reserves were thus automatically sterilized by increased borrowing at the discount window, unless the penalty rate was raised. It was a rather inflexible system also because decisions on interest rate changes could only be made by the governing board of the Riksbank, a body that meets regularly at most once a week, and because the Riksbank was reluctant to make too frequent changes in the penalty rate. All in all, this gave rise to a high degree of short-term interest rate smoothing and the short end of the yield curve tended to be flat. The fixed exchange rate was based on a target value relative to the basket index, but the Riksbank had not announced any boundaries for the index, i.e. the krona was allowed to vary within an unspecified target zone. At a later stage, the Riksbank disclosed that it had been working with a band of ±2.25%.

This system was far from ideal from the point of view of making a hard currency policy or a fixed exchange rate credible. First, the absence of a target zone made the exchange rate commitment seem vague. Second, the inflexibility of interest rate policy limited the ability to defend the krona against speculative attacks and reduced the market induced interest rate responses to losses of foreign exchange reserves. The preference for interest rate smoothing implicit in the penalty rate system was difficult to reconcile with the requirement to use interest rates to stabilize the krona. Third, the regulations were effectively structured so as to protect the government and the politically important housing sector from the adverse interest rate effects of inflation and currency market disturbances. The policy-makers thus had neither economic nor political incentives to aim for price stability. The government incurred losses on its foreign currency debt when devaluations were made, but this had had no restrictive effects in the past. Perhaps this was because these losses were more than offset by the resulting fall in the real value of the long-term krona denominated debt. Alternatively, it is possible that the krona value of the government foreign debt is too subtle a notion to have much influence on short-term economic policy, especially since the costs can be pushed far into the future. In any case, the weak incentives for a non-inflationary policy cannot have made the krona look more like a hard currency in the eyes of the public.

### 6.3.2   *Deregulation and Institutional Reform*

Over the past 10 years, most of these institutional features have been changed. In the rest of this section, we will try to chart the process through which these changes have been made. The general picture that emerges is a mixture of strategic moves, in particular in the deregulation of financial markets, and a stepwise adjustment of institutions and operational techniques as they have been found to be ineffective or inappropriate in the new environment.

As part of the strategic restructuring, a ban on net government borrowing in foreign currency was introduced in 1984. This meant that domestic interest rates had to be adjusted to make private foreign currency transactions balance. Gradually, starting in 1983, domestic credit market controls were lifted and by 1985 quantities and interest rates on both loans and deposits could be set without central bank involvement. Then attention was turned to international transactions and the last parts of the foreign exchange controls were repealed in 1989. In a parallel development, the regulatory policy instruments were replaced by conventional market-based techniques for controlling the supply of bank reserves. The marginal overnight lending rate to banks became the most important instrument of monetary policy.[8]

The result of the deregulation was that, to prevent capital flows from undermining the fixed exchange rate, krona interest rates consistently must be aligned to the rate of return private investors require on krona assets. In combination with the ban on net foreign currency borrowing, this implied that the government was forced to borrow at krona interest rates that reflect swings in the credibility of the exchange rate peg. In a deregulated environment, increases in interest rates are also transmitted to the private sector. Consequently, the government must bear both economic and political costs for policies that undermine the confidence in the krona. Although the primary driving forces were of a different kind, not least the erosion of the regulatory system and the need to develop new instruments, the deregulation led to a restructuring of the political incentive system. By exposing their actions to market scrutiny, policy-makers imposed penalties on themselves, should they fail to maintain the credibility of the fixed exchange rate.

The first opportunity to demonstrate the readiness to use interest rates to defend the krona occurred in early 1985.[9] After a period of losses of foreign exchange reserves, the Riksbank in January raised the overnight lending rate by four percentage points (p.p.). In addition, the currency basket index was for the first time since the devaluation allowed to rise well above the target value (Figure 6.6) which shows the deviations of the krona exchange rate from central parity for the period January 1982 to 19 November 1992. This depreciation was intended to create expectations of a future reversal towards the target value, making krona assets more attractive by promising capital gains, a strategy that is consistent with interest rate smoothing. It appears, however, that market participants had come to regard the target value as the upper bound of an implicit target zone.[10] When this was broken through, uncertainty about exchange rate movements increased, raising the required interest rate differential. This is illustrated in Figure 6.7, which shows the 3-month interest rate differential between Euro-deposits denominated in Swedish kronor and basket currencies. Similarly, the forward rate, shown in Figure 6.8 as the deviation from central parity, was well outside the unofficial target zone of $\pm 2.25\%$, indicating that investors did not exclude a depreciation beyond this limit.[11] Capital outflows accelerated and the Riksbank raised the overnight interest rate by an additional 2 p.p.

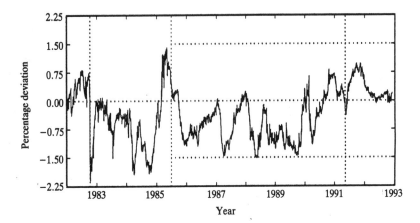

**Figure 6.6**   Exchange rate. The deviation of the Swedish currency index from central parity. Daily data from January 1982 to 19 November 1992. The exchange rate band is marked with horizontal lines. The devaluation 1982, the announcement of the ±1.5% band and the ECU peg are marked with dotted vertical lines. *Source*: Sveriges Riksbank.

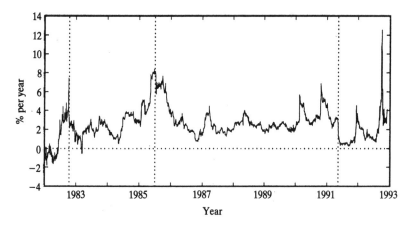

**Figure 6.7**   Interest rate differential (expressed as annualized rates of return) between Swedish krona Euro-deposits and basket-currency Euro-deposits carrying a fixed maturity of 3 months. Daily data from January 1982 to 19 November 1992. The devaluation 1982, the announcement of the ±1.5% band and the ECU peg are marked with dotted vertical lines. *Source*: The Bank for International Settlements (BIS) and Sveriges Riksbank

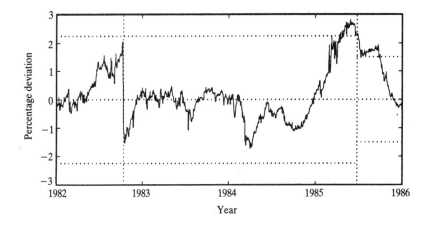

**Figure 6.8**  Forward exchange rate, 3 months. The forward exchange rate in terms of the basket currency, expressed as percentage deviation from central parity. Daily data from January 1982 to December 1985. The boundaries of the exchange rate band are marked with dotted horizontal lines. The devaluation 1982 and the announcement of the ±1.5% band are marked with dotted vertical lines. *Source*: The BIS and Sveriges Riksbank

Interest rates could be brought down after the Riksbank had announced an official target zone of ±1.5% around the benchmark value. This illustrates how credibility can be improved by making the policy rules more transparent. Apart from reducing the risks of policy signals being misinterpreted, this limits the discretion of the policy maker as it is more costly to break an explicit rule than to deviate from a pattern based on implicit conventions only.

These events had also pointed to the limitations in the Riksbank's techniques for short-term interest rate control. The automatic sterilization of losses of foreign exchange reserves in the penalty rate system tended to delay an upward adjustment of market interest rates. This gave a high degree of interest rate smoothing, but made capital flows more volatile, with potentially destabilizing effects on the foreign exchange reserves. The need for a more flexible system led to the introduction of the so-called interest rate scale in January 1986.[12] In this way, the Riksbank shortened its response time to swings in capital flows, effectively reducing the degree of sterilization and interest rate smoothing.

### 6.3.3   *The Divergence from the Hard Currency Path*

During the rest of the 1980s the need for such flexibility was not so apparent. The absence of major disturbances indicates that the exchange rate peg was seen as more or less credible (Figure 6.9) showing 90 and 100% confidence intervals for devaluation expectations.[13] One reason was the domestic economic situation, characterized by a strong boom. To understand this development it is necessary to consider the effects of the 1982 devaluation.

As Figure 6.3 indicates, the devaluation had made the krona strongly undervalued. As a result, exports and profits in the tradables sector picked up rapidly. Less progress was made in effecting the transfer of resources needed to achieve a commensurate expansion of capacity in this sector. One reason was that demand was buoyant also in the sheltered sectors. Instead of shedding resources, as it should according to the blueprint, the private non-tradables sector was expanding. In addition, the restructuring of the public sector went slower than anticipated, partly because the pressure for, and the political acceptance of, cut-backs in expenditure programmes was reduced as the economy expanded and government revenues increased.

Inevitably, general excess demand developed, in particular in the labour market, leading to increases in the rates of price and wage inflation, especially from 1987 and onwards (Figure 6.2). Such a development is at odds with the requirements of a hard currency. However, since a devaluation in an economy with no excess capacity makes little sense, the

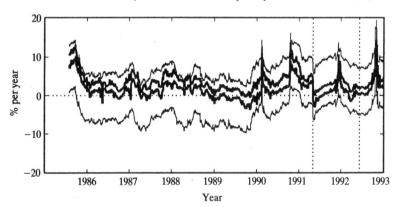

**Figure 6.9**   Expected rate of devaluation, 3 months. 100% and 90% confidence intervals. Daily data from 27 June 1985 to 19 November 1992. The ECU peg and the Riksbank's announcement of stronger preferences for exchange rate stability within the band in May 1992 are marked with dotted vertical lines. *Source*: Lindberg et al. (1993)

short-term credibility of the fixed exchange rate is not seriously impaired. Instead, real interest rates tend to fall, as nominal rates reflect (expected) international rather than domestic inflation rates. This spurs domestic demand by making credit cheap and savings unattractive. For example, in early 1989 a household mortgage loan cost around 12%, which implied a real rate before tax of around 5%.[14] Since nominal interest payments were deductible at a marginal tax rate of 50%, the real after tax interest rate was negative. Not surprisingly, credit expanded very rapidly, feeding both goods and asset price inflation.

There is little that a central bank firmly committed to fixed exchange rates—and thus unable to control interest rates and credit expansion—can do in this situation. Exploiting the potential for exchange rate movements within a target zone, the Riksbank tried to keep the interest rate differential as high as possible. As Figure 6.6 shows, the krona index was kept in the lower (stronger) part of the band. This creates a potential for a depreciation within the band, which, other things being equal, tends to raise short-term nominal interest rates. In addition, the Riksbank made sterilized net purchases of foreign currency, leading to a gradual increase in foreign exchange reserves.

Whatever the effects of these policies, they were insufficient to prevent general excess demand from developing and an inflation gap to the rest of the world opened up. This thwarted the plans for a balanced recovery, led by the tradables sector.[15] The record for the 1980s thus shows that Sweden—although sticking to the fixed exchange rate—failed to pursue a policy consistent with an inflation rate at par with the reference currency. It can be argued that active demand management is not the task of the government and that the fixed exchange rate shifted the responsibility for price and wage developments to private sector decision-makers. Although we basically agree with this position, the argument hardly carries much weight in this case. The time to abstain from 'tuning'—be it 'fine' or 'gross'—is not in the aftermath of a major policy-induced shock, with strong expansionary and inflationary effects. Quite apart from whether it was sensible, ex ante, to devalue the krona in 1982, policy-makers can be faulted for lack of consistency. As Henrekson (1991) shows they did not achieve the fiscal tightening necessary to make resources available to the tradables sector.

It has been argued that the credit expansion contributed to the overheating. As a factual statement this is correct. However, the fixing of the exchange rate and the deregulation of credit markets, decisions taken by the Riksbank but with support from the parliament and the government, disarmed monetary policy as a tool for demand management. The responsibility for containing the expansionary effects of the devaluation therefore rested with the fiscal authorities.[16] Irrespective of how the responsibility is to be shared, the result was that inflation got out of hand. As we mentioned in the introduction, this is the time when a hard currency policy is tested.

### 6.3.4  The Initial Tests of the Fixed Exchange Rate

The first test came in February 1990, when the government resigned after having failed to get support in the parliament for a set of fiscal austerity measures. This instigated a flight from krona assets and the Riksbank had to make substantial interventions to support the krona. To stop the losses of foreign exchange reserves, it raised the overnight interest rate by 3 p.p. This pattern was repeated in October 1990, when outflows were caused by rumours of an imminent devaluation, to be combined with a shift to an ECU peg. This time the Riksbank raised the overnight rate by altogether 5 p.p. to reverse capital flows. These incidents indicated that a credibility problem had emerged. This is also illustrated by the expected rates of devaluation reported in Figure 6.9. Innumerable declarations from the Riksbank and the government stating that the experiences from the previous devaluations showed the futility of such a policy were insufficient to root out these expectations.

In our opinion, it is useful—and plausible—to interpret the Swedish experience as an example of a policy-maker that has difficulties in conveying his actual policy targets to the public.[17] The policy-maker is determined not to accommodate inflationary disturbances. If competitiveness is eroded due to excessive price and wage increases, he will let the nominal adjustment run its course through a recession, on the assumption that accommodation would lead to more inflation and only temporary gains in employment. If this was known, private sector decision-makers would be cautious when setting wages and prices. However, due to past experiences of soft policies, they remain sceptical about the policy-maker's willingness and/or ability to stick to the announced strategy, creating self-fulfilling expectations of high inflation.

The extent to which such a divergence between actual and perceived policy goals has contributed to bringing Swedish inflation out of line is unknown. However, the development during the 1980s is consistent with a situation where private sector decisions are based on the belief that price and wage increases will be accommodated. Clearly, the actual inflation performance in the second half of the 1980s will not have made private agents more confident that the policy declarations would hold. The traditional emphasis on high employment will also have mattered, despite declarations that price stability was seen as a precondition for long-term full employment. We interpret this development, at least partly, as a result of an underestimation of the importance of making strong commitments or, given the difficulty for policy-makers to commit themselves in a credible way, of pursuing a policy that sticks closely to the announced targets.

Irrespective of whether confusion about the policy targets is a causal factor or not, under less than perfect credibility a recession will give rise to intermittent currency crises when the steadfastness of the policy-maker is tested. Somewhat paradoxically, a currency crisis can be seen as an opportunity for a central bank with a latent credibility problem. By actively contributing to the increase in short-term interest rates, it can show its determination and ability to stick to the announced policy, i.e. it is an 'investment in credibility' to successfully fight off a currency crisis. If market participants see that the central bank is willing to go to great lengths to defend the currency, not only will they take the opportunity to buy domestic assets, thus reversing the capital flow, but they may also feel more confident that the central bank will withstand future crises. The net effect of a drastic increase in short-term interest rates may therefore be that long-term rates fall; see the events marked with arrows in Figure 6.10.

However, this is clearly a case of making the best out of a bad situation. Interest rate shocks lead to increased volatility and, on average, higher interest rate differentials. Neither is conducive to economic recovery. Eventually, the true policy targets will be revealed, but recovery is

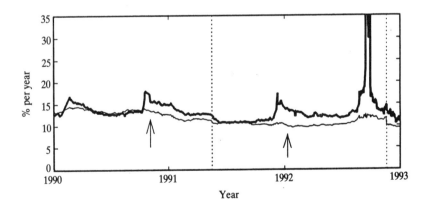

**Figure 6.10** Interest rates; 1-month Euro-deposits denominated in Swedish kronor and 5-year government bonds, expressed as annualized rates of return. The ECU peg and the shift to flexible exchange rates are marked with dotted vertical lines. Daily data for the period January 1990 to December 1992. *Source*: The BIS and Sveriges Riksbank.

delayed and the losses in terms of unemployment and output may be high. In these circumstances, the policy-maker has strong incentives to try to demonstrate his true policy targets by some other means.

### 6.3.5   The Search for 'Harder' Commitments

The fixed exchange rate being the most visible element of the Swedish hard currency policy, it is inevitable that the lack of credibility would show up in expectations of devaluations. Similarly, it is logical for policy-makers trying to signal their actual policy targets to strengthen the commitment to the fixed exchange rate. This led to a reconsideration of the currency basket as the reference point for the krona.

In this context, the difference between volatility of krona interest rates and the relative stability of the multilateral cooperation in the EMS was telling. The EMS was in practice not open to countries outside the EC, but new opportunities to demonstrate the commitment to the fixed exchange rate arose as a result of Sweden's decision in the fall of 1990 to apply for EC membership. In May 1991, following Norway's example from October 1990, the Riksbank announced a shift to a unilateral ECU peg.[18] The central rate was set so as to give an unchanged overall exchange rate and the band was maintained at ±1.5%.[19] To indicate that the decision was more than the replacement of one currency basket with another, the Riksbank announced that Sweden, as soon as such an option became available, would seek formal association with the EMS, the ultimate objective being to bring the krona into the ERM.

Unlike the earlier currency basket, the ECU did not reflect the currency mix in Sweden's foreign trade. The most important difference was the exclusion of the US dollar, which had a weight of around 21% in the basket. Thus, the Swedish exchange rate system is no longer designed to protect the real exchange rate against swings in the dollar/DM rate, i.e. the useful smoothing properties of the basket were lost. However, the ECU peg was a natural consequence of the Swedish application for EC membership. With Sweden as a member of the EC, the krona would one day be linked to the ECU, i.e. the question was not *if* but *when* the currency basket would be abandoned. This made it important to link the krona to the EMS at an early stage, to avoid concerns that this step would be combined with changes in the exchange rate. That the Swedish ECU peg was preceded by and explicitly linked to the membership application also meant that it was seen as a 'harder' commitment, although formally it was as unilateral as the peg to the basket.

The credibility of the fixed exchange rate increased as a result of the

ECU peg. There was a significant inflow of capital and interest rate differentials fell (Figure 6.7). A period with small but persistent outflows began. This was part of a plan to reduce the foreign exchange reserves, that were seen as excessively large following the inflows after the ECU peg. In response to the outflows, the krona/ECU rate was kept in the weaker part of the target zone, which given credible boundaries also made the required interest rate differential smaller. In general, the market situation in the months after the ECU peg was quite stable. As Figure 6.9 shows, however, the ECU peg had not completely cured the latent credibility problem. Some devaluation expectations remained, albeit at a much lower level.[20]

In the wake of the Finnish devaluation in November 1991, the credibility problem once more came to the fore. A priori, there seemed little reason for investors to draw parallels to Sweden as the differences between the Swedish and the Finnish economies were quite striking. For example, in Sweden the fixed exchange had almost unanimous support from political parties, unions, and industry representatives. In Finland, on the other hand, the important forestry industry demanded a devaluation and the government was not united in its rejection of these demands. Despite these differences, the Finnish devaluation did influence investor confidence in the krona and large outflows of capital were recorded. The Riksbank increased the overnight rate by 6 p.p. in early December. The pressure on the krona stopped and interest rates could gradually be brought down as the foreign exchange reserves were restored. The Riksbank also let the increased demand for kronor spill over into an appreciation of the krona/ECU rate towards the central parity (Figure 6.6).

These events made the Riksbank reconsider its guidelines for exchange rate movements within the band and, more generally, the importance assigned to interest rate smoothing. Meeting swings in the demand for krona assets with movements within the band and sterilized interventions, rather than interest rate adjustments, may in some circumstances have adverse effects. For example, the weakness of the krona at the time of the Finnish crisis may have contributed to investor uncertainty. In addition, the initial sterilized interventions made when the krona came under pressure delayed the interest rate response. It is also conceivable that market participants had interpreted the attempts to keep domestic interest rates down as indicating increased emphasis on short-run (employment) goals, at the expense of the long-run (exchange rate/price stability) target. By letting interest rates rise earlier, the Riksbank may have been able to avoid such a drastic hike of the overnight rate. It seems fair to say—of course, with the benefit of hindsight—that the Riksbank underestimated the risks of contagion from the Finnish devaluation.

Arguably, it was 'irrational', for the reasons mentioned above, to draw parallels to Finland, but a central bank defending a fixed exchange rate must respond to swings in market sentiments even if they are considered ill-founded.

The December events indicated that devaluation expectations and capital flows had become more sensitive to the position of the exchange rate within the band. This destroys the trade-off between exchange rate and interest rate levels and variability in a target zone.[21] The Riksbank's practical conclusion was to limit exchange rate variability within the band.[22] The other side of this policy was that the Riksbank was willing to respond earlier with changes in the overnight interest rate to swings in the demand for kronor. Thus, the effective degree of sterilization of foreign exchange market interventions declined.[23]

These policies were tested in April 1992, when—due to a shift in market sentiment of unclear origin—the Riksbank during a single day had to sell foreign currency corresponding to 22 billion kronor to defend the krona/ECU rate. The following market day the overnight interest rate was raised by 2 p.p. This led to an immediate reflow of currency and within days market interest rates were back to or—in the case of long-term rates—even below levels recorded before the outflows started.

This policy change can be seen as a continuation of the reforms during 1980s, such as the narrowing of the band and the introduction of the interest rate scale, resulting in a decline in exchange rate variability.[24] In parallel, there was less smoothing of interest rates at the very short end of the term structure. This implied that Sweden came closer to the textbook case of fixed exchange rates, losing the ability to influence the level as well as the variability of interest rates. However, it did not necessarily follow from this policy shift that the ex post facto variability of, for example, the 3-month rate would rise. By letting the overnight rate respond more rapidly to swings in capital flows, the Riksbank hoped to prevent speculative attacks and reduce the likelihood of interest rate shocks of the type seen in December 1991.

### 6.3.6   *The Collapse of the Fixed Exchange Rate Regime*

The situation for the krona was stable during the late spring and summer 1992 with the marginal overnight rate at 11.5 and 12%. However, the deterioration of the real economy continued with output falling and unemployment rising to record levels. Moreover, the budget deficit was revised upward with each new forecast. Part of this was business cycle related, but it was becoming clear that there was also a substantial structural deficit (Figure 6.5). Concerns for the sustainability of the budget were being voiced. At the same time, the support for radical consolidation measures in the parliament appeared uncertain.

It was in this environment that, in late August, a slow and steady capital outflow began. The Riksbank responded by raising the overnight rate by 1 p.p., but outflows continued. The marginal rate was then increased from 13 to 16% and small reflows were recorded.

On 8 September, when markets were about to open in Stockholm, Finland announced that the markka would float. The krona immediately came under pressure. The Riksbank raised the overnight rate to 24% in the middle of trading. This level was insufficient to stop the outflows, however, and the following morning the marginal rate was increased to 75%. It was also announced that the Riksbank would borrow the equivalent of 15 billion ECUs in foreign currencies to strengthen the foreign exchange reserves and would be prepared to borrow another 16 billion ECUs if necessary. The krona market stabilized, but at the same time the tensions were rising in Europe. During the weekend, the ERM countries made at realignment (involving an effective 7% devaluation of the lira) and the Bundesbank announced that it would lower interest rates. Hoping that tensions would ease, the Riksbank brought the overnight rate down to 20% and during the first day it seemed that a stabilization was under way. However, on 15 September the turmoil began all over again. The overnight rate was increased to 75% in the morning of the 16 September, but there was chaos all over Europe's currency markets, Sweden's included. The Riksbank took the extreme measure of raising the overnight rate to 500%. Italy and the United Kingdom, under similar pressures, decided to float their currencies.

A 500% interest rate is not sustainable even if applied only to the overnight rate. However, by making it extremely expensive to go short in kronor, it achieved its goal, namely to stop the speculative outflows. Thereby, the Riksbank bought time for the government and the opposition to finalize a crisis package, primarily designed to reduce the budget deficit, as mentioned above, one of the major factors behind the concerns for the stability of the Swedish economy.

After 4 days at 500%, it was possible to lower the overnight rate, first to 50% and then to 40% the following week. However, the currency markets were still unstable. The government and the opposition presented a second joint proposal, this time designed to improve the competitiveness of Swedish industry through a fully financed cut in pay-roll taxes. The repeated demonstration of the political will to take fiscal measures to come to terms with the economic imbalances improved market sentiment and the Riksbank could gradually reduce the overnight rate to the pre-crisis level, 11.5%.

The step to hike the overnight interest rate to 500% proved sufficient to prevent continued outflows. However, in contrast to experience from previous, less severe crises, there were quite limited reflows, despite the extreme interest rate differentials. This may be attributed to lingering exchange rate uncertainty, but it is relevant to consider also the effects of interest rate shock.

Undoubtedly, the September events changed the perception of what the peak interest level might be. The interest rate volatility in connection with currency crises makes fixed income securities seem more risky, irrespective of the perceived risk of an exchange rate change. This is problematic if, as in the Swedish case, the circumstances in which the currency crisis arose remain or reappear. Investors may stay away from the domestic currency out of fear for a renewed interest rate shock or, what amounts to the same thing, because they expect to make profits by buying krona assets after interest rates have been raised to levels from which they are bound to fall back again. Thus, for currency outflows to arise it may be sufficient that investors expect that the central bank will be compelled to raise interest rates. In this regard, having a strong reputation for being willing to go great lengths to defend the exchange rate may in effect be destabilizing. In principle, an increase in market interest rates unrelated to any change in the fundamental evaluation of the krona could be sufficient to set off self-fulfilling expectations of a currency crisis. If investors interpret the change as a signal that others have revised their expectations they may, especially in a generally uncertain environment, choose to move in the same direction.

It was awareness of these mechanisms that made the Riksbank try to counteract disturbances that could put upward pressure on market interest rates during October and November. For example, attempts were made to make the money market function more smoothly and to help investors cope with interest rate risks related to year-end effects. However, in mid-November, the market interest rates started to rise from their bottom level after the September crisis. As expected, the krona came under substantial pressure and the Riksbank responded with sterilized interventions. The first rounds of outflows came from domestic investors. Once the process came under way, foreign investors jumped on the bandwagon and outflows increased even further. On 19 November, the Riksbank increased the overnight rate to 20%, but the pressure did not ease. The Riksbank had then lost over 160 billion kronor of the foreign reserves in 6 days. The ability to use further increases of the overnight rate to defend the fixed exchange rate were considered as exhausted. In the afternoon of 19 November, the Riksbank announced that the krona was floating.

During the following weeks, the krona fell significantly in value. By year-end, it had depreciated approximately 15% relative to the ECU. As

Figure 6.3 shows, this implied that the real effective exchange rate was at the same level as immediately after the 1982 devaluation. The depreciation is a cause for concern for future price developments, but Swedish policy-makers have continued to emphasize the importance of the long-term price stability target. Monetary policy will be conducted in such a way that an increase in the price level resulting from higher import prices will not be transmitted into a permanent rise in inflation.

### 6.3.7    *On the Feasibility of Fixed Exchange Rates*

The Swedish experience can be said to confirm that the ability to use high interest rates to defend a fixed exchange rate is exhaustible, especially if the fundamentals are weak to begin with. Persistently high and volatile interest rates have detrimental effects on the real economy and on the financial sector. In order to succeed with this kind of policy, it is important, perhaps necessary, that the conditions giving rise to the crisis disappear. In the Swedish case, policy-makers were not so lucky. The fiscal measures taken proved insufficient to allay the concerns for the government budget, the recession continued to deepen, etc. The experience from September, when several currencies were brought down by speculative attacks, and remaining tensions on the international foreign exchange markets contributed to the uncertainty. In such circumstances, a speculative process is likely to come under way. The central bank is then limited to making sterilized intervention. Given the potential size of capital flows this is a weak instrument that, unless the speculative process is broken by some 'good news', can only delay the collapse of the exchange rate regime.

This does not warrant the conclusion that the actions taken to defend the krona in September were in vain. First, they included budgetary changes that were necessary irrespective of the exchange rate regime. Second, the decisiveness with which the krona was defended can be expected to influence the perception of policy in the new regime, that is the credibility of the low inflation target is presumably stronger than if the fixed exchange rate had been abandoned without a fight.

The difficulties in maintaining exchange rate pegs encountered by Sweden and other European countries have led some commentators to raise doubts about the feasibility of fixed but in practice adjustable exchange rates. Although documenting the difficulties that may arise in such a system, the experience in the Swedish case does not warrant such a pessimistic conclusion. The speculations against the krona were conditioned by fundamental imbalances in the Swedish economy, in particular the structurally weak budget position in an economy also hit by a deep recession, not by random events. Rather than indicating that fixed exchange rates are impossible to maintain, the events in Sweden (and elsewhere) in the fall of 1992, the major lesson for a hard currency strategy based on a fixed exchange rate seems to be the importance of keeping the economy on a balanced path. For policy-makers this implies that the constraints imposed by the chosen exchange rate regime, both on all parts of economic policy and on overall economic developments, will have to be observed more rigorously, also in the short and medium term. In the Swedish case, it was the failure to keep the economy on a balanced path and to pursue budgetary policies seen to be consistent with the requirements of a fixed exchange rate that created the environment in which the international foreign exchange market turbulence was sufficient to bring the krona down.

## 6.4   Some Observations on Central Bank Behaviour

In this section, we will try to broaden the perspective by using the Swedish experience from the struggle to establish the krona as a hard currency as a basis for some observations on the behaviour of the Riksbank. Both in the policy strategies pursued and in the institutional adjustments, it is possible to identify characteristics with general relevance for positive analyses of central bank behaviour. Our review can be seen as a complement to Bernanke and Mishkin's (1992) case studies of six central banks working under flexible exchange rates.[25]

### 6.4.1   *Policy-making*

The first observation is that the Riksbank—like all central banks—is concerned with more than one target variable. At the level of ultimate targets, inflation dominates. Instances when the Riksbank has put weight also on output can be identified, but it is significant that the price stability target has become more important over time. In the short term, the fixed exchange rate—an intermediate target established to help achieve the ultimate target(s)—has been the most important variable, but the Riksbank has also been concerned with the behaviour of interest rates, including the instrument variable, the overnight rate. A second characteristic that the Riksbank shares with other central banks is a preference for continuity—smoothness—in all its targets. This is seen most clearly in the techniques used to smooth interest rates and exchange rates, in the latter case primarily using sterilized interventions.

With just one instrument available, it is impossible to meet all targets at all times. Consequently, the Riksbank has from time to time been forced to make trade-offs between its targets, for example, between the exchange rate and a smooth path for interest rates. In this context, it is important to recognize that a central bank rarely, if ever, commits itself in a strictly binding way concerning any of its target variables. In the Riksbank's case this is illustrated by the exchange rate target zone and by the revocability of the exchange rate peg.[26] As noted in section 6.3, a target zone makes it possible to let the exchange rate absorb disturbances that otherwise would have their entire impact on interest rates. Depending on the width of the target zone, an appreciation within the band may also be made to offset excess demand pressures, i.e. the central bank can use the target zone to trade-off (short-term) exchange rate stability against the ultimate targets of price and output stability.[27]

By abstaining from strict commitments, the central bank makes room for short-term discretion. The distinction between the short and the medium or long run is crucial for discretion to work. A case in point is the use of the target zone to smooth nominal interest rates. This mechanism presupposes that agents expect the exchange rate to display mean-reversion. Assuming that the entire target zone is used, the average exchange rate (measured over sufficiently long periods) must therefore equal the target value. Although not based on a strict commitment, the fixed exchange rate is still a binding constraint in this average sense. Bernanke and Mishkin (1992) refer to this type of behaviour, which they find to be very common in the central banks' use of monetary targets, as a 'hybrid strategy', characterized by discretion in the short run, but constrained by rules in the long run.

The absence of commitments creates trade-offs that can be exploited in a purposeful way. It is purposeful in the sense that the weights assigned to the different targets depend on the perceived urgency of rectifying a deviation from some desired position. The importance of a target may depend on the economic situation. In a boom, for example, the fixed exchange rate target may 'look after itself', allowing the central bank to use interest rate policy partly for other purposes, as in the 1988–9 period in Sweden.

One drawback of the absence of binding rules is that the central bank is forced to signal its intentions in more indirect ways. If these signals are misinterpreted, for example, because a secondary target is given priority, doubts about the validity of the commitment to the ultimate target may arise and the central bank is faced with a 'crisis'.[28] Then a drastic shift of attention to the ultimate target must be made. In the Swedish case, this is illustrated by the interest rate shocks made to defend the fixed exchange rate, in some case when disturbances occurred in connection with periods of interest rate smoothing.[29]

At the level of the ultimate target and partly beyond the realm of the Riksbank, the disinflation that Sweden has recently experienced can be interpreted in similar terms. The discretion exercised when inflation got out of hand in the 1980s—not least as a result of the failure to adjust fiscal policies to domestic demand developments—sowed doubts about the commitment to price stability, making a drastic turnaround necessary. This was inevitable, but it has made actual inflation fall far below expected rates, with adverse real effects and medium-term costs in the form of output instability.

The Swedish experience also illustrates that the smoothing ambitions inherent in the fixed exchange rate in some circumstances can be difficult to reconcile with price stability. For example, a revaluation of the krona in, say, 1985, would have reduced excess demand and, perhaps, held back inflation, helping to keep the krona on the hard currency course. However, it is not so obvious that such a managed exchange rate policy would have been advisable seen in a wider perspective. When the fixed exchange rate is the most visible part of the hard currency strategy, any deviation, even in an anti-inflationary direction, could be misinterpreted as a return to a 'manipulative' policy. This would have raised the perceived risk of future devaluations, with detrimental long-term effects. In the absence of some other (credible) commitment to price stability, the fixed exchange rate takes on an importance not normally accorded to an intermediate target.

### 6.4.2   *Institutional Arrangement*

The process reviewed in this paper has gradually tightened the constraints on policy-makers. Market deregulation and integration have set forces in motion that leave little room for discretion or even hesitation.[30] In these circumstances, it is essential, first, to have flexible policy instruments and to use them in such a way that potentially destabilizing disturbances can be contained. Second, to prevent disturbances from arising, ambiguities in the policy targets must be eliminated. The common theme in the Swedish institutional reforms is the ambition to devise such a system.

The Swedish institutional reform process has several interesting characteristics. First, it is marked by an overall ambition to maintain as much scope for discretion and for smoothing as possible, subject to the constraint that credibility is not impaired. This is consistent with the hybrid strategy outlined above. Second, and related to the first point, the reforms have been made defensively rather than according to some planned scheme.[31] Rules and practices creating scope for trade-offs between targets have thus been retained until they are found to be incompatible with the new environment. For example, the target zone was kept secret until the events in 1985 showed the risks involved. The same pattern is seen in the reduced emphasis on interest rate smoothing and in the decision to forgo the benefits of the currency basket.

In a sense, this indicates that the preference for continuity extends also to the institutional structure. This is certainly not unique. The idea of 'optimal policy rules' derived once and for all, starting with a clean slate, is patently unrealistic. Rules and institutions develop gradually, in an interplay with the changing (internal and external) environment. This is not always a well charted process and—not least with the benefit of hindsight—it is often possible to point to instances when changes could have been made earlier. However, interpreted as an attempt to retain scope for a hybrid strategy, it is rational not to give up more discretion than necessary. Under a hybrid strategy, making binding commitments is a means to an end, not something done for its own sake. If the same degree of stability of expectations can be achieved without commitments, there is no reason to forgo the option to exercise discretion. It must be acknowledged that the optimal degree of commitment cannot be determined on theoretical grounds and that empirical information is also of limited value. Many of the arguments in this area tend to be counterfactual—'This would never have happened under a different set of rules!'—statements that can be neither proved nor disproved.

Inertia in policy reform follows also from another principle readily and, considering the uncertainty described above, perhaps sensibly adopted by real world policy-makers. Laidler (1993, p. 352) expresses it succinctly: 'In matters of policy, it is more important to be right than original'. Not least given the difficulty in determining—ex ante or even ex post—what is 'right' in matters of economic policy, sticking to what you have until it is seen to be 'wrong' is often a natural strategy.

More generally, it must be acknowledged that virtually all human activities work on the principle expressed vernacularly as: 'If it ain't broke, don't fix it'. In formal economic terms, this is captured in adjustment cost models, in which changes are made only if the deviation from the desired position exceeds a certain threshold, so-called (S,s) models.[32] We conjecture that economic policy-makers—just like other decision units—face (non-convex) adjustment costs of various kinds, making it rational not to respond instantaneously to shocks.[33] Many observations on central bank behaviour are consistent with this hypothesis. It could, for example, explain interest rate smoothing in settings where interest rates are used as instruments.

It should be added that policy adjustments, in particular those involving institutional reforms, typically are significantly more complex than those described in conventional adjustment cost models. For example, the 'desired position' in terms of the institutional structure may often be impossible to determine, as the success of a reform will depend, among other things, on the expectational responses of the private sector. In these circumstances, the policy-maker may be acting under pure uncertainty. Complex though they may be, it seems to us that a worthwhile task for positive analyses of economic policy-making— potentially with normative implications—would be to try to understand the nature of such adjustment costs.

It is beyond the scope of this paper to attempt either a positive or normative analysis of these behavioural characteristics. Taking the difficulty of achieving change as an empirical fact, what we find most striking in the Swedish development over the past 10 years, however, is the extent to which the basic premises of monetary policy decision-making have been changed. Perhaps it is in the willingness to adjust policies and institutions that have turned out to be irreconcilable with the aim of maintaining credibility of the fixed exchange rate that the strongest evidence of the commitment to the krona as a hard currency is found.

## 6.5   Concluding Comments

The Swedish krona was a 'soft' currency in the 1970s and early 1980s, with persistent high inflation accommodated by repeated devaluations. An attempt to break with these patterns was made in the early 1980s. However, policy-makers only gradually realized the requirements—in terms of actual policies and commitments—of a successful hard currency policy. This contributed to bringing the krona off the hard currency course, but as the problems became evident, policy-makers were willing to adapt. A real depreciation of the krona was under way during 1992, as Swedish inflation has fallen below the average (ECU-weighted) EC rate. This is how a hard currency responds to an inflationary period. The adjustment came too late, however, and in too turbulent an environment, to make it possible to defend the fixed exchange rate.

The Riksbank has strongly emphasized that the collapse of the fixed exchange rate regime does not mean that the ultimate target of monetary policy has changed. To this end, the governing board at the Riksbank has announced that price stability remains the overriding objective for monetary policy under the flexible exchange rate. In the absence of an explicit intermediate target, the ultimate target has thus been given greater prominence. The Riksbank has specified that the objective of monetary policy is to limit the annual increase in the consumer price index in 1995 and onwards to 2% (±1 percentage point).[34]

The Swedish experience illustrates the difficulties of achieving credibility. Adjustments of policy institutions and practices of the type made throughout the period is one essential element in this process. However, important though they may be, the institutional rules just make up the skeleton of economic policy. By adjusting institutions, policy-makers can signal their intentions, but in the end it is the decisions made—or not made—that determine the outcome.

In this paper we have focused on monetary and exchange rate policy. However, the Swedish experience also illustrates that credibility of a hard currency strategy cannot be based entirely on monetary and exchange rate policy and the institutional framework governing the central bank. This is obviously the case under fixed exchange rate, but also in a flexible rate system fiscal policy matters for inflation. In particular, it is inevitable that budgetary developments play a role for the expectations of long-term economic policies and future inflation. Sweden, in common with a number of other industrialized countries, currently has substantial budget deficits. It has become clear that many countries have structural deficit problems that will not go away when the recession is over. This situation is, by definition, not sustainable, i.e. current paths for expenditures and incomes are inconsistent with the intertemporal government budget constraint.[35] It is inevitable that the elimination of the structural components of the deficits is an important part of the continued efforts to establish the currencies of future as well as current EC countries as hard currencies also in a long-term perspective.

# Notes

Paper prepared for the CEPR/Bank of Finland conference 'Exchange Rate Policies in the Nordic Countries' in Helsinki, 22–22 September 1992. The paper was originally, at the suggestion of the organizers, entitled 'Has the Swedish Krona Turned into a Hard Currency?'. We are grateful to Zhaohui Chen, Marvin Goodfriend, Christina Lindenius, Yngve Lindh, Jonny Nilsson, Pentti Pikkarainen, Paul Söderlind, Lars Svensson, Niels Thygesen, Anders Vredin and participants at the conference for comments. The opinions expressed are solely those of the authors and should not be seen as reflecting Sveriges Riksbank's views on the matters concerned.

1. For example, this is the notion used when referring to an entity that would never depreciate relative to any ERM currency as 'the hard ECU'.
2. For discussions of the relevance of credibility aspects for Swedish exchange rate policy, see Agell and Vredin (1991a,b) and Hörngren (1991).
3. The Swedish currency basket system is described by Franzén et al. (1980).
4. As Sweden later had reason to reconsider the choice of exchange rate peg, we will return to these issues below.
5. Provided that PPP is approximately upheld in the long run, such disturbances will primarily have temporary effects. This indicates that the choice of a trade-weighted basket may also reflect stronger concern with short- and medium-term stability than a hard currency peg.
6. These events have recently been documented by Bergström (1991). The confusion was

concerned with whether Sweden could introduce a unilateral DM peg without formal approval from the Bundesbank. Uncertainty on this point made policy-makers stick to the trade-weighted basket.

7. See Englund et al. (1989) for details.

8. Englund (1990) discusses the deregulation in more detail. The new policy procedures are presented by Englund et al. (1989), and Hörngren and Westman-Mårtensson (1991).

9. For detailed discussion of this episode, see Hörngren and Viotti (1985a,b) and Franzén (1985).

10. Edin and Vredin (1993) analyse the determinants of devaluation in the Nordic countries. On the basis of their results, it is difficult to explain this incident with reference to a 'fundamental' weakening of the Swedish economy.

11. This is a version of the so-called simplest test of target zone credibility presented by Svensson (1991).

12. See Englund et al. (1989) and Hörngren and Westman-Mårtensson (1991) for details.

13. The expectations are calculated according to the drift adjustment method suggested by Bertola and Svensson (1993) and a version of the simplest test presented by Svensson (1991), respectively. The drift adjustment method is implemented empirically on Swedish data by Lindberg et al. (1993).

14. It is not self-evident that current inflation gives the best estimate of the expected real interest rate. However, as will become evident below, it is not unlikely that many at this time expected inflation to rise even further.

15. It is ironic that a large part of the real investments in this period went into commercial real estate, about as far from tradables as one can get. That credit losses from real estate lending recently have created severe problems in the Swedish banking industry does not make the record any more favourable.

16. One driving force behind the credit expansion was, as illustrated by the numerical example above, the tax system. Sweden made a major tax reform in 1990–1, including reductions in the deductibility of interest rate costs to 30%. It has been claimed—with hindsight—that credit market regulations should have been retained until a proper tax system had been put in place. However, it can also be argued that the deregulation may have made way for the tax reform by revealing the inequities and inefficiencies of the old tax system.

17. In formal terms, the policy-maker would be said to have a reputational problem. For a review of the relevant literature, see Persson and Tabellini (1990).

18. Exchange rate policy in Sweden—including the choice of exchange rate system—is the exclusive responsibility of the central bank. Some aspects of the Riksbank's legal position are discussed by Hörngren and Westman-Mårtensson (1991).

19. See Lindberg and Lindenius (1991) for details about the ECU peg and its implications for krona exchange rates.

20. According to Lindberg et al. (1993), the expected time to devaluation increased from 2 to 38 years.

21. See Svensson (1992) for a study—with applications to Sweden—of the trade-off between exchange rate and interest rate variability in an exchange rate target zone.

22. This is similar to the target zone policy pursued in Norway since late 1988; *cf.* Mundaca (1990).

23. The Riksbank's intervention policy and its implications for the basic target zone model are studied by Lindberg and Söderlind (1994a).

24. See Lindberg and Söderlind (1994b) for data on exchange rate variability and other statistics on the krona exchange rate.

25. This section is also inspired by some thought-provoking remarks by Marvin Goodfriend at the conference 'Transmission of Monetary Policy in Open Economies' at Studienzentrum Gerzensee, 19–20 March 1992. See also Goodfriend (1993).

26. The ERM has the same characteristics. It can be noted that European monetary union, with its common currency, would lead to an unprecedented degree of central bank commitment, as the members would agree to link their exchange rates irrevocably (short of secession from the union).

27. Korkman and Åkerholm (1991) point out that this form for monetary policy independence may be a reason to work with a relatively wide band provided that overall credibility can be maintained.
28. Goodfriend (1993), discussing the US experience, refers to such a situation as an 'inflation scare'.
29. Bernanke and Mishkin (1992) cite the shift in US monetary policy in October 1979 as an analogous drastic switch from interest rate smoothing to the inflation target.
30. As an illustration, we can compare the cumulative loss of foreign exchange reserves of less than 10 billion kronor during the first 5 months of 1985—then considered a serious crisis—with the 22 billion recorded in one single day in April 1992 or the 160 billion during the last 6 days of the fixed exchange rate regime.
31. One exception to this pattern is the deregulation process.
32. See, for example, Caballero and Engel (1992).
33. This is not to say that this behaviour is necessarily fully optimal in a normative sense. The costs may, for example, be related to public choice aspects or inefficient agency relations between the policy-maker and the electorate.
34. For a review of some of the issues facing Swedish monetary policy in the new flexible exchange rate regime, see Sveriges Riksbank (1992).
35. See Blanchard et al. (1990) for a discussion of conceptual and empirical issues related to sustainability problems.

# References

Agell, J. and Vredin, A. (1991a), 'Normer eller diskretion i stabiliseringspolitiken?' [Rules or discretion in stabilization policy?], *Ekonomisk Debatt*, **19**, 336–50.

Agell, J. and Vredin, A. (1991b), 'Spelregler är bra, normer dåliga' [Rules are good, norms are bad], *Ekonomisk Debatt*, **19**, 615–22.

Bergström, H. (1991), 'Devalveringens politiska tillkomst och logik' [The political background and logic of the devaluation], in L. Jonung (ed.), *Devalveringen 1982—Rivstart Eller Snedtändning?*, SNS Förlag, Stockholm.

Bernanke, B. and Mishkin, F. (1992), 'Central Bank Behavior and the Strategy of Monetary Policy: Observations from Six Industrialized Countries', in *NBER Macroeconomics Annual 1992*, MIT Press, Cambridge, MA.

Bertola, G. and Svensson, L. E. O. (1993), 'Stochastic Devaluation Risk and the Empirical Fit of Target Zone Models', *Review of Economic Studies*, **60**, 689–712.

Blanchard, O., Chouraqui, J. C., Hagerman, R. P. and Sartor, N. (1990), 'The sustainability of fiscal policy: new answers to an old question', *OECD Economic Studies*, **15**, 7–36.

Caballero, R. J. and Engel, E. M. R. A. (1992), 'Microeconomic adjustment hazards and aggregate dynamics', Working Paper No. 4090, National Bureau of Economic Research.

Edin, P. A. and Vredin, A. (1993), 'Devaluation risk in target zones: evidence from the Nordic countries'. *Economic Journal*, **103**, 161–75.

Englund, P. (1990), 'Financial deregulation in Sweden', *European Economic Review*, **34**, 385–93.

Englund, P., Hörngren, L. and Viotti, S. (1989), 'Discount window borrowing and money market interest rates', *Scandinavian Journal of Economics*, **91**, 517–33.

Franzén, T. (1985), 'Currency flows in spring 1985', *Skandinaviska Enskilda Banken Quarterly Review*, **14**, 110–13.

Franzén, T., Markowski, A. and Rosenberg, I. (1980), *Effective Exchange Rate Index as a Guideline for Exchange Rate Policy*, Occasional Paper No. 1, Sveriges Riksbank.

Goodfriend, M. (1993), 'Interest rate policy and the inflation scare problem: 1979–1992', *Federal Reserve Bank of Richmond, Economic Quarterly*, 1–23.

Henrekson, M. (1991), 'Devalveringarnas effekter på den svenska ekonomins struktur' [The effects of the devaluations on the structure of the Swedish economy], in L. Jonung (ed.), *Devalveringen 1982—Rivstart Eller Snedtändning?*, SNS Förlag, Stockholm.

Hörngren, L. (1991), 'Normer eller diskretion? Om möjliga och omöjliga val i stabiliseringspolitiken' [Rules or discretion? On possible and impossible choices in stabilization policy]. *Ekonomisk Debatt*, **19**, 489–501.

Hörngren, L. and Viotti, S. (1985a), Foreign exchange movements and monetary policy: an analysis of the outflow of foreign currency from Sweden in the spring 1985', *Skandinaviska Enskilda Banken Quarterly Review*, **14**, 46–55.

Hörngren, L. and Viotti, S. (1985b), 'Reply to Thomas Franzén', *Skandinaviska Enskilda Banken Quarterly Review*, **14**, 113–15.

Hörngren, L. and Westman-Mårtensson, A. (1991), 'Swedish Monetary Policy: Institutions, Targets, and Instruments', Arbetsrapport nr 2, Sveriges Riksbank.

Korkman, S. and Åkerholm, J. (1991), 'Sveriges växelkurspolitik i internationell belysning' [Sweden's exchange rate policy in an international perspective], In L. Jonung (ed.), *Devalveringen 1982—Rivstart Eller Snedtändning?*, SNS Förlag, Stockholm.

Laidler, D. (1993), 'Price Stability and the Monetary Order', in K. Shigehara (ed.), *Price Stabilization in the 1990s*, Macmillan, London.

Lindberg, H. and Lindenius, C. (1991), 'The Swedish Krona Pegged to the Ecu', *Sveriges Riksbank Quarterly Review*, **3**, 14–23.

Lindberg, H. and Söderlind, P. (1994a), 'Intervention Policy and Mean Reversion in Exchange Rate Target Zones: The Swedish Case', *Scandinavian Journal of Economics*, forthcoming.

Lindberg, H. and Söderlind, P. (1994b), 'Testing the Basic Target Zone Model on Swedish Data, 1982–1990', *European Economic Review*, forthcoming.

Lindberg, H., Söderlind, P. and Svensson, L. E. O. (1993), 'Devaluation Expectations: The Swedish Krona 1985–1992'. *Economic Journal*, **103**, 1170–9.

Mundaca, B. G. (1990), 'Intervention decisions and exchange rate volatility in a target zone', Mimeo, Norges Bank.

Persson, T. and Tabellini, G. (1990), *Macroeconomic Policy, Credibility and Politics*, Harwood Academic Publishers.

Svensson, L. E. O. (1991), 'The simplest test of target zone credibility', *IMF Staff Papers*, **38**, 655–65.

Svensson, L. E. O. (1992), 'Why exchange rate bands? Monetary independence in spite of fixed exchange rates', Working Paper No. 4207, National Bureau of Economic Research.

Sveriges Riksbank (1992), *Monetary Policy under Flexible Exchange Rates*, Sveriges Riksbank, Stockholm.

# Discussion

## Zhaohui Chen
*London School of Economics*

The Swedish experience is important for the literature in general since it covers different historical episodes—from a high inflation era to a booming period, then to a recession, and it also contains the (sometimes dramatic) use of different policy instruments, from 'soft peg' to 'hard peg', from implicit band to explicit band, from over devaluation to interest rate shocks. The Swedish experience can serve as a reference point for various hypotheses concerning the crises in the EMS. The fact that Sweden as a non-EC member suffers the same problem as the EMS members in recent currency crises suggests something more fundamental than the EC/EMS/EMU-specific reasons.

The paper by Hörngren and Lindberg not only provides an informative description of the extraordinary historical experience of the Swedish monetary authorities, it also presents a comprehensive evaluation of the hard currency strategy, the institutional reform, and central bank behaviour.

The Swedish experiment begins with a process for the government shifting its policy targets as it gradually realizes the importance of the vertical Phillips curve. It was then followed by a process in which the monetary authorities struggle to convince the public of their policy stance through harder and clearer choices of targets. The lesson here, according to the paper, seems to be that tighter commitment to refraining from monetary policy manipulation is important for building-up credibility. This is consistent with the experience of most EMS countries.

However, the recent crises in the European currency market suggests that credibility gains in the past did not matter much to the market in a situation where the economy is in a recession, the central bank has been trying to clear off its responsibility on non-monetary policies, and the financial markets have become more integrated. Hörngren and Lindberg correctly point out that a truly credible regime should also meet the requirements not only on nominal monetary targets, but also on other fundamentals such as fiscal deficit (and unemployment). The question whether such non-monetary targets should be the responsibility of the central bank is open to debate, but at least to the market, they are just as important as monetary targets. This problem becomes more acute when adjustment of the fundamentals takes time but speculative attacks do not. So even when the high interest policy bought the Swedish government some time to change the fiscal policy, it could not convince the market that the course will change completely in the short run.

So what can be done about it? The paper does not directly answer the question. Instead, it shifts its focus to an examination of central bank behaviour, under the Benanke–Mishkin theme of 'crises mentality', and the practical constraints of the government described by the phrase 'If it ain't broke, don't fix it'. The hard currency option was initially motivated by the inflation—a variable that was then 'in crisis'. Such an option had been pursued until the market broke the currency parity and presented another 'crisis' related to weak fundamentals. In the Swedish case, the remedy seems to be less controversial—strengthening the fiscal discipline, as it does not undermine the monetary reform. It would be a more difficult problem if the solution to unemployment requires the use of short-term Phillips curve trade-off.

It would be interesting to further test empirically whether the notion of 'crisis mentality' is supported by the data. That is, whether the government, or the market, has assigned different weights to various targets over time, or was it simply the targets themselves that have been changing. Such a test can be done in the framework of the Lucas Critique.

The paper documented the experience of using high interest rates to defend the exchange rate parity. It shows that sometimes the high interest rate was successful in reversing the capital outflow, but sometimes it merely halted the speculation, but the money did not flow back. This is an interesting issue that requires further explanation. It is interesting because it has an implication on the effect of the interest rate policy in general. My conjecture is that whether the capital outflow can be reversed depends on the type of agents who are dominating the market at the time. If the market is dominated by bystanders who jump into the market to reap the gains of high interest rates, the reflow may occur. If the market is dominated by speculators who have strong convictions on the weak fundamentals of the economy and are determined to win the 'one-way bet', then they will not view the high interest rate offer as attractive compared with the possible gains in the event of a successful attack. So the direction of capital flow will not be reversed. However, the high interest rate represents a high cost of market activities by both the central bank and the speculators, so the market activity tends to slow down, or halt. In such cases, high interest rate only serves as a measure to 'buy time', so that the government can do something about the fundamentals.

Another interesting issue raised in the paper is the 'contagion' with Finland, and with the EMS. In particular, the fundamentals in Finland are described as being drastically different from Sweden's. Then why was

Sweden also attacked in the turmoil? This is a question for further investigation.

# Discussion

## Niels Thygesen
*University of Copenhagen*

Hörngren and Lindberg have provided an informative and detailed account of Swedish monetary and exchange rate policy in the 1980s. The focus of the paper is narrow in the sense that the valiant efforts to peg the exchange rate for more than a decade and to defend it energetically by means of high interest rates was undermined less by technical deficiencies in the conduct of monetary and exchange rate policies than by the failure to back up these efforts by budgetary and other domestic policies, which are not discussed in the paper. Inadequate efforts to restrain the rise of wages and weak budgetary policies allowed Swedish inflation to remain higher than in the group of Sweden's trading partners to whose currencies the krona remained pegged. The initial sizeable competitive advantage brought about by the two large devaluations of the krona in 1981 and 1982—amounting to a total of 26%—was first allowed to erode and then to be replaced by a sharp worsening of the competitive position in the late 1980s as the economy overheated and the Swedish inflation rate diverged further from the international average. This ominous course of events is evident in Figures 6.2 and 6.3 of the paper, but not discussed further in the text. For a more detailed analysis of the increasing degree of overvaluation of the krona one has to turn to other papers, notably Lindbeck et al. (1993a,b) and Eichengreen and Wyplosz (1993); the latter also brings a comparison with other currencies which came under attack in the currency markets in 1992 and had to be devalued in a major way, notably sterling, the lira and the peseta.

From about 1985 the Swedish economy was visibly on a collision course: prices and wages accelerated while the trend was towards lower inflation elsewhere, particularly in Europe. The effects of the loss of competitiveness on output and employment were offset by higher public expenditures and an expansion of public sector employment. When the international recession hit Sweden from 1990 onwards, the economy was in a very exposed position and the decline in first external demand, then overall demand was sharper than anywhere else with the exception of Finland (which had a further unfavourable shock in the shape of the collapse of markets to the East). Although Swedish inflation then dropped very sharply, it was too late to save the exchange rate. Sweden became a prototype of an economy where high interest rates—and short-term rates were pushed up more vigorously than elsewhere—could not credibly be used for any length of time to defend the parity. Private market participants were well justified in believing that the political will to sustain tough monetary policies would not last long in the face of rapidly mounting unemployment and a budget deficit threatening to become the largest in the OECD area.

This comment accepts the self-imposed limitation in the paper not to discuss the underlying factors which eroded confidence in the krona and turned the struggle by the authorities to pursue a hard currency strategy not only into an uphill fight, but into one that could not be won. The subject of how to conduct monetary and exchange rate policy, taking other policies as given, is large enough, and the authors should not be blamed for sticking to that. Within that area I shall take up three elements which all tended to increase further the difficulties of conducting a credible hard currency policy: (i) the initial situation in 1982, including the previous unstable history of the krona; (ii) the special nature of the pegging arrangement; and (iii) the role of deregulation and the slow removal of capital controls. Throughout I shall make comparisons with countries which have participated in the EMS. Finally, some comments on options for the krona after the floating in November 1992 in the light of the experience of the preceding decade would seem in order, even though the authors do not address that issue.

*The inheritance in 1982.* The paper does mention that the transition to a firm exchange rate policy in October 1982 was a reversal of past Swedish policy, but their account understates the difficulties of bringing about a successful reversal.

In the 1970s and in 1981–2 the Swedish krona had dramatically failed to become a hard currency in either of the two senses—preservation of domestic and external value—which the authors usefully discuss. Like the other two Scandinavian currencies, the krona stuck initially to the DM in the snake, even though Sweden was not an EC member. In retrospect, it was probably harmful that the rate remained firmly pegged to the DM until September 1976 despite the cost explosion of the mid-1970s. The dike finally burst in 1976–7 with three devaluations of cumulatively nearly 20% and exit from the snake. Instead the Swedish authorities introduced a policy of attaching the krona to an effective rate index. Sweden did not seriously consider associate status for the krona in the EMS when the new system was set up in 1978–9.

As the authors point out, the next round of devaluations in 1981–2 of cumulatively 26% was provoked less by past losses of competitiveness than by a desire to combine an expenditure-reducing budgetary policy with a significant shift of demand towards the tradeables sector. Sweden became the prime example in the European OECD area of an aggressive exchange rate strategy to shorten the recession of the early 1980s (Australia providing another example outside Europe). This example provided a strong temptation for some other smaller European economies, not least Sweden's Nordic neighbours. The temptation was resisted, as the final realignment of the early EMS period in March 1983 showed.

Given this history of two rounds of massive devaluations over little more than 6 years it was clearly going to be an uphill fight to turn the krona into a hard currency, although it could initially be argued that there would now be no need for further adjustments for a lengthy period. However, the expenditure-reducing parts of the policy package turned out to be rather weak and the rise in profits in the tradables sector was so strong that inflationary risks became apparent sooner rather than later. In this context the deficiencies of the pegging arrangement assumed considerable importance.

*The pegging arrangements.* Three aspects of the pegging arrangements did not inspire confidence. First, the pegging remained a unilateral commitment. Whereas the EMS currencies derived some credibility from the mutual obligations to intervene and to coordinate interest rate policies, the Swedish krona could be viewed as being still on its own. This was significant, since the EMS had proved, already in 1982, that it was capable of modifying national policies, denying to some participants (Belgium, Denmark) the extent of devaluation which they had sought, and pushing them towards stronger domestic adjustment than they would have opted for individually (France). Second, no margins of fluctuations for the krona were announced early on in contrast to the EMS rules and the practice in the Bretton Woods system. Third, the krona was pegged to an average of other currencies rather than to individual ones as in a bilateral parity grid. The latter facilitates convergence of interest rates towards the lower levels prevailing in the least inflationary partner countries.

All these three deficiencies might have been repaired, if Sweden had pursued the option of associate status in the EMS, which would probably have been difficult to reject for the EC countries participating in the system at the time, since the EMS agreement explicitly provides for such a status—and because use of this provision in the period of the Snake was still fresh in the minds in 1982. Furthermore, at that time the ambition to move towards monetary union which later complicated the acceptance of associate currencies in the EMS, was far beyond the horizon. As Bergström (1991), whom the authors refer to, has recorded a half-hearted exploration of this option was undertaken by the then Swedish Finance Minister, but it was not pursued with the vigour which some proponents of a switch towards a hard currency policy would have liked. Pegging to the DM from 1982 could, in retrospect, have made an important contribution to introducing a shift to a tough exchange rate policy through the gradually increasing pressure on domestic policies which participation in the EMS would have implied during the disciplining period of 1983–7 and into the years of the rigid EMS after that. There is, of course, no way of knowing how Swedish policy-makers would have responded to such constraints, but my presumption is that the effect would have been in Sweden's long-term interests by modifying somewhat the imbalances which developed later in the 1980s.

Whatever the evaluation of the inadequate efforts to link up with the EMS currencies in order to remedy the deficiencies and turn the krona into a hard currency, when an effort was finally made in 1991 it was too late—both for Sweden and for the EMS participants. Overheating and inflation in the late 1980s had by then made EMS participation more hazardous, and the EC had put monetary union on the agenda which changed the attitude to the system's desirable degree of openness for associate currencies. The Swedish authorities switched to an ECU peg in May 1991 following the lead of Norway some months earlier. The switch preceded the application for EC membership in mid-1991 and was clearly linked to this step. Sweden would have preferred to join the EMS with the same rights and obligations as the EC participants, but their determined bid was first stalled by the competent bodies in the EC—the Monetary Committee and the Committee of Governors—and then firmly rejected by the Council of Finance Ministers in Bath in early September 1992. This rejection, though understandable in terms of the more advanced state of monetary integration than 10 years earlier, no doubt contributed, along with the floating of the Finnish markka, to the onslaught on the krona in mid-September.

Pegging to the ECU with announced margins of fluctuation around a central rate only marginally repaired the deficiencies of Sweden's pegging arrangements which, above all, remained unilateral and without firm links to monetary conditions in any particular country. The ECU became unattractive as a peg as the EMS began to unfold in September 1992, when two important currencies with a combined weight of nearly one-quarter in the ECU basket floated and depreciated strongly. The anchor chosen by Sweden, faute de mieux, had started to drift.

*The role of deregulation and the slow removal of capital controls.* Sweden was a latecomer to the process of deregulating financial markets domestically and removing capital controls. While this may have facilitated monetary management at times in the post-1982 period the Swedish reluctance also denied to Sweden the credibility-building impact on the exchange rate of lifting regulations. Such effects were visible initially as other small countries, notably Denmark, which moved in this direction in 1983–5. Closer financial integration there speeded up the convergence of interest rates towards the low levels which prevailed in Germany throughout most of the 1980s and reinforced the efforts by other economies to improve the credibility of a firm attachment to the DM. When Sweden finally joined the process of liberalization and deregulation, the strong boom of the late 1980s was well under way and the steps taken contributed to the domestic imbalances. The sequencing of Sweden's policy steps could clearly have been more conducive to stability.

In conclusion, what are the lessons of this decade of largely failed efforts to turn the krona into a hard currency? What are the mains efforts required to make such a policy more successful in the future?

Given the very sizeable imbalances now prevailing in the Swedish economy and the reluctant adoption of a floating exchange rate since November 1992 it is obvious that the main emphasis in efforts to build credibility for a stable and healthy krona must lie in domestic policies and reforms along the lines suggested in Lindbeck et.al. (1993). There is no easy short-cut available in the form of early pegging of the krona to one or more foreign currencies. This conclusion is inevitable simply because of the disappearance of alternative forms of implementing such a policy. The ECU remains unreliable for some time with important currencies outside the system of central rates, even though these currencies may now be more likely to strengthen than to weaken in the shorter term. Pegging to the DM is also less attractive than before in view of the isolation of the German currency and the uncertain prospects for the German economy in deep recession. Having burnt her fingers trying to peg unilaterally, Sweden would anyway be very hesitant to engage in any effort before the latter can be multilateral and underpinned by mutual intervention obligations.

Sweden is already moving in the direction of the second and more basic notion of what is implied by the notion of a hard currency, namely to provide a krona with nearly stable purchasing power domestically. The Council of the Riksbank has set 2% inflation for the next few years as the objective of monetary policy. Though this aim will seem ambitious for a country which has recently devalued by more than 20%, success can not be excluded in view of the modest pass-through to import prices of the devaluation and the very considerable slack in the Swedish economy. If inflation remains near this figure even as the economy emerges from the trough of the recession, the option of pegging the exchange rate once more can be considered. By that time Sweden will probably have become a member of the European Union, though the EMS is unlikely to have restored its former rules of operation before that happens. The current wide margins in the System would present few dangers then to Sweden, but also few benefits. Whether Sweden could participate in a monetary union with some of the current EC members towards the end of the decade—if that remains a feasible alternative—remains to be seen, but it may be difficult given the current budgetary outlook—even if the inflation rate remains close to that of a hard core of EC members.

# References

Bergström, H. (1991), 'Devalveringens politiska tillkomst och logik' [The political background and logic of the devaluation], in L. Jonung (ed.), *Devalveringen 1982—Rivstart Eller Snedtändning?* SNS Förlag, Stockholm.

Eichengreen, B. and Wyplosz, C. (1993), 'The unstable EMS', *Brookings Papers on Economic Activity* 1993:1, Brookings Institution, Washington, DC, pp. 51–143.

Lindbeck, A. et al. (1993a), 'Options for economic and political reform in Sweden', *Economic Policy*, **17**, 219–63.

Lindbeck, A. et al. (1993b), *Nya villkor för ekonomi och politik*, Ekonomikommissions förslag, SOK 1993:16, Allmänna Förlaget, Stockholm, translated and updated as *Turning Sweden Around*, MIT Press, Cambridge, MA, 1994.

# 7

## Disinflation Experience in Finland Compared with other OECD Countries

### Palle S. Andersen
*Bank for International Settlements, Basle*

### 7.1    Introduction

During the 1980s virtually all OECD countries adopted policies to reduce inflation though so far only Canada and New Zealand have introduced specific inflation targets and timetables for their central banks.

As a result of these policies the OECD area experienced a substantial fall in the rate of inflation, with the average rate—measured by the GDP-weighted private consumption deflator—falling by almost nine percentage points (p.p.) in the course of only 6 years. The principal features of this process may be summarized in four points:

- The origin can be traced to decisions taken in late 1979 when most countries agreed not to repeat the accommodating policies adopted after the first oil shock. Led by a change in the operating procedures of the Federal Reserve Board, monetary policies were the key instrument in the anti-inflation stance and both nominal and real interest rates rose substantially.
- Although more restrictive monetary policies provided the largest contribution to reducing inflation,[1] the process was also helped by the terms-of-trade gains[2] related to the steep fall in oil prices in 1985–6 and by the weakness of non-oil commodity prices during most of the decade. Regardless of whether the terms-of-trade improvements are regarded as exogenous or as partly induced by the weaker demand growth in the OECD area, the resulting gains in real disposable income mitigated distributional issues, which in earlier years had been one of the main sources of inflationary pressure.
- Nominal and real wage restraint was also instrumental in reducing

173

inflation and in preventing a re-acceleration of inflation during the
second half of the decade, when output growth was stronger. This was
especially evident in the manufacturing sectors, where the deceleration of nominal wages in almost all countries was more pronounced
than that of prices (see Figure 7.1). In other sectors, and especially in
the services sector, the degree of nominal and real wage moderation
was less pronounced and when wages are measured by aggregate
wages and salaries per employee, there is little evidence of lower real
wage growth (see Table 7.1).[3] Finland deviates markedly from the
general trend as real wage growth has been very high in both
manufacturing and the aggregate economy.

● A unique feature of the disinflation process was its uniformity, despite
variations in the policy mix across countries and volatile nominal and
real exchange rates. Since countries entering the 1980s with a
comparatively poor inflation performance tended to see a more
pronounced decline in price inflation than traditional low inflation

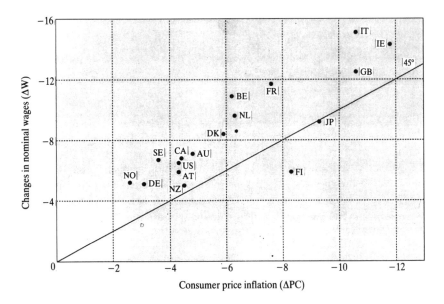

**Figure 7.1**  Deceleration in nominal wage and price inflation 1973/9–1986/9
*Note*: US = United States; JP = Japan; DE = Germany; FR = France;
GB = United Kingdom; IT = Italy; CA = Canada; AU = Australia;
AT = Austria; BE = Belgium; DK = Denmark; FI = Finland; IE = Ireland;
NL = Netherlands; NZ = New Zealand; NO = Norway; SE = Sweden.
The asterisk represents the average of these countries.

countries, the decline in the area's average inflation rate was accompanied by a marked convergence of inflation rates across countries (see Figure 7.2). In addition, the year-to-year variability of inflation declined,[4] so that the ambiguous price signals typical of a high inflation economy were significantly reduced.

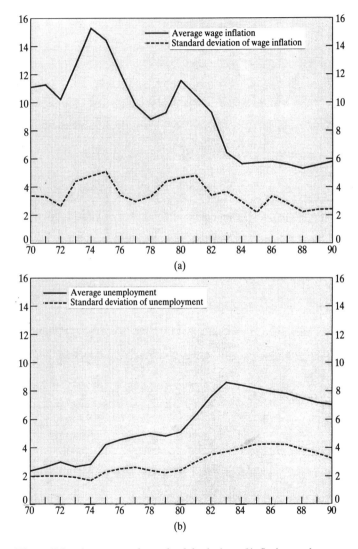

**Figure 7.2**   Average and standard deviation of inflation and employment. (a) Rate of inflation (nominal wages, aggregate economy); (b) Unemployment (as % of the labour force)

**Table 7.1**  Developments in consumer prices (PC) and wages (W): % change, annual average

| Countries | | 1973–9 | 1979–81 | 1981–6 | 1986–9 | 1990 | 1991[a] | Peak (year)[b] | Trough (year)[b] |
|---|---|---|---|---|---|---|---|---|---|
| United States | W | 7.2 | 9.0 | 4.8 | 4.1 | 4.4 | 4.0 | 9.2 (1980) | 3.3 (1989) |
| | PC | 7.8 | 10.0 | 3.7 | 4.3 | 5.0 | 4.1 | 10.8 (1980) | 2.4 (1986) |
| Japan | W | 11.4 | 7.2 | 4.7 | 4.7 | 5.2 | 4.5 | 7.9 (1980) | 3.5 (1987) |
| | PC | 8.0 | 5.6 | 1.7 | 0.6 | 2.6 | 2.6 | 7.1 (1980) | −0.2 (1987) |
| Germany | W | 6.6 | 5.6 | 3.3 | 2.8 | 4.3 | 5.8 | 6.4 (1980) | 2.8 (1989) |
| | PC | 4.3 | 5.9 | 2.5 | 1.4 | 2.5 | 3.6 | 6.2 (1981) | −0.5 (1986) |
| France | W | 13.2 | 13.7 | 7.2 | 4.4 | 4.9 | 4.6 | 13.9 (1980) | 3.5 (1987) |
| | PC | 10.9 | 13.4 | 6.9 | 3.2 | 3.0 | 2.9 | 13.5 (1980) | 2.9 (1988) |
| Italy | W | 17.7 | 20.0 | 11.3 | 8.3 | 8.6 | 8.1 | 20.2 (1981) | 7.3 (1986) |
| | PC | 16.6 | 19.3 | 10.9 | 5.3 | 6.2 | 6.2 | 20.5 (1980) | 5.0 (1987) |
| United Kingdom | W | 14.5 | 14.6 | 8.1 | 8.1 | 10.0 | 8.5 | 18.5 (1980) | 5.6 (1984) |
| | PC | 14.0 | 12.6 | 5.3 | 4.8 | 5.6 | 7.4 | 15.3 (1980) | 4.3 (1987) |
| Canada | W | 9.4 | 9.9 | 4.9 | 6.3 | 6.3 | 4.7 | 11.0 (1981) | 3.2 (1986) |
| | PC | 8.5 | 10.6 | 5.1 | 4.2 | 4.2 | 4.8 | 11.2 (1981) | 3.7 (1985) |
| Austria | W | 8.6 | 6.7 | 5.1 | 3.6 | 7.2 | 5.1 | 7.6 (1980) | 2.9 (1990) |
| | PC | 6.2 | 7.0 | 3.7 | 1.6 | 3.1 | 3.3 | 7.6 (1981) | 0.9 (1987) |
| Belgium | W | 9.8 | 8.2 | 4.9 | 1.7 | 5.5 | 5.0 | 11.5 (1980) | 0.9 (1987) |
| | PC | 7.2 | 7.4 | 4.0 | 2.2 | 3.5 | 3.3 | 8.7 (1981) | 0.7 (1986) |

|  |  |  |  |  |  |  |  |
|---|---|---|---|---|---|---|---|
| Denmark | W | 11.0 | 10.0 | 5.1 | 4.5 | 3.6 | 12.0 (1982) | 2.5 (1984) |
|  | PC | 10.4 | 11.7 | 6.1 | 4.6 | 2.1 | 12.0 (1981) | 2.1 (1990) |
| *Finland* | *W* | *14.8* | *13.3* | *9.7* | *9.3* | *7.9* | *14.5 (1981)* | *6.5 (1991)* |
|  | *PC* | *12.8* | *11.7* | *6.8* | *4.5* | *5.8* | *11.9 (1981)* | *3.1 (1986)* |
| Republic of Ireland | W | 17.1 | 17.8 | 8.8 | 5.7 | 4.5 | 19.1 (1980) | 3.3 (1991) |
|  | PC | 14.5 | 19.1 | 7.4 | 3.2 | 3.2 | 19.6 (1981) | 2.5 (1988) |
| Netherlands | W | 9.1 | 4.2 | 1.8 | 2.2 | 3.0 | 6.0 (1982) | 0.5 (1984) |
|  | PC | 6.8 | 6.3 | 1.8 | 0.9 | 3.4 | 7.0 (1980) | −0.9 (1987) |
| New Zealand | W | 12.4 | 17.3 | 3.9 | 7.8 | 3.0 | 17.7 (1981) | 0.3 (1983) |
|  | PC | 14.2 | 16.1 | 10.9 | 8.4 | 2.8 | 17.8 (1980) | 2.8 (1991) |
| Norway | W | 8.5 | 10.0 | 8.5 | 6.1 | 4.4 | 10.9 (1981) | 3.9 (1989) |
|  | PC | 8.4 | 11.6 | 7.7 | 6.0 | 3.6 | 13.4 (1981) | 3.6 (1991) |
| Sweden | W | 9.5 | 8.5 | 7.6 | 8.8 | 6.3 | 11.3 (1990) | 2.8 (1991) |
|  | PC | 10.3 | 12.4 | 7.8 | 6.0 | 10.4 | 12.4 (1980) | 4.6 (1986) |
| Australia | W | 11.7 | 12.1 | 7.5 | 6.3 | 3.5 | 12.3 (1980) | 3.5 (1991) |
|  | PC | 11.9 | 9.6 | 8.1 | 6.9 | 3.5 | 10.9 (1982) | 3.5 (1991) |
| Average[c] | W | 11.3 | 11.1 | 6.3 | 5.5 | 5.0 | 11.2 | — |
|  | PC | 10.2 | 11.2 | 5.8 | 4.0 | 4.3 | 12.1 | — |

*Notes:* [a] Preliminary figures. [b] After 1979. [c] Unweighted.
*Sources:* OECD Economic Outlook (PC), OECD Historical Statistics (W for Austria); IMF International Financial Statistics (W for the Republic of Ireland and New Zealand) and OECD National Accounts (W for other countries)

However, while the process of disinflation was impressive and also unparalleled in the post-war period,[5] it was not without costs. During the first half of the 1980s real output growth for the OECD area was less than 2·5% per year, compared with 3·5% for the previous 5 years. Moreover, unemployment in the area rose sharply (Figure 7.2) and, particularly in Europe, remained high well after output growth had returned to a stronger trend.

This raises a number of questions about the costs of disinflation and their principal determinants and these will be discussed in section 7.2, starting with theoretical issues and then turning to empirical measures based on the experience of 17 OECD countries. Against this background, section 7.3 looks at recent developments in Finland which in several respects have deviated from those of other OECD countries. In analysing the reason for the deviation, this part discusses policy changes and institutional factors, paying particular attention to exchange rate policies, changes in financial regulations and balances and the role of incomes policies. Section 7.4 summarizes and draws some general conclusions while details of the empirical estimates used in section 7.2 are presented in the Appendix.

## 7.2    The Costs of Disinflation

### 7.2.1    *Theory*

There is a general consensus that, while the benefits of lower inflation are permanent, the costs associated with reducing inflation are only transitory. It is also commonly recognized that two important determinants of the transitory costs are lack of credibility and slow adjustment of prices and wages.[6] The former view is associated with the New Classical School and the latter with the New Keynesians, but both can be regarded as essential to the transitory costs.[7] At the same time, a number of other factors should be added, in particular the initial conditions, terms-of-trade developments, the policy instruments used as 'nominal anchors', the speed with which the policies are implemented and the 'mix' of macroeconomic policies. Below we briefly discuss some features of these fundamental determinants before turning to their actual influence on measures of the costs of disinflation in section 7.2.2.

### Credibility[8]

It goes without saying that anti-inflation policies which are not credible to economic agents will either fail to reduce inflation or will do so only at great cost. Conversely, a credible policy can, by affecting expectations directly, considerably reduce the costs of disinflation. Yet despite its potentially crucial role the concept of credibility is not well defined in macroeconomics[9] and the empirical literature in this area is still in its infancy.

According to Blackburn and Christensen (1989), the factors most likely to have an adverse influence on credibility may be classified into three broad groups: (i) technological constraints, including reliability of the data, controlability of the policy instruments and the relevance of the economic theory used by the policy-makers; (ii) administrative constraints, which relate to the ability of the government to implement the required legislative changes; and (iii) strategic constraints, which refer to the interdependence between the behaviour of private agents and policy-makers and by most authors have been analysed within a game-theoretic framework. One issue of particular interest in this respect is the time inconsistency dilemma which can arise when the policy-makers pursue several targets and the optimal policy strategy changes over time. As stressed by Blackburn and Christensen, the three sets of constraints are not independent of each other and frequently the single most important determinant of credibility is the coherence or consistency of the overall macroeconomic programme and especially whether fiscal policies support an anti-inflation monetary policy stance.

Empirical studies of credibility effects have relied on analysing economic relations before and after a given policy change or deriving a parameter hypothesized to capture credibility effects. The first method may be seen as a special application of the Lucas critique and its reliability obviously depends on the stability of the underlying behavioural or reduced-form equations. Moreover, to the extent that credibility effects gradually build up (or decay) over time, models with time-varying coefficients would be required. Direct measures of credibility variables have mostly been derived from exchange rate or interest rate equations using a Bayesian approach (Baxter, 1985; Weber, 1991). One problem appears to be that the variables or parameters do not measure credibility alone. For instance, credibility parameters are often derived by decomposing a specific error process and may combine policy reaction parameters with coefficients from price and wage equations (Takeda, 1992).

## Wage and Price Rigidities and Unemployment Persistence

There are two major reasons why prices and wages do not immediately adjust to the inflation targets announced by the authorities. First, because of built-in habits and the costs associated with obtaining new information, expectations tend to be backward-looking (or adaptive) rather than forward-looking. Second, even in a case of perfect credibility and forward-looking expectations, coordination failures (Fortin, 1991) and institutional factors such as staggered contracts (Fischer, 1977, 1986a; Taylor, 1980) would prevent expectations from immediately affecting actual price and wage changes. Because of these lags (*nominal rigidity*), the adoption of anti-inflation policies will be accompanied by excess supply in labour and product markets and the transitory costs will not only depend on the length of the lags but also on the sensitivity of price and wage changes to a given degree of slack (*real rigidity*).[10]

Table 7.2 shows empirical estimates of the nominal and real rigidities[11] using a model (for details see the Appendix) which, to ease the exposition, can be simplified to:

$$dw = -\eta\, u_{-1} + dp^* \qquad \text{and} \qquad (7.1)$$
$$dp^* = \beta dp + (1-\beta)dw_{-1} \qquad (7.2)$$

All variables are measured in logs and $w$ denotes nominal wages, $p$ consumer prices (with $*$ denoting expected values), $u$ the rate of unemployment and $d$ the first difference operator.

**Table 7.2**   Sources of labour market rigidities and unemployment persistence

| Country | Hysteresis $(\alpha)^a$ | Real wage rigidity $(\eta)^a$ | Nominal wage rigidity $(1-\beta_1)^a$ | Unemployment persistence $(o_1 + o_2)^b$ |
|---|---|---|---|---|
| United States | 0.00 | −0.23 | 0.73 | 0.75 |
| Japan | 0.68 | −1.84 | 0.46 | 0.94 |
| Germany | 0.76 | −0.45 | 0.47 | 0.94 |
| France | 0.00 | −0.15 | 0.14 | 0.98 |
| Italy | 0.00 | −0.38 | 0.26 | 0.96 |
| United Kingdom | 0.91 | −0.15 | 0.20 | 0.92 |
| Canada | 0.00 | −0.26 | 0.35 | 0.89 |
| Austria | 0.62 | −0.94 | 0.78 | 0.91 |
| Belgium | 0.00 | −0.29 | 0.37 | 0.96 |
| Denmark | 0.00 | −0.19 | 0.31 | 0.97 |
| *Finland* | *0.70* | *−0.48* | *0.10* | *0.81* |
| Republic of Ireland | 0.00 | −0.19 | 0.12 | 0.94 |
| Netherlands | 0.36 | −0.35 | 0.33 | 0.95 |
| New Zealand | 0.42 | −0.09 | 0.38 | 1.07 |
| Norway | 0.00 | −0.20 | 0.37 | 0.93 |
| Sweden | 0.69 | −0.50 | 0.66 | 0.66 |
| Australia | 0.00 | −0.18 | 0.00 | 0.95 |

*Notes:* [a] Derived from a nominal wage equation specified as: $d\ln W = \mu + \eta$ $(\ln U - \alpha\ln U_{-1}) + \beta_1 d\ln PC + \beta_2 d\ln PC_{-1} + (1-\beta_1-\beta_2)d\ln W_{-1}$; see the Appendix
[b] Derived from an autoregressive unemployment equation: $U = o_1 U_{-1} + o_2 U_{-2}$; see the Appendix

Inserting equation (7.2) into equation (7.1) then gives:

$$dw = -\eta u_{-1} + \beta dp + (1-\beta)dw_{-1} \qquad (7.1')$$

where $\eta$ can be used as an indicator of real rigidity and $(1-\beta)$ as a measure of nominal rigidity. The model may be extended to include a labour demand equation with a real wage elasticity of $-1$, a price adjustment function where price changes equal changes in money supply (i.e. $dp = dm$) and constant labour supply. On these assumptions, a tightening of monetary policy aimed at lowering the long run rate of inflation by 1 p.p. would initially reduce $dw$ by only $\beta$ points and increase real wages and the rate of unemployment by $1-\beta$ points. A convenient measure of the intermediate or historical costs (Cozier and Wilkinson, 1990) of reducing inflation is $(1-\beta)/\eta$, which may be interpreted as the number of unemployment years required to reduce the rate of wage inflation by 1 p.p. and is usually referred to as the 'sacrifice ratio'. Nominal and real rigidities enter symmetrically, with $(1-\beta)$ measuring the gap between the actual and the targeted wage inflation rate and $1/\eta$ the rise in $u$ required to eliminate this gap. In more realistic models additional variables may be included. Thus, to allow for hysteresis the unemployment term in equation (7.1) can be written as $-\eta u + \eta \alpha u_{-1}$, with $\alpha$ a parameter between 0 and 1. The presence of hysteresis reduces the sensitivity of $dw$ to $u$ from $\eta$ to $\eta(1-\alpha)$ and in the extreme case of $\alpha = 1$ the costs of disinflation become permanent. Moreover, since strongly backward-looking schemes raise the numerator in the sacrifice ratio, the weighting pattern of the expectation formation process is often extended to include several lagged terms.[12]

## Initial Conditions

Depending on their nature, these can directly influence the transitory costs but may also have important indirect effects, either through the shape of the trade-off curve or by affecting the extent to which anti-inflation policies are credible to the general public. Table 7.3 presents three sets of factors and their likely influence may be summarized as follows:

● the initial levels of inflation and unemployment[13] affect the costs when the trade-off is non-linear and/or when the weights assigned to inflation and unemployment in the welfare function of the general public change along the trade-off curve.[14] On the basis of survey evidence and empirical estimates, it is frequently argued that at low rates of inflation and high rates of unemployment the costs of reducing inflation further rise disproportionately as the trade-off curve is very

**Table 7.3**   Initial conditions[a]

| Countries | 'Domestic' indicators | | | | Fiscal position | | | | External indicators | | |
|---|---|---|---|---|---|---|---|---|---|---|---|
| | CPI | U | PRO | Bal | Pbal | Gdebt | Sust | BoP | Fdebt | REXCH | PMR |
| United States | 10.0 | 7.4 | 1.7 | -1.2 | -0.5 | 20.8 | 1.5 | 0.1 | 0.6 | 107.2 | -2.2 |
| Japan | 6.0 | 2.1 | -6.9 | -4.1 | -2.3 | 22.0 | 2.6 | -0.3 | 2.2 | 97.2 | -4.9 |
| Germany | 6.1 | 3.9 | -1.6 | -3.3 | -1.7 | 18.6 | 1.5 | -1.1 | 3.3 | 94.0 | -4.3 |
| France | 13.2 | 6.9 | -7.4 | -1.0 | -0.2 | 16.0 | 1.6 | -0.7 | 4.2 | 97.7 | -4.1 |
| Italy | 19.3 | 8.1 | 0.3 | -10.1 | -5.5 | 60.3 | 5.4 | -2.2 | 2.2 | 88.3 | -7.2 |
| United Kingdom | 13.8 | 7.3 | -2.0 | -3.0 | -0.8 | 46.3 | 1.0 | 1.9 | 1.3 | 133.8 | -2.9 |
| Canada | 10.6 | 7.5 | -0.3 | -2.1 | -1.0 | 14.0 | 1.5 | -1.0 | -29.0 | 94.6 | -5.0 |
| Austria | 7.0 | 2.2 | -0.9 | -1.7 | -0.4 | 40.5[b] | 1.4 | -2.1 | -3.8 | 98.2 | -5.6 |
| Belgium | 7.5 | 9.0 | -12.5 | -11.1 | -4.5 | 85.2 | 10.6 | -4.1 | -5.8 | 80.9 | -11.6 |
| Denmark | 11.3 | 8.3 | -4.9 | -5.1 | -3.9 | 21.5 | 7.9 | -3.5 | -31.2 | 80.7 | -7.2 |
| *Finland* | *11.7* | *4.8* | *-3.0* | *0.8* | *1.0* | *-5.4* | *-1.1* | *-1.8* | *-14.1* | *99.0* | *-9.1* |
| Republic of Ireland | 19.1 | 8.6 | -4.5 | -12.7 | -8.0 | 88.0[b] | 7.7 | -13.1 | -49.6 | 96.9 | -8.3 |
| Netherlands | 6.6 | 7.3 | -0.5 | -4.7 | -2.5 | 29.4 | 4.0 | 0.1 | 6.4 | 89.5 | -10.3 |
| New Zealand | 16.2 | 3.1 | -13.3 | -7.9[c] | -3.1[c] | 48.3[c] | 1.4[c] | -4.7 | -26.7 | 111.0 | -12.0 |
| Norway | 11.7 | 1.8 | 11.9 | 5.3 | 5.2 | 2.6 | -4.3 | 2.8 | -26.5 | 101.1 | -4.4 |
| Sweden | 13.4 | 2.3 | -3.6 | -4.7 | -4.7 | -0.4 | 5.2 | -3.8 | -15.5 | 92.9 | -6.5 |
| Australia | 9.9 | 5.8 | -3.6 | -0.3 | -0.0 | 22.2[b] | 0.4 | -3.8 | -7.9 | 103.0 | -3.3 |

*Notes:* [a] Average 1980–1.   [b] Estimated.   [c] Central government only. Notation: CPI, consumer prices, percentage change; *U*, unemployment as a percentage of total labour force; PRO, change in profit share (operating surplus/GNP in factor prices), 1970/4–1980/1 (in percentage points); Bal, general government net lending as a percentage of GNP; Pbal, general government net lending less interest payments, as a percentage of GNP; Gdebt, general government net debt, as a percentage of GNP; Sust, indicator of sustainability, calculated as 0.01 Gdebt. (IR−Y) − Pbal. IR−Y is the long-term bond rate less change in nominal GNP (3-year moving average) and a positive sign indicates a need for raising taxes and/or reducing expenditure; BoP, current external account as a percentage of GNP; Fdebt, net foreign assets as a percentage of GNP; REXCH, real effective exchange rate (unit labour costs) as a percentage of 1970–9 average; PMR, change in ratio of import prices to consumer prices (1982–9), scaled by ratio of imports to GNP (1985) flat and inflation has a low weight in the general welfare function. The profit share might also be included among the initial conditions on the assumption that when profits are relatively high, enterprises are able to lower prices without reducing labour demand or cutting investment plans.[15]

- The fiscal position can influence the costs of disinflation in at least two ways: first, an unfavourable position, measured by the overall balance, the level of public debt or the sustainability of current policies, is likely to reduce the credibility of an anti-inflation monetary policy. Second, a large initial deficit narrows the scope for offsetting the contractionary impact of a more restrictive monetary policy through a fiscal stimulus.
- The external position can affect the costs along the same lines as the initial fiscal balance: a large external imbalance, measured by the current account or the net asset position, would tend to reduce credibility and an unfavourable competitive position narrows the scope for offsetting the fall in domestic demand growth through net exports. Table 7.3 also includes the terms of trade among the external indicators, measured as changes in relative import prices scaled by the ratio of imports to GNP. For all countries this indicator shows a marked decline which, to a large extent, explains the trough of consumer price inflation in 1986. In addition to this one-time effect of the fall in import prices, the associated terms-of-trade gains are likely to have had a permanent effect on the sacrifice ratios by reducing the degree of slack required to solve the problem of inconsistent income share claims.

## Policies

This is potentially the most important influence on the costs of disinflation but also the one that is most difficult to evaluate. Some features of the policies adopted are summarized in Table 7.4, and four issues deserve further elaboration.

The first concerns the choice of nominal anchors and, more specifically, whether a monetary aggregate target or a fixed nominal exchange rate is the most effective instrument for anchoring inflation expectations.[16] There is general agreement that in periods of large shifts in the demand for money function a fixed exchange rate will be a more effective anchor, but it is also recognized that fixing the exchange rate before the rate of inflation has declined entails a high risk of leading to an appreciation of the real rate.[17] Generally it is difficult to use monetary aggregate targets and a fixed exchange rate as complementary anchors, whereas several countries (Austria, Belgium, Denmark, Finland, Norway, France and, more recently, the Republic of Ireland) have combined a fixed exchange

**Table 7.4** Policies and disinflation[a]

| Countries | Fiscal policy[b] (Change in balances) (% of GNP/GDP) | | | Monetary policy (Change in bond rates) | | | Exchange rate policy (Change in effective rates) | | | Incomes policy | |
|---|---|---|---|---|---|---|---|---|---|---|---|
| | Actual | Non-cyclical | Primary | Nominal | Real[c] | Differential[d] | Arrangement[e] | Nominal[f] | Real[g] | General | Disindexation |
| United States | -1.3 | -1.1 | 0.6 | -4.0 | 1.0 | 2.1 | Flexible | -10.0 | -25.0 | No | No |
| Japan | 6.8 | 6.1 | 5.6 | -1.5 | 2.0 | 0.5 | — | 61.0 | 34.5 | No | No |
| Germany | 0.8 | 4.3 | 1.1 | -0.6 | 2.1 | 1.9 | ERM | 27.0 (35.0) | 12.5 | No | No |
| France | -0.7 | 1.4 | 1.1 | -4.6 | 4.7 | -1.0 | ERM | -13.2 (-12.5) | -7.0 | (Yes) | Yes |
| Italy | -0.6 | 1.8 | 4.0 | -5.5 | 6.8 | 0.0 | ERM | -20.5 (-20.0) | 26.5 | No | (Yes) |
| United Kingdom | 2.3 | 2.1 | 2.3 | -2.2 | 5.4 | -2.5 | Flexible | -20.0 | -7.5 | No | No |
| Canada | -1.7 | -2.3 | 2.6 | -3.0 | 2.5 | -0.5 | Flexible | -1.5 | 10.2 | No | No |
| Austria | -0.4 | -0.5 | 1.6 | -1.2 | 2.1 | 1.0 | DM | 16.8 | -5.0 | Yes | No |
| Belgium | 5.6 | 7.9 | 9.9 | -3.0 | -0.8 | 2.2 | ERM | -4.5 (-4.5) | -20.5 | Yes | (Yes) |
| Denmark | 3.5 | 4.2 | 5.8 | -8.5 | -0.7 | -2.5 | ERM | 2.5 (-1.0) | 14.0 | (Yes) | Yes |
| *Finland* | *0.6* | *-0.7* | *1.0* | *0.9* | *7.1* | *2.7* | *Basket* | *6.0* | *15.0* | *Yes* | *No* |
| Republic of Ireland | 10.4 | 14.9 | 12.6 | -6.0 | 8.0 | -1.0 | ERM | -4.5 (-2.0) | -27.5 | Yes | No |
| Netherlands | -0.6 | 1.9 | 2.2 | -1.8 | 1.6 | 0.7 | ERM | 20.5 (20.0) | -9.0 | No | No |
| New Zealand[h] | 12.0 | NA | 13.2[i] | -0.5 | 9.8 | -3.0 | Flexible | -35.5 | -1.5 | (Yes) | No |
| Norway | -3.0 | -5.3 | -6.4 | -0.5 | 7.9 | -1.5 | Basket | -15.0 | 0.0 | Yes | No |
| Sweden | 8.6 | 6.9 | 9.4 | 0.9 | 7.0 | 0.3 | Basket | -23.5 | 1.0 | No | No |
| Australia | 1.5 | 1.8 | 3.1 | 0.4 | 3.8 | -0.5 | Flexible | -39.5 | -13.5 | Yes | No |

*Notes:*

a  Unless otherwise indicated all changes refer to the period 1980/1–1990

b  All figures refer to general government; + (–) indicates smaller (larger) deficit or larger (smaller) surplus. The second column is the cumulative change (1982–9) in the cyclically adjusted budget balance and the third column is the inflation-corrected change in the fiscal impact index (1981–9), assuming forward-looking behaviour by households; see Chouraqui et al. (1990), Tables 4, 13 and 14

c  Nominal rate less current and lagged change (unweighted average) in consumer prices

d  Nominal bond rate less representative short-term rate

e  Refers to the period in general and does not include recent changes in ERM participation

f  Nominal effective exchange rate against 21 most important trading partners: + (–) denotes appreciation (depreciation). Figures in parentheses denote change vis-à-vis ERM partners

g  Deflated by unit labour costs; + (–) indicates a deterioration (improvement) in competitiveness

h  Central government, fiscal year (April to April)

i  1982–8

rate target with permanent or transitory incomes policies.[18] Australia appears to be the only one of the countries included in Table 7.4 which relies on both monetary policy and a permanent incomes policy (the 'Wage Accord') as the principal means of reducing inflation.

A second issue is the policy mix. According to Mundell's (1971) assignment rule, a country with a floating exchange rate should combine a tight monetary policy with an expansionary fiscal policy to minimise the sacrifice ratio. The United States successfully applied this combination during the first half of the 1980s (Sachs, 1985) but the strategy is not without problems. A large proportion of the fall in the rate of inflation may be only temporary as it results from an appreciation of the exchange rate, which will eventually have to be wholly or partly reversed to improve the external position. Moreover, growing fiscal and external imbalances can adversely affect the credibility of anti-inflation monetary policies and a number of countries which in the past adopted Mundell's rule experienced a depreciation and not an appreciation of the exchange rate. Finally, the strategy is obviously not feasible on a worldwide basis and in the early 1980s fiscal consolidation was a primary objective in most countries with the use of fiscal measures to influence aggregate demand being assigned a rather low priority on the policy agenda.

A third issue concerns the speed of implementation, or whether a shock ('cold turkey') approach or a gradual approach produces the lowest sacrifice ratio. According to Kahn and Weiner (1990), the gradual approach taken by the US authorities in the late 1950s entailed the same sacrifice ratio as the more drastic tightening of monetary policy in late 1979. More recently, a consensus seems to have emerged that the speed of implementation should be geared to the lags in the price and wage formation process.[19] As shown by Taylor (1983) and also in several simulations reported in Chadha et al. (1991) such a 'matching' can reduce inflation with virtually no output and employment costs. However, a major problem is that the initial speed of disinflation is very slow,[20] which is likely to adversely affect the credibility of the announced inflation targets.

A fourth but separate issue relates to the interpretation of changes in monetary aggregates which are distorted by shifts in portfolio preferences in response to regulatory changes or the availability of new financial instruments. Countries experiencing the re-entry problem mentioned above not only face the problem of interpretation but even more a problem of selecting an appropriate strategy. When, for instance, the rate of inflation and the nominal interest rate decline as a result of a credible anti-inflation monetary policy, the demand for money will rise,[21] creating a dilemma for the monetary authorities: on the one hand, if the rise in demand is accommodated and the aggregate target is overshot, credibility is likely to suffer; on the other hand, if the demand rise is not accommodated, the adjustment will have to come through alternative channels (higher nominal and real interest rates, lower output growth or an unsustainably steep fall in the rate of inflation), which may be equally damaging to credibility and the costs of disinflation.[22]

### 7.2.2  *Empirical Measures*

Because some of the determinants discussed above are difficult to quantify or their presumed influence on the costs of disinflation interact with those of other determinants, it is not possible to appraise all potential issues. However, relying on 'snapshot empiricism' (Blackburn and Christensen, 1989), cross-country comparisons and econometric estimates we shall attempt to answer three questions, which are also relevant to analysing developments in Finland: (i) Do the initial conditions as shown in Table 7.3 influence the transitory costs? (ii) What is the role of labour market rigidities? and (iii) Is a fixed exchange rate helpful for anchoring inflation expectations and reducing the costs? Tentative answers are given below, following a brief discussion of methodology and of some shortcomings of the measures applied.

*Methodology*

As mentioned above, the transitory costs are usually presented as sacrifice ratios and three methods have been used to derive such ratios.[23] They can give quite different results[24] and each has its own particular advantages and shortcomings.

*Slope of short-run Phillips curve (or aggregate supply curve)*  This is the method applied by most researchers and merely requires estimates of the Phillips curve or the aggregate supply curve. The precise definition varies as some use the real rigidity coefficient ($1/\eta$), while others combine nominal and real rigidities ($(1-\beta)/\eta$). The ratios are easy to derive, but are only partial measures and, in particular, cannot take account of shifts induced by changes in expectations or credibility effects. Special problems are also encountered when the trade-offs are non-linear and the range of estimates is particularly wide in studies which combine trade-offs from the Phillips curve with slopes of the Okun curve in order to derive a sacrifice ratio based on foregone output. Two examples illustrate this point and, at the same time, provide some perspective to the disinflation of the 1980s. In a well-known review of the 1970s Tobin (1980) concluded with a Figure, using the wage-price model generally accepted for the United States at that time. Although Tobin is careful to point out that the Figure is not intended to be a forecast but a path against which actual developments should be compared, it is instructive to note that the unemployment-based sacrifice ratio using Tobin's figures for the period 1980–1 to 1986–9 would be 2.5, or three times the value given in Table 7.5. A comparison with actual developments also shows that the more favourable outcome can mainly be ascribed to a much faster adjustment of inflation than predicted by the model.[25] As a second example, assume that the Phillips curve is linear with a slope equal to '$a$' and that the Okun curve is also linear with a slope equal to '$b$'. A one point rise in the rate of unemployment would then be accompanied by an '$a$' point decline in the rate of inflation and a '$b$' point deceleration in real output growth, with the ratio of real to nominal output changes equal to $b/(a+b)$ (Fortin, 1990). A consensus view would probably put '$a$' at around 0.5 and '$b$' at 2.5 for all OECD countries on average, producing a ratio of 0.85. However, as can be seen from the bottom lines of Table 7.3 in the Appendix, the actual change

**Table 7.5** Sacrifice ratios[a]

| Countries | $U$ | Y1 | Y2 | Y3 |
|---|---|---|---|---|
| United States | 0.85 | 1.35 | 0.40 | 0.30 |
| Japan | 0.70 | 0.50 | 0.10 | −0.30 |
| Germany | 6.40 | 2.20 | 1.20 | 1.60 |
| France | 2.15 | 0.50 | 0.50 | 0.20 |
| Italy | 1.40 | 0.65 | 0.45 | 0.20 |
| United Kingdom | 3.40 | 0.90 | 0.60 | 0.20 |
| Canada | 2.75 | 1.50 | 0.80 | 0.15 |
| Austria | 2.05 | 4.65 | 0.90 | 0.90 |
| Belgium | 3.00 | 6.10 | 0.90 | 0.50 |
| Denmark | 1.25 | 0.90 | −0.15 | 0.15 |
| *Finland* | *0.05* | *1.25* | *0.75* | *0.30* |
| Republic of Ireland | 3.35 | 0.30 | 0.50 | 0.50 |
| Netherlands | 4.95 | 1.85 | 0.80 | 1.10 |
| New Zealand | 2.05 | 0.25 | 0.55 | 0.85 |
| Norway | 1.05 | 2.00 | −0.00 | 0.50 |
| Sweden | 1.20 | 0.65 | 0.00 | −0.40 |
| Australia | 6.00 | 1.25 | 0.25 | −0.15 |
| Average[b] | 2.50 | 1.60 | 0.50 | 0.40 |

*Notes:* [a] The first column is calculated as the *cumulative* rise in the rate of unemployment between 1979–81 and 1986–9 divided by the change in the rate of consumer price inflation over the same period. The next three columns are calculated as the *cumulative* output losses between 1979 and 1982, 1985 and 1988, respectively, divided by the change in the rate of consumer price inflation between 1979–81 and 1984, 1987 and 1990, respectively. In calculating the output losses trend or potential output was approximated by a cubic trend (see the Appendix) except for New Zealand where the 1960–79 trend was extrapolated into the 1980s
[b] Unweighted

between 1973–9 and 1979–81 produced a ratio of only 0.35 and between 1979–81 and 1986–9 the ratio was *negative* as real output growth increased while nominal output growth declined. It was only during 1990–1, when output growth became negative in several countries, that the ratio reached 0.85.

*Counter-factual model simulations*    Analytically, this is by far the most satisfactory method as it is comprehensive and exogenous factors are isolated. The sensitivity of costs to changes in the lag structure of the price and wage formation process can be estimated and it is also possible to illustrate the effect of changes in credibility (Selody, 1990; Chadha et al., 1991; Murphy, 1991). Nonetheless, the cost measures may be subject to a bias—though the size as well as the sign of the bias is unknown—as virtually all macromodels are based on the assumption that in the long run all real variables are neutral with respect to changes in monetary policy and in the rate of inflation and thus do not include the benefits of lower inflation.

*Actual developments*    This is the easiest method as it merely requires the calculation of cumulative changes in unemployment (or lost output) over a certain period and the division of this figure by changes in the rate of inflation over the same period. It also has the advantage that credibility gains or changes in the expectation formation process are included, though not quantified. An obvious disadvantage, however, is that the influence of factors (especially supply shocks) which are entirely exogenous to the anti-inflation policy is difficult to exclude and the ratios are very sensitive to the period chosen. Another problem is whether to measure the cumulative output and employment losses relative to some potential (or equilibrium) level or rate of change or to base the comparisons on the actual values observed just prior to the implementation of anti-inflation policies. Most empirical studies have applied potential levels and rates, which requires that such values have to be estimated in advance and may lead to biases if the initial year is far away from the equilibrium position. The measures discussed below rely on deviations from actual values in the initial period, but this procedure is also problematic, especially if there are trend changes in the underlying equilibrium values.

## The Costs of Disinflation in the 1980s

Table 7.5 shows sacrifice ratios based on actual developments. The first column measures cost in terms of unemployment, while the next three show output losses calculated for different time horizons. The ratios are only intended as broad indicators, but, nevertheless, may be used to highlight certain general features, provide a preliminary ranking of the seventeen countries and give some tentative answers to the questions posed above.

In most cases the unemployment-based ratios shown in the first column give a more 'pessimistic' picture of the transitory costs than evaluations based on output developments. In several countries the cumulative output losses become very small (or even negative) for the longer time horizon, whereas only four countries (the United States, Canada, Finland and Sweden) had managed to reduce unemployment to (or below) the initial level by 1989 and this was only temporary as in all four cases the unemployment rates of 1991 exceeded those of the initial period. One reason for the discrepancy in the cost measures[26] may be that the equilibrium rate of unemployment has increased relative to the level of potential output. Alternatively, labour markets could have adjusted more slowly than output markets, so that unemployment had to be kept high over an extended period to obtain the required degree of wage restraint. Yet another possibility is that a cubic trend understates potential output for the 1980s, thus also understating the output losses. Both the IMF and the OECD have revised their assessments of potential growth rates and ascribe most of the revisions to the favourable impact of the supply-side policies pursued in many countries. On the other hand, if lower inflation has had a positive impact on potential output growth,[27] the use of higher rates would overstate the sacrifice ratios, since one of the expected benefits of lower inflation would be counted as a current cost.

Another feature of the measures shown is that the output losses tend to fall or to be reversed as the period is extended. This supports the assumption that the costs are only transitory but also poses a problem regarding the choice of the time horizon for the calculation. On the one hand, if the period is too short the lags in the wage–price adjustment process would tend to dominate and overstate the costs. On the other hand, as the time period is extended the risk of including factors which are entirely exogenous to the policy of disinflation increases.

## Preliminary Ranking and Some Tentative Answers

Tables 7.6a and 7.6b rank the countries using the sacrifice ratios of Table 7.5 and Table 7.7 attempts to link the sacrifice ratios to the principal determinants by regressing the four sacrifice ratios—across the 17 countries—on the initial conditions, the relative change in import prices over 1982–9 and the rigidity parameters given in Table 7.2. The most satisfactory results are obtained for the unemployment-based sacrifice

**Table 7.6a**   Ranking based on sacrifice ratios[a]

| Countries | U | Y1 | Y2 | Y3 | Average[b] |
|---|---|---|---|---|---|
| United States | 3 | 11 | 6 | 9 | 5 |
| Japan | 2 | 4 | 4 | 2 | 1 |
| Germany | 17 | 15 | 16 | 17 | 17 |
| France | 10 | 4 | 8 | 6 | 8 |
| Italy | 7 | 6 | 7 | 6 | 7 |
| United Kingdom | 14 | 8 | 11 | 6 | 13 |
| Canada | 11 | 12 | 13 | 4 | 11 |
| Austria | 9 | 16 | 15 | 15 | 14 |
| Belgium | 12 | 17 | 15 | 11 | 15 |
| Denmark | 6 | 8 | 1 | 4 | 3 |
| *Finland* | *1* | *10* | *12* | *9* | *4* |
| Republic of Ireland | 13 | 2 | 8 | 11 | 10 |
| Netherlands | 15 | 13 | 13 | 16 | 16 |
| New Zealand | 8 | 1 | 10 | 14 | 9 |
| Norway | 4 | 14 | 2 | 11 | 6 |
| Sweden | 5 | 6 | 3 | 1 | 2 |
| Australia | 16 | 10 | 5 | 3 | 12 |

Notes: [a] For all measures countries with the lowest ranks are those with the lowest costs

[b] Calculated assigning a weight of 3 to U and 1 to each of Y1, Y2 and Y3

**Table 7.6b**   Correlations of sacrifice ratios

| | U | Y1 | Y2 | Y3 |
|---|---|---|---|---|
| U | 1.00 | 0.25 | 0.53 | 0.33 |
| Y1 | 0.16 | 1.00 | 0.50 | 0.41 |
| Y2 | 0.48 | 0.49 | 1.00 | 0.65 |
| Y3 | 0.45 | 0.37 | 0.70 | 1.00 |

Note: Figures above (below) the diagonal indicate rank (simple) correlation coefficients

**Table 7.7**   Sacrifice ratios and the principal determinants[a]

| | U | U[b] | Y1 | Y2 | Y3 |
|---|---|---|---|---|---|
| C | 4.93 (1.2) | 4.64 (1.6) | — | — | −1.28 (0.8) |
| dPC | −0.35 (2.8) | −0.37 (4.1) | −0.27 (3.1) | −0.07 (2.2) | −0.05 (1.4) |
| GDEF | −0.28 (2.1) | −0.31 (3.4) | −0.12 (1.5) | −0.04 (2.0) | −0.03 (0.9) |
| REXCH | 0.30 (0.8) | 0.35 (1.3) | — | 0.11 (3.3) | — |
| dPM | 0.20 (1.1) | 0.25 (1.9) | — | — | — |
| $\eta$ | 2.69 (2.4) | 2.68 (3.5) | 1.26 (1.5) | 0.28 (1.2) | 0.62 (1.9) |
| $(1-\beta)$ | — | — | 2.35 (1.7) | — | 1.01 (1.5) |
| $o_1 + o_2$ | — | — | 4.17 (3.3) | — | 2.22 (1.6) |
| $R^2$ | 0.25 | 0.64 | 0.34 | 0.07 | 0.17 |
| SE | 1.6 | 1.1 | 1.2 | 0.4 | 0.5 |

Notes: [a] Notation: dPC, percentage change in consumer prices, 1980–1; GDEF, general government net lending as a percentage of GDP, 1980–1; REXCH, real exchange rate, 1980–1 as a percentage of 1970–9 average; dPM, change in the ratio of import prices to consumer prices, 1982–9; $\eta$, indicator of real wage flexibility (see the Appendix); $(1-\beta)$, indicator of nominal wage flexibility (see the Appendix); $o_1 + o_2$, indicator of unemployment persistence (see the Appendix); $t$- values given in parentheses

[b] Also includes a dummy variable coefficient 2.85 (3.5)) which equals −1 for the United States, 1 for Australia and 0 for other countries

ratio when the deviations for the United States and Australia are removed.[28] However, even for the uncorrected equation the coefficients have rather high $t$-ratios and support some of the various hypotheses discussed above. In terms of explanatory power, the equations based on output costs are less satisfactory and the low $R^2$ for Y2 is particularly puzzling.

*Do the initial conditions influence the costs of disinflation?* The debt ratios had no effect and the primary fiscal deficits—separately or combined with the debt ratio and IR−Y—were also insignificant. The same applies to the external position and the profit share, while the rate of unemployment was marginally significant in the U-equation but not at all significant in any of the Y-equations. At the same time, for some of the other factors given in Table 7.3 a significant influence could be identified:

- A high initial rate of inflation seems to reduce the sacrifice ratio, thus suggesting that inflation is more costly to reduce when it is already very low. This may be one of the principal reasons why Germany[29] receives such a poor rank in Table 7.6a and a low initial rate of inflation may also have contributed to the unfavourable rankings of Austria, Belgium and the Netherlands.
- A large fiscal deficit tends to raise the transitory costs, but due to the crude nature of the estimates it is not possible to say whether this effect is transmitted through lower credibility or a subsequent tightening of the fiscal stance. For Belgium and Ireland a high initial deficit combined with a tighter policy stance during the 1980s, probably helps to explain the poor ranking, whereas for Italy the effect of a high initial deficit seems to have been offset by other factors.
- An initially high level of the real effective exchange rate (i.e. an unfavourable competitive position) also raises the sacrifice ratios, probably by narrowing the scope for increasing net real exports to offset the fall in domestic demand growth. On the other hand, a fall in relative import prices (scaled by the ratio of imports to GNP) obtains the expected positive sign, but only affects the unemployment-based sacrifice ratio. This may indicate that distributional issues are more important in the wage bargaining process than in the determination of prices and that the terms-of-trade gains have prevented an even steeper rise in the rate of unemployment.

*What is the role of labour market rigidities?* Among the labour market measures shown in Table 7.2, the hysteresis parameter ($\alpha$) was never significant when entered separately and $(1-\eta)\alpha$, which in theory provides the most satisfactory measure of the long run real rigidity, always produced less satisfactory results than $\eta$ alone. It is also slightly surprising that nominal rigidities only affect the output-based measures and $(1-\beta_1)$ actually obtained the wrong sign when included in the U-equation. Similarly, the indicator proposed by Alogoskoufis and Manning (1988) (see the Appendix) as an overall measure of unemployment persistence only affects the output-based measures.

At the same time, all four equations support the hypothesis that a low sensitivity of wages to increases in unemployment tends to raise the transitory costs and from the output-based equations, it is also interesting to note that while the influence of the initial conditions progressively declines as the time horizon is extended, the structural labour market parameters either increase or become more significant. The favourable ranking for Japan can probably be ascribed to the high sensitivity of nominal wages to labour market. For the United States the estimates in Table 7.7 could indicate a behavioural change which reduced the transitory costs. Several studies have emphasised the high degree of flexibility characterising the US labour market compared with those in Europe and, as a consequence, its ability to adjust smoothly to various shocks. The contrasting performances of Denmark and the Republic of Ireland are also worth noting. Thus, Denmark shares the lowest average rank with Japan and Sweden, whereas Ireland obtains a rather poor rank, even though since 1978 the Deutschemark (DM) has been used as a nominal anchor for anti-inflation policies. The particularly high costs in terms of unemployment, suggest that the performance of Ireland is partly explained by labour market rigidities and such rigidities also appear to have influenced the rank obtained by the United Kingdom whereas supply-side policies have reduced rigidities in output markets and thus helped to lower the transitory output costs. Sweden, by contrast, has a flexible labour market and obtains a favourable ranking regardless of the measure used. Nonetheless, this may be more indicative of the quality and limitations of the indicators applied than of Sweden's actual performance. During much of the period Sweden continued to give high priority to the unemployment target and the same applies to Norway where the deceleration in wage and price increases has been comparatively modest.

*Is a fixed exchange rate helpful to anchoring inflation expectations and to reducing the transitory costs?*   Germany and several of the countries which throughout the 1980s have linked their currencies closely to the DM (Austria, Belgium, France and the Netherlands) obtain a rather low ranking. Among the ERM countries with looser links to the DM, Italy is slightly better placed than France even though the initial fiscal and external positions were much less favourable and, as noted above, Denmark is favourably placed. The rather poor ranking of the countries with close currency links to the DM is one of the more surprising results, as it might have been expected that such a linkage would strengthen credibility and lower the transitory costs.[30] Relatively high sacrifice ratios for ERM countries have also been observed in other empirical analyses of inflation and labour market adjustments, and two recent studies go some way towards explaining the puzzle or at least identifying the source of the problem.

- Relying on pooled time series and cross-country data for ERM countries, Van Poeck (1989) estimates price change and unemployment equations using money supply developments and measures characterising the wage formation process as explanatory variables. From his results three conclusions emerge: first, money supply growth only affects price changes and has no effect on unemployment, suggesting that the convergence of inflation rates can mainly be ascribed to a convergence of monetary policies; second, measures of the wage formation process, (real rigidities, proxies for indexation and features of the bargaining structure) only affect the rate of unemployment and have no influence on the rate of inflation, suggesting that the observed divergences in unemployment can mainly be ascribed to institutional differences and divergent labour market policies; and third, average unemployment in the ERM area has been subject to a trend rise independent of monetary policies and labour market characteristics.
- Artis and Ormerod (1991) first estimate price expectation equations (using an autoregressive process) and find that the German rate of inflation enters significantly into price expectations in other ERM countries after 1979.[31] At a second stage they enter price expectations as an explanatory variable in structural wage adjustment equations while at the same time searching for parameter shifts and structural breaks. They find little evidence of changes in their definition of real rigidities but some evidence of lower long run real wage aspirations after 1979, except for Germany and the Netherlands, where real wage aspirations appear to have strengthened. From their results it may be concluded that the link to the DM clearly helped to dampen inflation expectations in other ERM countries. However, it also appears that in the absence of specific changes in the wage formation process and in the natural rates of unemployment other ERM countries were forced to follow the German rise in unemployment to validate the lower rates of inflation.

The overall conclusion which can be drawn from these two studies would thus seem to be that the exchange rate commitment was instrumental in generating a convergence of monetary policies and rates of inflation. Because of differences in the characteristics of the wage formation process and only marginal changes in the structural para-meters,[32] the exchange rate commitment, however, did not help to reduce the transitory costs. In fact, the sacrifice ratios may have been influenced by a trend rise in the natural unemployment rate of the key currency country.

## 7.3  A Case Study of Finland

We left Finland out of the previous discussion as Finland's general performance and position in Table 7.5 and Figure 7.3 call for a separate analysis. Judging by the unemployment-based sacrifice ratio Finland has clearly outperformed other countries and there are several factors

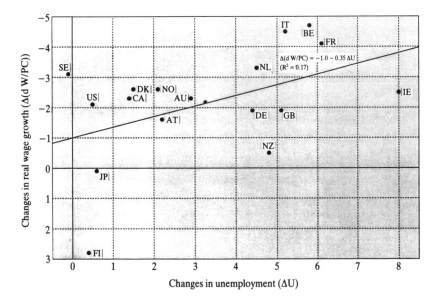

**Figure 7.3**  Changes in real wage growth and unemployment: 1973/9–1986/9
*Note*: US = United States; JP = Japan; DE = Germany; FR = France;
GB = United Kingdom; IT = Italy; CA = Canada; AU = Australia;
AT = Austria; BE = Belgium; DK = Denmark; FI = Finland; IE = Ireland;
NL = Netherlands; NZ = New Zealand; NO = Norway; SE = Sweden.
The asterisk represents the average of these countries.

supporting the low sacrifice ratio, such as a high degree of real (notably when hysteresis is disregarded) and nominal wage flexibility, low unemployment persistence, large terms-of-trade gains and a favourable initial fiscal position. The output-based sacrifice ratios are less favourable, possibly suggesting that product markets are more rigid than the labour market.[33] In addition, the ratios decline over time which, considering the comparatively moderate fall in inflation until 1989 and especially in view of the recent problems, give reasons to believe that neither unemployment nor output-based sacrifice ratios tell the whole story. For one thing, the periods chosen may be particularly favourable to Finland. More importantly, however, the sacrifice ratios provide a too narrow basis for evaluating the general economic performance since they leave out developments where Finland is much less favourably placed[34] and where the roots of the current problems can be found.

Consequently, the following will be a rather broad analysis of major trends in Finland during the 1980s with particular attention given to the period 1986–9 when the process of disinflation moved off track.

### 7.3.1  Major Trends and Policies: an Overview

In several ways developments and the policies pursued in Finland during the last 15–20 years have differed from those of most other countries.

● Although the volatility of real output changes has fallen compared with earlier years, Finland's business cycle has continued to be 'out of phase' with that of other European countries.[35] During the second half of the 1970s when OECD Europe was recovering from the first oil shock Finland had to apply rather restrictive policies to prevent a further deterioration in the external position and when other countries tightened policies in the early 1980s growth in Finland recovered. During 1982–6 output growth in Finland declined while in other countries a cyclical upswing was getting under way. This period of unusual stability for Finland was, however, followed by 3 years with GDP growth averaging 5% per year and the economy approaching a state of severe overheating. Finally, induced by restrictive policies and a slowdown in private spending to correct for earlier excesses and reinforced by the collapse of exports to the former USSR the Finnish economy 'nosedived' in 1990–1 while most other countries managed a 'soft landing' (see Table 7.8).
● Like most other OECD countries Finland has seen a rise in the actual as well as the 'natural' rate of unemployment.[36] However, except for the late 1970s and the last 2 years the rise has been less steep than in

**Table 7.8**  Changes in real output, unemployment, consumer prices and the current account in Finland and OECD Europe

| Item | 1975–9 | 1979–82 | 1982-6 | 1986–9 | 1989–91 |
|---|---|---|---|---|---|
| *Output$^a$* | | | | | |
| Finland | 2.4 | 3.5 | 2.9 | 4.7 | −2.9 |
| OECD Europe | 3.4 | 0.8 | 2.4 | 3.3 | 1.9 |
| *Unemployment$^b$* | | | | | |
| Finland | 3.8 | −0.4 | 0.0 | −1.9 | 4.2 |
| OECD Europe | 1.4 | 3.2 | 1.3 | −1.6 | 0.2 |
| *Consumer prices$^c$* | | | | | |
| Finland | 10.3 | 11.0 | 6.2 | 4.5 | 5.5 |
| OECD Europe | 10.3 | 12.1 | 6.2 | 4.5 | 5.6 |
| *Current account$^d$* | | | | | |
| Finland | 7.2 | −1.5 | 0.9 | −4.0 | 0.4 |
| OECD Europe | 0.0 | −0.2 | 1.7 | −1.1 | −0.8 |

*Notes:* $^a$ GDP, average percentage change
$^b$ Change in rate of unemployment during period
$^c$ Private consumption deflator, average percentage change
$^d$ Change in current account relative to GDP during period

other countries and in periods of faster output growth Finland has also been more successful in reducing unemployment.[37]

- As regards inflation Finland managed to eliminate the differential vis-à-vis OECD Europe in the early 1980s but during the period of excess demand the differential tended to widen again it was not until last year that inflation in Finland fell below the OECD average.[38] It is also worth noting that during the early 1980s, when disinflation was most pronounced, almost 40% of the deceleration of the domestic demand deflator in Finland (see Figure 7.4) was the result of changes in foreign prices, compared with only 20% in the rest of Europe.

- The current account is highly sensitive to changes in Finland's relative cyclical position[39] and shows a marked improvement in the late 1970s when growth in Finland was relatively low. During 1986–9, on the other hand, the external position deteriorated sharply.

- Policies in Finland have also differed from those of most other countries and Finland has not yet found a satisfactory solution to the assignment problem. Traditionally, fiscal policy was aimed at balancing the budget every year, generating a pro-cyclical policy stance but also leaving Finland with a relatively low level of public debt. In the early 1980s when most other countries took steps to consolidate budget imbalances, reform taxes and reduce the size of the public sector, Finland adopted the principle of balancing the budget over the cycle. Major tax reforms were also implemented late in the period but the public sector has increased relative to total GDP. With the Currency Act of 1977 Finland reinforced an exchange rate

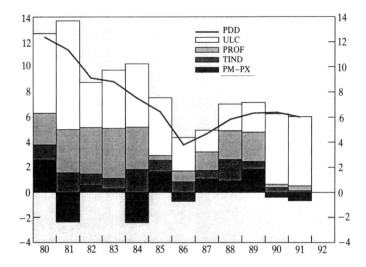

**Figure 7.4**  Changes in the domestic demand deflator in Finland, by contributing factor (in %)
The changes and contributions are calculated from national accounts data, using the equation:
dPDD = $a_1$dULC + $a_2$dPROF + $a_3$dTIND + $a_4$d(PM − PX) + Rest
with:
PDD = domestic demand deflator
ULC = compensation per unit of domestic demand
PROF = operating surplus (including depreciations) per unit of domestic demand
TIND = indirect taxes less subsidies per unit of domestic demand
PM − PX = imports less exports per unit of domestic demand
Rest = residual items, mainly reflecting changes in composition
d = first difference operator
$a_i$ = share (previous year) of component $i$ in domestic demand

policy whereby the markka was to be kept stable relative to a trade-weighted basket of other currencies. This marked a further step in a gradual process towards breaking with earlier policies of accommodating excess inflation and deteriorations in international competitiveness by rather large devaluations. Monetary policy in the early 1980s was based on controls of domestic lending rates and capital flows and the principal policy instrument were the conditions set for banks' borrowing at the central bank. Later in the period as capital flows were liberalized and domestic money and credit markets deregulated, the scope for conducting an independent monetary policy narrowed considerably. Instead the principal target of the Bank became the maintenance of a stable exchange rate which it attempted to meet through variations in domestic interest rates relative to those abroad. Finally, unlike most other countries Finland has continued to rely on incomes policies to influence price and wage increases. In fact, Finland is one of the few countries in the world which has applied tax concessions as a means to reducing nominal wage claims.[40]

Against this background an analysis focusing on disinflation and the output costs incurred would clearly be too narrow. In fact, a more relevant and appropriate question would seem to be why disinflation has not been as prominent a feature as in most other countries. More precisely, the following is an attempt to find out whether the absence of a higher degree of disinflation can be explained by the policies pursued or has resulted from factors of a more exogenous nature. In this context special attention will be given to the wage formation process and the possible influence of tax-based incomes policies. We shall further look at terms-of-trade changes and their effect on the real exchange rate, domestic output and inflation and a subject of principal importance will be the process of financial liberalisation and deregulation which has significantly changed the conditions for monetary policy and may have released pent-up demand pressures in the private sector.

### 7.3.2   *Macroeconomic Policies and Changing Assignments*

*Exchange Rate Regime*

Given the openness of the Finnish economy exchange rate changes are obviously important to the development of domestic prices and output. Moreover, given the gradual removal of restrictions and controls of interest rates and capital flows, policy decisions with respect to the exchange rate regime have implications for the independence of monetary policy and for the assignment of macroeconomic policies in general.

Unfortunately, attempting to evaluate the role and influence of the exchange rate is not an easy task. Even though Finland has formally had a fixed exchange rate since the breakdown of the Bretton Woods system, there have been several discrete changes. In 1978 the nominal rate was devalued by about 10% and following the Swedish currency change in 1981–2 the markka was devalued by another 5%. During the next 6–7 years the central bank frequently had to resist strong upward or downward pressures on the markka. The nominal rate was stable (see Figure 7.5) until March 1989, when the Bank, in an attempt to tighten policies, shifted the intervention margins equivalent to an appreciation

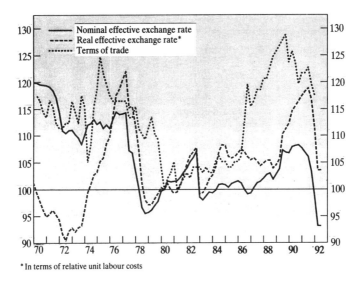

**Figure 7.5** Effective exchange rates and terms of trade in Finland: 1970–92. Quarterly data, first quarter 1980 = 100

of 4%. In July 1990 the Bank took a further step towards 'cementing' the fixed-rate regime by linking the markka to the ECU, but last year in November, following strong downward pressures on the markka, the Bank was forced to devalue the markka by 12.5% against the ECU. After renewed pressure in September this year, the markka was floated, leading to another 15% depreciation against the ECU. When the discrete changes are combined with the influence of autonomous movements in the exchange market there is no clear evidence that the growing consensus in favour of a fixed regime has been accompanied by greater stability of the actual rate.[41]

Another problem is that the choice of an 'optimum regime' appears to be more difficult in Finland than for most other industrialized countries. On the one hand, given the relatively underdeveloped state of money, credit and bond markets until well into the mid-1980s a fixed rate would probably be a more effective anchor than a money or credit aggregate target.[42] When applying the criteria proposed in the literature on optimum currency areas[43] Finland would also seem to be better off with a fixed exchange rate and the growing evidence of the failure of past devaluations together with signs of an evolving 'devaluation psychology' in the 1970s would point in the same direction. On the other hand, like other countries (Canada, Australia and New Zealand) with a high export share of raw materials and semi-finished goods Finland has been exposed to large and frequent terms-of-trade changes (Figure 7.5)[44] and thus faces the dilemma of finding an exchange rate regime which minimizes the domestic repercussions of such shocks. Consequently, the literature which chooses the optimum regime on the basis of the nature of stochastic shocks may be particularly relevant to the case of Finland. Unfortunately, the various contributions to this literature come to rather contrasting results, depending on policy objectives and assumptions made with respect to structural and behavioural parameters. As pointed out by Blundell-Wignall and Gregory (1990), a flexible regime is to be preferred when terms-of-trade shocks dominate monetary shocks and the authorities have the objective of stabilizing and the rate of inflation.

As a crude test of this hypothesis we estimated the model proposed by Blundell-Wignall and Gregory, using the Engle–Granger two-step procedure on quarterly data (1970, Q1, 1992, Q1) for the terms of trade (tot) and two measures of the real exchange rate (rexch). As a first step the order of integration of the three series was determined and in all three cases an $I(1)$ process could not be rejected, implying that the real exchange rate series do not display any tendency to revert towards a constant purchasing power parity (PPP) equilibrium. On the further assumption that the principal cause of shifts in the long-run equilibrium rate are terms-of-trade changes we then estimated the cointegration equation:

$$\text{rexch} = a + b\,\text{tot}$$

with the results shown in Table 7.9 columns 1 and 3. The corresponding error correction equations are presented in columns 2 and 4 with $EC_{-1}$ denoting the coefficients for the error correction terms.

The results only partly support the hypothesis that fluctuations in the terms of trade are the main source of changes in the equilibrium real exchange rate. The ADF-statistics are significant and the coefficients on the error correction terms have the correct (negative) signs and are also significant. On the other hand, the EC-coefficients point to a rather slow adjustment of the real exchange rate and the $R^2$ and DW values in the cointegration equations are too low to reject the null hypothesis of no cointegration. Together with the relatively large coefficients on the lagged dependent variable in the error correction equation the overall impression from Table 7.9 is that terms of trade changes may be one of the causes of changes in equilibrium real exchange rates. They are not, however, the only one and the model does not include other possible causes.

Even if the evidence had provided stronger support for the hypothesis proposed by Blundell-Wignall and Gregory, one should not draw the

**Table 7.9** Real effective exchange rates and the terms of trade

|  | Dependent variable | | | |
|  | ULC | | CPI | |
| Independent variables | (1) rexch | (2) drexch | (3) rexch | (4) drexh |
|---|---|---|---|---|
| C | 0.66 (5.8) | 0.02 (0.1) | 0.50 (4.2) | — |
| tot | 0.35 (3.4) |  | 0.50 (4.6) |  |
| dtot |  | 0.08 (1.0) |  | 0.14 (1.8) |
| $dtot_{-1}$ |  | — |  | −0.06 (0.8) |
| $drexch_{-1}$ |  | 0.37 (3.5) |  | 0.25 (2.3) |
| $drexch_{-2}$ |  | −0.10 (3.1) |  | −0.06 (2.1) |
| $ec_{-1}$ |  | −0.10 (3.1) |  | −0.06 (2.1) |
| $R^2$ | 0.11 | 0.24 | 0.19 | 0.09 |
| DW (H) | 0.11 | (1.00) | 0.09 | (−0.17) |
| ADF | −2.96 | — | −2.47 | — |

*Note*: ULC and CPI refer to real exchange rate indices using, respectively, unit labour costs and consumer prices in deflating nominal rates. Figures in parentheses after the coefficients are *t*-ratios (biased in the cointegration equation) and the values given for ADF refer to an augmented Dickey–Fuller test

conclusion that the Finnish authorities would have been better off by adopting a more flexible regime. The model entirely ignores the expectational effects referred to above and it provides no guidance to the authorities for evaluating the nature of future shocks and for deciding whether such shocks should be accommodated through exchange rate adjustments or resisted. On the other hand, the influence on inflation of terms-of-trade changes cannot be ignored[45] and in the absence of a clear break with past policies, memories of past devaluation cycles[46] have lingered and made it difficult to realize the hoped for dampening effect of a fixed regime on inflation expectations. Although the progressive liberalisation of money, credit and capital markets do not permit firm conclusions,[47] it is quite striking that between 1980–1 and 1986 when the rate of inflation declined by more than 8 p.p., short-term rates remained largely unchanged while long-term rates declined. Over the next 5 years long-term rates fell further while the short-term rate rose, thus generating a steeply inverted yield curve and an interest premium vis-à-vis German rates which seems to be largely insensitive to the narrowing and recent reversal of inflation differential. On the whole, the development in long-term rates may be indicative of some decline in inflation expectations but the short-term rates show no evidence of credibility gains.

## Incomes Policies and Real Wages

With monetary policy increasingly constrained by the exchange rate target and no apparent dampening of inflation expectations coming from the fixed exchange rate regime, the primary instrument for keeping inflation under control has been incomes policies. In fact, Finland is one of the few countries which has relied on incomes policies throughout most of the post-war period and applied income tax reductions as well as frequent adjustments of employers' social security contributions as means to reduce nominal wage claims and preserve international competitiveness.[48] The reaction of wage earners and employers to such measures is, therefore, of crucial importance to the effectiveness of anti-inflation policies since, in the absence of a wage response, there is a high risk that fiscal policy will become too expansionary.

Unfortunately, the empirical evidence is rather mixed. Eriksson et al. (1991) obtain results which strongly support the hypothesis that wage earners are concerned about post-tax real wages as they find that changes in income taxes and employers' contributions are entirely shifted back onto pre-tax earnings. Tyrvainen's (1991) results are less favourable as he finds only a partial effect of changes in income taxes and social security contributions and almost complete shifting of indirect taxes into earnings. Our own estimates are the least favourable as we obtained the following results (annual data 1960–91, $t$-ratios in parentheses) when estimating a real wage equation for the aggregate economy:[49,50]

$$d\log W = -5.92 - 0.054 \log U_{-1} + 0.90\, d\log PC + 0.88\, d\log Q -$$
$$(4.0) \quad (9.0) \qquad (12.2) \qquad\qquad (6.5)$$
$$0.52 \log((W/PC)/Q)_{-1} - 0.20\, d\log(1-t_2) + 0.37 \log(P(1-t_1)/$$
$$(5.5) \qquad\qquad (1.7) \qquad\qquad (4.9)$$
$$PC) + 0.66\, d\log(1-t_3). \qquad R^2 = 0.93,\ DW = 1.79.$$
$$(2.2)$$

The specification may be interpreted as a compact version of the Engle–Granger procedure where a long-run relation between real earnings, productivity and the role of unemployment is included as error-correction terms in a first-difference wage equation without any prior parameter constraints. On this interpretation, a main feature of the above equation is that changes in income taxes and employers' social security contributions are taken into account by wage earners, but the effect is only transitory. In other words, nominal wage claims are scaled down following a reduction in income taxes or an increase in employers' taxes, but unless the tax adjustments are followed by further changes wage inflation will return to its initial rate and the level of long-run pre-tax real earnings will not be affected.[51] It would be presumptuous to argue that our own results are superior to those obtained by Finnish researchers. Nonetheless, there are reasons to be sceptical of strong tax absorption effects.

● Tri-partite agreements cover only contractual wages and wage drift is an important component of total wage increases especially in conditions of excess demand. Moreover, none of the agreements involving tax concessions have included ex post facto sanctions for 'excessive' wage increases.

- Although the general agreements have usually comprised 75–85% of all workers, there is a 'free rider problem' with respect to those preferring separate negotiations as they also benefit from the tax concessions. Because of a rising tendency towards decentralised bargaining this free rider problem and the risk of excess demand have increased during the period considered.

Three additional features of the above equations are also worth noticing briefly.

- The cyclical sensitivity of nominal and real wages is relatively high[52] and in level form the wage equation is not suggestive of any hysteresis effects.[53]
- Productivity gains are fully reflected in nominal wage changes and in long run real earnings. Consequently, one reason for the relatively high rate of nominal wage inflation and real wage growth in Finland (see Table 7.1 and Figures 7.1 and 7.3) has been the exceptionally strong productivity growth. At the same time, given our measure of productivity and the absence of any adjustment for changes in the capital/labour ratio, the 1:1 relation between real earnings and productivity may indicate that labour has obtained more than its contribution to value added growth.
- Nominal wages appear to be more affected by output prices than by consumer prices. This points to a strong bargaining position for the employers and is helpful in periods of rising import prices. It also implies that with a fixed exchange rate terms-of-trade gains are quickly reflected in higher wage claims.[54]

## Fiscal Policy

Fiscal policy in Finland during the 1980s has been significantly influenced by the adoption of the 1977–82 medium-term stabilization programme which inter alia assigned a higher priority to stable economic growth and, in particular, changed fiscal policy from annual balancing to balancing the budget over the business cycle. The programme undoubtedly removed a source of earlier instabilities but the combination of an overall strategy of balancing the budget over the cycle with the use of tax concessions to moderate wage claims entails a certain risk of generating a too expansionary policy stance. The strength of economic forces is perhaps underestimated when the budget is prepared and subsequent restrictive measures may come too late. The tax concessions might also fail to moderate wage claims and leave a net stimulus to aggregate demand. Overall, the general government budget improved by 2.5% of GDP between 1979 and 1989, the net debt turned into a net asset position and despite relatively high nominal interest rates sustainability of the government budget was never in doubt. There are, therefore, good reasons to assume that the initial position as well as the fiscal changes during the 1980s strengthened credibility and reduced the transitory costs of disinflation. Nonetheless, on two crucial occasions fiscal policy appears to have exacerbated excess demand pressures and thus retarded the process of disinflation.

• When the 1987 budget was prepared, the strength of real GDP was seriously underestimated and the fact that general elections were to be held in March probably provided the budget a further stimulus (OECD, 1990–1, Graph 10). As a result, the cyclically corrected budget balance went into deficit to the tune of 1.5% of GDP and for the 1986–9 period as a whole discretionary measures had a net expansionary effect, even though average GDP growth at nearly 5% was well above the potential rate of 3–3.5% (Table 7.10).
• The incomes policy agreement concluded in the autumn of 1988 may also have provided a stimulus to a budget that was already too expansionary. Moreover, the agreement included a clause which committed the Central Bank to lower the base rate by 0.5 p.p. by early 1989. Although the influence of the base rate on the overall interest rate structure has declined over time, a wide range of loan rates were still adjusted in step with the base rate. In addition, given more and more evident signs of overheating, the timing of the interest cut did not seem appropriate and was probably one reason for the subsequent tightening of monetary policy through the appreciation of the markka in March.

During the last 2 years the budgetary situation has dramatically changed, to some extent confirming the view that policies had not been

**Table 7.10**   Changes in general government net lending (in % of GDP)

| Items | 1979–86 | 1986–9 | 1989–91 |
|---|---|---|---|
| Actual balance | 0.4 | 2.1 | −8.2 |
| Discretionary changes | 3.9 | −0.7 | −2.9 |
| Changes due to cycle | −3.5 | 2.8 | −5.3 |
| *Memo item: real GDP* | | | |
| *annual rate of change* | *3.1* | *4.9* | *−3.1* |

sufficiently tight during 1986–9. Influenced by the severe cyclical downturn as well as discretionary measures the general government budget balance deteriorated by more than 8% of GDP and it is officially estimated that net debt may increase to 25% of GDP by 1996. It is rather unlikely that the discretionary measures have worsened the prospects for further disinflation in the current situation but it cannot be excluded that the sudden loss of sustainability eventually could affect credibility and inflation expectations.

## Monetary Policy

This is not the place to review in detail the process of financial deregulation in Finland and its implications for the conduct of monetary policy and the transmission of policy changes. Nor shall we discuss possible distortions due to tax exemptions for interest incomes, preferential treatments of certain investment and the remaining relatively high degree of segmentation. Instead this section will attempt to evaluate the implications for inflation of the changes in the financial system and monetary policy that have taken place during the 1980s.

Traditionally, banks have played a dominating role in the intermediation process.[55] During the 1970s bank lending was controlled through banks' borrowing conditions at the central bank and by a ceiling on average lending rates linked to the base rate. Credit controls were not applied but capital inflows and outflows were subject to controls though the Bank often applied a liberal interpretation of the regulations. Because of the capital controls it was in theory possible for the Central Bank to control credit growth, interest rates and the exchange rates, but for mainly three reasons the system contained an inflationary bias:

- despite the small public debt and the low share of interest payments in total public expenditure political constraints made it difficult for the Bank to use variations in interest rates to contain credit growth;
- because the principal instruments of control were based on banks' net indebtedness with the Bank, periods of rapid growth in export earnings tended to be accompanied by an increase in credit availability which eventually led to excess demand and higher inflation;
- high priority assigned to rapid growth and low unemployment meant that deteriorations in international competitiveness due to excessive inflation were met by devaluations rather than by a tightening of policies.

The growing resistance to exchange rate adjustments as a means to remove imbalances has gradually reduced devaluation as a cause of inflation, but also narrowed the scope for an independent monetary policy in step with the phasing out of domestic credit regulations and capital flow controls. As a result of deregulation the call money market replaced central bank borrowing as the primary source of bank liquidity and in the course of the 1980s the Bank's principal instruments became changes in the call money rate and in banks' reserve requirement combined with interventions in the forward exchange market. At the same time, the gradual removal of capital flow controls increasingly linked domestic interest rates to international rates and appears to have left the Bank with no effective instruments for influencing domestic credit expansion. Though partly influenced by tax revenues, this problem was particularly evident during the crucial period 1986–9 when the rate of domestic credit expansion accelerated to almost 30% (see Figure 7.6), before restrictive steps were taken in early 1989.

### 7.3.3 Developments in Financial Balances and Aggregate Demand

While the acceleration of money and credit aggregates during 1986–9 is unlikely to have affected inflation directly, there are clear signs that it was accompanied by and associated with a marked shift in financial balances and a strong rise in aggregate demand relative to potential output.

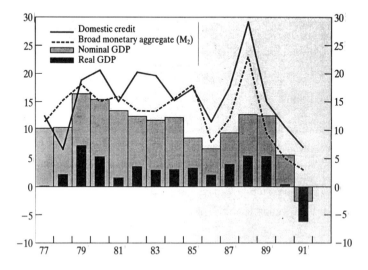

**Figure 7.6** Developments in domestic credit, money supply and income in Finland (% change)

## Financial Balances

Traditionally the financial balance of the private sector in Finland has been in deficit and throughout the post-war period a primary aim of the authorities has been to prevent this deficit from destabilizing the external position. During 1986–9, however, the deficit was allowed to rise from less than 2 to over 7.5% of GDP and despite a rise in the public sector saving surplus the current account deficit rose from 1 to almost 5% of GDP. As can be seen from Figure 7.7 both households and non-financial enterprises moved heavily into deficit and when looking separately at saving and investment it appears that the financial deterioration was mainly the result of a marked rise in investment whereas the private saving rate was largely stable. According to the calculations shown in Table 7.11, which updates the equations presented in Andersen (1990), the strengthening of economic activity increased the private sector saving deficit by almost 4% of GDP and the lagged effect of the fall in long-term interest rates and in the real effective exchange rate added another 0.75 points. In addition, almost 60% of the rise in public sector net saving was offset by lower private saving, while the net effect of the EC-terms, which may be interpreted as the cumulative effect of deviations from the long run trends, was only minor. On the whole it thus appears that the greater availability of credit allowed non-financial enterprises and households to finance an unprecedented expansion of investment by debt financing and

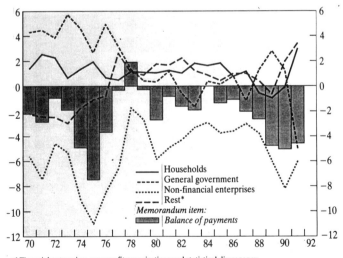

* Financial enterprises, non-profit organizations and statistical discrepancy.

**Figure 7.7** Financial balances in Finland (in % of GDP)

**Table 7.11**   Developments in saving and investment by causal factor (in % of GDP)

| Item | 1979–86 | | | 1986–9 | | | 1989–91 | | |
|---|---|---|---|---|---|---|---|---|---|
| | IP | SP | GDEF | IP | SP | GDEF | IP | SP | GDEF |
| GAP | 0.05 | -0.05 | 0.95 | 2.20 | -1.40 | 0.65 | -3.70 | 2.40 | 0.10 |
| dY | 0.45 | 0.55 | -2.30 | 0.85 | 1.00 | 1.45 | -2.00 | -2.40 | -5.10 |
| dP | -1.25 | -0.50 | -0.90 | 0.75 | 0.30 | 0.50 | -0.95 | -0.30 | -0.65 |
| REXCH | — | -0.45 | — | — | 0.10 | — | — | -0.95 | — |
| INT | -0.10 | — | -0.15 | 0.85 | — | 0.60 | 0.35 | — | -0.05 |
| GDEF | — | -0.20 | — | — | -1.20 | — | — | 4.65 | — |
| EC | -2.10 | -3.45 | 2.75 | 1.75 | 1.80 | -1.10 | 0.00 | -1.30 | 2.50 |
| Total | -2.95 | -4.10 | 0.35 | 6.40 | 0.60 | 2.10 | -6.30 | 2.10 | -8.20 |

| | BoP | BoP | BoP |
|---|---|---|---|
| DD | -6.75 | -6.85 | 3.35 |
| CDD | 4.20 | 4.15 | 0.35 |
| REXCH | -0.25 | -0.10 | -0.15 |
| EC | 2.00 | -0.90 | -3.35 |
| Total | -0.80 | -3.70 | 0.20 |

*Note:* The calculations are based on the following equations (annual data, 1960–91, intercept terms for IP and SP not shown and *t*-ratios in parentheses):

$$IP = 0.34\ GAP + 0.40\ dY_{-1} + 0.32\ dP - 0.27\ INT_{-2}$$
$$\quad\ (2.7)\qquad\ (2.7)\qquad\quad (4.3)\qquad (1.3)$$

$$SP = -0.22\ GAP + 0.48\ dY_{-1} + 0.16\ dP_{-1} - 8.68\ REXCH_{-1} - 0.56\ GDEF$$
$$\qquad (1.8)\qquad\ (3.5)\qquad\quad (2.2)\qquad\quad (2.4)\qquad\qquad (4.5)$$

$$GDEF = 0.21\ GAP_{-1} + 0.44\ dY + 0.21\ dP - 0.18\ INT_{-1}$$
$$\qquad\quad (1.6)\qquad\quad (4.1)\qquad (2.4)\qquad (2.0)$$

$$BoP = -0.36\ DD + 0.38\ CDD - 3.01\ REXCH + 2.72\ DUM$$
$$\qquad\ (5.6)\qquad (5.3)\qquad (2.5)\qquad\qquad (3.2)$$

| | | |
|---|---|---|
| $R^2 = 0.73$ | DF = 4.75 | DW = 1.82    ECV = -1.05 |
| $R^2 = 0.52$ | DF = 5.47 | DW = 2.04    ECV = -1.11 |
| $R^2 = 0.42$ | DF = 3.05 | DW = 1.06    ECV = -0.40 |
| $R^2 = 0.49$ | DF = 2.98 | DW = 1.07    ECV = -0.57 |

Notation: IP, private investment (current prices, including inventory changes) as a percentage of GDP; SP, private saving as a percentage of GDP; GDEF, general government net lending as a percentage of GDP; GAP, actual relative to trend output, calculated as a quadratic trend (in logs); dY, percentage change in real GDP; dP, percentage change in GDP deflator; REXCH, real effective exchange rate (in logs); INT, long-term bond rate; BoP, current account as a percentage of GDP; DD, real domestic demand (in logs); CDD, trade weighted index of real demand in major trading partners (in logs); DUM, dummy variable with 1 for 1980–91 and otherwise 0; $R^2$, coefficient of determination; DW, Durbin–Watson statistic; DF, Dickey–Fuller statistic; EC, residual in level equations, used (lagged) as an explanatory variable [...] with ECV denoting the estimated co-efficient on the lagged EC-term even though the public sector reduced its net debt, Finland's net foreign debt rose from less than 14 to more than 21% of GDP. The controls on lending rates and capital flows in force during 1979–86 may have entailed some degree of excess or unsatisfied demands for credits, although the cumulative EC-terms largely cancel out. Mostly, however, exceptionally high investment growth during 1986–9 was the result of stronger overall demand combined with more favourable borrowing conditions.

### Aggregate Demand

This brings us to the contribution of overall demand to the rise in price and wage inflation. Based on the equations shown in the Appendix (Tables 7.1 and 7.4) the direct effect of the rise in actual relative to potential output may account for about one-half of the more than 2 points acceleration of the GDP deflator, while the fall of unemployment explains about 45% of the 3.6 points acceleration of nominal wages. When lags and interactions between prices and wages are also taken into account, the overall demand contribution to the rise in wage inflation increases to more than 3 points or about 85% of the total increase. On the other hand (see Table 7.12), shifts in relative wage increases and a possible breakdown of the Scandinavian model of inflation have not been a major source of inflation. As the table shows there was some rise in wage gains in the sheltered sectors relative to sectors more exposed to foreign trade. The changes were, however, rather small and do not appear to have affected profits of the exposed industries and thus their ability to compete with foreign enterprises.

## 7.4    Summary and Conclusions

Some partial and tentative conclusions regarding successful anti-inflation policies have already appeared earlier in this paper, and in the space remaining we first recall these conclusions. We then turn to areas of uncertainty before concluding with some observations on Finland's experience.

There is some, albeit weak, support for the view that a central bank should stop short of full price stability. A high initial rate of inflation *does* seem to lower the sacrifice ratios and the non-linear trade-off worked well for the estimates given in the Appendix. The effect of the initial inflation rate, however, weakens over time and the non-linear form was chosen in the light of recent international practice and not dictated by econometric tests. Large budget deficits seem to have damaged the credibility of monetary policies in Canada and the Republic of Ireland

**Table 7.12**   Finland: Changes in sectoral wages and profits

| Industry | 1980 compensation index, total manufacturing = 100 | Compensation per employee (% change, annual rate) | | | Operating profits/GDP (%) | | | Indicators of openness, 1980 (%) | |
|---|---|---|---|---|---|---|---|---|---|
| | | 1976–9 | 1979–86 | 1986–9 | 1976 | 1980 | 1989 | Exports/ output | Imports/ domestic sales |
| Wood | 86.9 | 10.0 | 9.8 | 9.4 | −3.8 | 29.7 | 23.1 | 55.3 | 6.1 |
| Paper | 117.7 | 9.7 | 10.5 | 8.3 | −15.5 | 27.6 | 23.9 | 46.0 | 3.6 |
| Basic metals | 123.0 | 15.4 | 9.1 | 6.8 | −5.4 | 19.7 | 41.2 | 25.9 | 33.6 |
| Engineering | 104.2 | 9.3 | 10.2 | 9.0 | 25.0 | 14.8 | 26.8 | 25.1 | 58.0 |
| Textiles | 72.7 | 8.9 | 10.5 | 7.7 | 17.2 | 24.1 | 13.5 | 31.7 | 49.5 |
| *Average** | *101.6* | *9.9* | *10.1* | *8.5* | *5.1* | *21.0* | *25.5* | *37.9* | *31.6* |
| Food | 96.1 | 11.6 | 10.1 | 9.2 | 29.7 | 22.9 | 25.4 | 5.9 | 11.1 |
| Chemicals | 107.8 | 10.2 | 10.4 | 9.5 | 28.5 | 45.0 | 36.3 | 18.5 | 36.9 |
| Minerals | 98.5 | 9.2 | 9.2 | 10.6 | 16.2 | 29.5 | 39.3 | 11.4 | 17.1 |
| Electricity and water | 117.8 | 8.9 | 10.5 | 7.9 | 17.0 | 21.8 | 17.6 | NA | NA |
| Construction | 113.0 | 7.3 | 10.2 | 12.7 | 16.9 | 18.9 | 28.6 | NA | NA |
| Trade | 93.2 | 10.7 | 10.7 | 9.6 | 10.6 | 12.8 | 14.4 | NA | NA |
| Transport | 103.0 | 12.2 | 9.9 | 8.9 | 8.7 | 13.2 | 22.0 | NA | NA |
| *Average** | *104.0* | *10.2* | *10.1* | *9.9* | *15.5* | *19.2* | *22.0* | *NA* | *NA* |
| Financial institutions | 114.9 | 11.8 | 10.7 | 10.3 | 35.0 | 33.7 | 42.4 | NA | NA |
| Insurance | 137.7 | 10.3 | 10.8 | 8.9 | 30.8 | 36.2 | 3.0 | NA | NA |
| Real estate | 115.6 | 8.9 | 11.0 | 9.8 | 49.0 | 42.7 | 39.7 | NA | NA |
| Services | 88.3 | 9.9 | 9.9 | 8.7 | 27.5 | 30.9 | 39.1 | NA | NA |
| *Average** | *111.2* | *9.6* | *10.8* | *9.6* | *41.5* | *38.6* | *38.2* | *NA* | *NA* |
| Memo: Manufacturing | 100.0 | 10.0 | 10.4 | 9.2 | 15.1 | 25.3 | 27.7 | NA | NA |

*Note:* * Weighted average using 1980 GDP weights

*Sources*: OECD National Accounts, Volume II and OECD Working Paper No. 60

and the initial budget positions were also found to affect the sacrifice ratios. On the other hand, Italy has done comparatively well and while the US authorities have attracted much national and international criticism for failing to reduce the federal deficit, there is little evidence that this has made reducing inflation more costly. There are no convincing empirical reasons for adopting a gradualist approach. Unemployment rates seem to follow a random walk, but this feature is not—except for the United Kingdom—the result of hysteresis in the wage formation process. Moreover, even though the review does not include many episodes of shock treatment those that *are* included show marked reductions of inflation at rather low costs: the Danish broad-based approach in the early 1980s was clearly successful, and the surprisingly low sacrifice ratio found for the United States could be the result of the 1979 change in the conduct of monetary policy and the subsequent surge of the US dollar. Finally, going back to the 1970s, the dramatic tightening of fiscal and monetary policies in Japan following the first oil price shock produced quick inflation gains at low costs and left a permanent impact on the behaviour of trade unions and enterprises. The Thatcher stabilization programme of 1979 seems to be an exception as the costs in terms of unemployment were quite high. This merely underlines the fact that an essential condition for a successful shock treatment is that labour and product markets respond flexibly.[56] In the United Kingdom this was the case for output markets but not for the labour market.

There is also evidence to suggest that countries without a medium-term nominal anchor for inflation have done less well than countries using either monetary aggregate or exchange rate targets. The performance of Canada has been rather poor, and the relatively high sacrifice ratios experienced by Australia and New Zealand could also in part reflect the absence of a nominal anchor. On the other hand, it is not clear whether monetary aggregate or exchange rate targets are more effective as nominal anchors. The United States and Japan, which have relied on monetary aggregate targets, have incurred rather low transitory costs while Germany, which has experienced fewer distortions in the targeted aggregate (M3) than most other countries, obtains a very poor ranking.

In this context it is important to recall the rather high sacrifice ratios found for countries that have linked their currencies closely to that of a country with a well established reputation for persistently pursuing anti-inflation policies.[57] The most convincing explanation might be that such a linkage leads to a convergence of inflation rates through a convergence of monetary policies towards that of the key currency country. The costs, however, will not be lower than for countries outside the currency arrangement unless the structure and institutions of the wage and price formation process also converge. In fact, the costs could even rise if the natural unemployment rate of the key currency country is subject to a trend rise.[58]

Incomes policies could provide some temporary relief in this respect but cannot be relied upon as the only anti-inflation policy instrument and tend to create distortions if maintained for too long. This risk is even greater for wage and price controls, though some countries have achieved some success in using such controls as a short cut to reducing expectations—or the degree of inertia—during the initial phase of stabilization programmes. The Austrian experience is the most puzzling with respect to the usefulness of long-term incomes policies as it is hard to find a wage adjustment process which is better adapted to the exchange rate target. And yet Austria's sacrifice ratio is one of the highest among the 17 countries reviewed. Finland's very low sacrifice ratios might suggest tax-based incomes policies are helpful. As discussed in section 7.3, however, we did not find convincing[59] evidence in support of this view.

A major uncertainty concerns the reliability of the sacrifice ratios applied in this paper and the extent to which policy implications can be drawn from the ranking suggested by these ratios. Finland's low sacrifice ratio combined with its recent problems clearly shows that sacrifice ratios can provide a misleading impression of economic performance. It is also well known that ratios derived from actual developments are influenced by factors unrelated to the policies pursued, and a particularly disturbing result in this respect is that sacrifice ratios based on unemployment give a more pessimistic picture than ratios based on output losses. The random walk nature of unemployment could suggest that equilibrium unemployment has been subject to a trend rise which biases the estimated transitory costs. It is also possible that rigidities in output markets are much smaller than in labour markets, thus forcing up unemployment relative to potential output. However, further exploration of this possibility requires a much more rigorous analysis than undertaken in this paper.

Another open question is the influence of credibility, as we have not used any indicators nor attempted to quantify references to the presence or absence of credibility effects. There is no need to stress that this is an area in need of further research because an impressive amount of theoretical and empirical work has already been done. Consequently, we shall merely add a few observations on the type of work that might be particularly important for analyses of countries' experience with disinflation.

- Given the role of monetary policy, empirical measures derived from the relationship between short and long-term interest rates could provide useful additional information. Takeda's (1992) preliminary estimates look promising in this respect, though one problem, is that policy parameters cannot be separated from structural parameters.

- Although risking a further blurring of the distinction between reputation and credibility, it is important to recognize that economic agents have long memories with respect to tax policies and do not easily forgive slippages in an otherwise impeccable anti-inflation stance. The Swedish authorities have faced major difficulties in convincing economic agents of their commitment to a fixed exchange rate regime and in some other countries not surveyed in this paper recent attempts to reduce inflation and re-establish a generally accepted anchor appear to have entailed high costs in terms of both output and employment.

- Only few credibility models consider the timing of anti-inflation measures. There is some evidence that stabilization programmes undertaken in periods of severe economic stress enjoy a higher degree of credibility than programmes proposed when conditions are less gloomy. Hence delaying anti-inflation measures may reduce the transitory costs but the optimum delay is as yet not well known.

- One short-cut to directly influencing inflation expectations and creating favourable ex ante conditions for a credible programme might be to pre-announce a time path for the inflation target. Canada and New Zealand have recently embarked on such a course, but it is still too early to evaluate its effects on the actual rate of inflation and the costs of reaching the target.

It goes without saying that inflation cannot be reduced without an appropriately tight monetary policy. What is perhaps less obvious is that monetary policy alone is not enough if the transitory costs are to be kept low. The best that can be achieved through monetary policies is a reduction in nominal income growth, but how the slowdown is 'split' between lower inflation and lower real growth (and thus higher costs) depends on other factors and policies. As already mentioned a clearly defined nominal anchor is important in this respect and a crucial condition for creating a credible nominal anchor is that policies and policy instruments be assigned to the principal targets in an efficient and transparent way. This seems to be one problem to which policy makers in Finland have not yet found a solution. The fixed exchange rate could serve as an effective nominal anchor and with nominal and real wage rigidities relatively low the output costs associated with anti-inflation policies would also be low. The commitment has to be credible, however, and this condition is not yet satisfied in Finland. Tax-based incomes policies could also help to reduce inflation (though they cannot serve as a nominal anchor), but the tax reductions have to be accompanied by a permanent reduction in nominal wage increases or they will eventually only lead to stronger growth of domestic demand. This appears to have happened in Finland during the crucial years 1986–9 when fiscal policy became too expansionary and the proportion of employees opting for separate wage negotiations and still benefiting from the tax concessions reached 25%. During this period it also became evident that with monetary policy 'tied to' the fixed exchange rate and incomes policies not working as expected there were no instruments available to effectively offset the surge in private demand.

Fiscal policy was, however, not the only reason for excessive demand growth during 1986–9. Terms-of-trade gains were large and were fully reflected in domestic real income and subsequently in inflation. It is also worth noting, though perhaps only as a coincidence, that the start of the 1986–9 boom coincided with the removal of the ceiling on average bank lending rates and a significant liberalisation of capital controls. As can be seen from Figure 7.6 the exceptionally strong rise in nominal income growth was accompanied by an acceleration of domestic credit growth and by a sharp rise in private sector debt. Given the internationalization of money and capital markets there was no way that Finland could have maintained its earlier system of controls and the choice of a gradual deregulation process as opposed to an overnight elimination of all regulations would also seem appropriate. On the other hand, deregulating in conditions of rapid private demand growth entails a major risk of excessive credit expansion, especially if the deregulations are not backed up by a strengthening of the supervisory authorities. In addition, the effects of distortions to private saving and investment may take on much larger proportions in a system where most controls have been removed. Whatever the precise causes there is no doubt that by 1989 the process of disinflation had come to a halt and that the Finnish economy was in a state of severe overheating and disequilibrium.

The question remains whether disinflation will resume once the current crisis is over. Influenced by the fall in domestic demand and output, the rate of price inflation has already fallen to below the OECD average and nominal wage increases are also decelerating rapidly. Moreover, following the devaluations, the competitive position of Finnish enterprises has substantially improved and a marked rise in the household savings rate suggests that adjustments in private sector financial balances are not only absorbing the steep rise in general government borrowing but also 'making room' for a strengthening of the current account. Yet this is all taking place in a situation of severe recession and the critical issue is how large the cumulative output and employment costs will be and whether the gains will be consolidated once the economy starts growing again. The moderate wage behaviour so far looks promising and is consistent with econometric evidence of a high degree of nominal and real wage flexibility. The announcement of a medium-term fiscal consolidation plan is also a positive sign. The most vital question with respect to future inflation is whether a new ECU linkage of the markka will be regarded as credible and on this issue it is still too early to make any predictions.

## Appendix: Sources of Rigidities and Persistence

### Wage and Labour Market Rigidities

One important paradigm of New Keynesian economics is that changes in monetary policy are accompanied by short run real effects due to rigidities in the wage and price formation process. When price and wage expectations partly depend on past developments (*nominal rigidities*) a more restrictive monetary policy will tend to reduce real demand as well as the rate of inflation. Moreover, since price and wage changes do not clear output and labour markets instantaneously (*real rigidities*), real demand will remain below the initial level until prices and wages have fully adjusted to the change in monetary policy, with the size of the decline and the length of the period during which real demand remains depressed depending on both nominal and real rigidities.

In order to get an approximate idea of the size of rigidities and their possible role in explaining the sacrifice ratios discussed in the text nominal wage equations were estimated for 17 countries, using the following general specification:

$$d\ln W = \mu - \eta \ln U + \eta \alpha \ln U_{-1} + \beta_1 d\ln PC + \beta_2 d\ln PC_{-1} + \beta_3 d\ln W_{-1} \tag{7.3}$$

$W$, aggregate nominal wages per employee; $U$, rate of unemployment; $PC$, private consumption deflator; ln, natural logarithm; and $d$, first difference operator.

Assuming that the equations satisfy the long run neutrality condition ($\beta_3 = 1-\beta_1-\beta_2$) and that a change in monetary policy has an immediate effect on price inflation, the degree of nominal rigidity may be measured by $1-\beta_1$. If the lagged term in $U$ is disregarded for the moment, the degree of real rigidity is captured by $\eta$ or $1/\eta$ (i.e. the rise in $\ln U$ required to generate a 1 p.p. fall in the rate of wage inflation). However, since equilibrium unemployment may be partly dependent on the historical path of actual unemployment (hysteresis), equation (7.3) also includes a hysteresis parameter ($\alpha$). In the case of extreme hysteresis ($\alpha = 1$), wage inflation only depends on changes in $\ln U$ and the costs of disinflation will be permanent rather than transitory. On the other hand, for $0 < \alpha < 1$, the deceleration of wage inflation depends on the level of $\ln U$ as well as its change and, ceteris paribus, the degree of real wage rigidity will be higher than in the absence of hysteresis.[59]

Estimates of equation (7.3) are presented in Table 7.1 and in most cases the assumption of a long run vertical Phillips curve holds. For some countries, though, there is a need for further experiments with the lag structure or for introducing additional variables. Thus, for the United States and Japan the neutrality condition is doubtful, and the condition is clearly rejected for Italy and Sweden. The result for Italy could be due to a major change in the indexation system in 1985,[60] while for Sweden all alternative formulations implied money illusion and a high degree of nominal rigidity.[61]

For Finland, the neutrality condition is easily satisfied but the adjustment pattern looks rather odd. The latter was also found in the initial estimates for the United Kingdom and Australia and plausible coefficients were only obtained after imposing additional constraints and including dummy variables.

Leaving aside these less satisfactory aspects, which partly arise from using a uniform specification for all countries, the following results are worth noting.

• A rather high measure of real wage flexibility is found for three of the major countries and for Austria, Finland and Sweden. However, when the hysteresis parameter is taken into account only Japan, Austria and to some extent also Finland, remain in the high-flexibility group while in Sweden and Germany the unemployment coefficient falls to or below 0.15.
• A comparatively high degree of nominal flexibility is obtained for France, Italy, the United Kingdom, Finland, the Republic of Ireland and Australia, which are all countries with above-average inflation during most of the period. By contrast, and in line with earlier studies, nominal wages adjust slowly to price changes in the United States and Austria and, as noted above, Sweden is also characterised by high nominal rigidity.

### Real Wage and Unemployment Persistence

As an alternative to evaluating labour market rigidities from nominal wage equations, the constrained version of equation (7.3) may be rewritten as a real wage adjustment equation:

$$d\ln(W/PC) = \mu - \eta \ln U + \eta \alpha \ln U_{-1} + \beta_3 d\ln(W/PC)_{-1} - (1-\beta_1)(d\ln PC - d\ln PC_{-1}) \tag{7.4}$$

with $\beta_3$ indicating the degree of real wage persistence and $(1-\beta_1)$ the short run impact of inflationary surprises. This is the approach adopted by Alogoskoufis and Manning (1988),[62] who also include persistence in the labour demand equation and estimate overall persistence from a compact expression based on an autoregressive equation for unemployment:

$$U = \rho_0 + \rho_1 U_{-1} + \rho_2 U_{-2} \tag{7.5}$$

It can be shown that the particular case of $\rho_1 = 1$ and $\rho_2 = 0$ occurs when $\eta = \infty$ and $\alpha = 1$ and $\rho_1$ and $\rho_2$ will sum to unity when $\eta = 0$ and $\beta_3 = 1$ or when $\alpha$ and $\beta_3$ are both equal to 1. Table 7.2 presents our own estimates of equation (7.5), with $\rho_1 + \rho_2$ included in Table 7.2 of the text. The estimates are generally satisfactory,[63] and for 14 of the countries both $\rho_1$ and $\rho_2$ are significant and of the expected signs. The estimated values for $\rho_1$ range from 1.6 to 1, with most of the ERM countries located towards the higher end of the range while Austria comes close to the case of $\rho_1 = 1$ and $\rho_2 = 0$. $\rho_2$ is always negative and for 10 of the countries $\rho_1 + \rho_2 \geqslant 0.94$. Only the United States, Finland and Sweden show an overall degree of persistence which is significantly below 1, while for the remaining countries $\rho_1 + \rho_2$ is around 0.9.

When combining the results of Table 7.1, which reject the hypothesis of extreme hysteresis except for the United Kingdom, with those of Table 7.2, where the hypothesis that $U$ follows a random walk process cannot be rejected for any of the seventeen countries, two tentative conclusions can be derived:

- on the one hand, there is a risk that anti-inflation policies will result in a permanent rise in the rate of unemployment, though the transmission channels of this effect remain unknown until the process making $U$ a random walk is further analysed;[64]
- on the other hand, even though the forces generating the random walk process do not seem to be embedded in the wage formation process, the results of Table 7.2 imply that the estimated unemployment coefficients in the wage equations may be biased and that sacrifice ratios calculated from the trade-off coefficients should be interpreted with some caution.

### Price and Output Market Rigidities

Evaluating rigidities from wage or unemployment functions clearly involves a bias since rigidities are equally important in product markets and in the adjustment of output prices. It may also be argued (Gordon, 1988, 1990) that focusing on the wage equation is misleading and irrelevant because wage changes only affect the share of wages and have no influence on the rate of price inflation. Mehra (1991) also disputes the validity of the traditional mark-up model for the United States, and a recent study by Cozier (1991) finds a similar result for Canada. On the other hand, experience shows that it is difficult to estimate real and nominal rigidities from price equations as the sensitivity of price changes to output slack is low and the homogeneity condition is not easily satisfied. Moreover, in the case of Australia Fahrer and Myatt (1991) show that the wage equation is the key relation for anti-inflation policies.

Nonetheless, as a supplement to the estimates discussed above we have included Table 7.3, showing developments in the 'split' between nominal and real changes in GDP. Corresponding to Table 7.1 of the text, there is a marked improvement between the 1970s and the 1980s. Even for 1990, when inflation accelerated in several countries, it was still the case that for the seventeen countries on average a rise in nominal GDP of 5·75% was split between a real change of 2·5% and a price change of just over 3%. On the other hand, as nominal GDP growth fell to 3·5% last year (partly because of restrictive monetary policies) most of the deceleration appeared as lower real growth.

This recent episode might be used to illustrate the nature of price rigidities and their relevance to the disinflation process.[65] Denoting annual changes in log nominal GDP by $dy$, real growth by $dq$ and changes in the output deflator by $dp$, the following identities hold:

$$dp \equiv a\,dy \quad \text{and} \tag{7.6}$$
$$dq \equiv (1-a)\,dy$$

In this set-up the crucial question is why '$a$' is not close to unity and a preliminary answer can be obtained by assuming that price changes are determined by two factors: the degree of excess supply in the product market and inertia. Using $\hat{Q}$ to indicate the ratio of actual to potential output and letting inertia enter via adaptive price expectations, an equation for the changes in output prices can be specified as:

$$dp = b\hat{q} - bc\hat{q}_{-1} + dp_{-1} \quad \text{or as}$$
$$dp = bd\hat{q} + b(1-c)\hat{q}_{-1} + dp_{-1} \tag{7.7}$$

As a second step the national accounting identity ($dy \equiv dq + dp$) may be rewritten as:

$$dy \equiv d\hat{q} + dq^* + dp \tag{7.8}$$

With $dq^*$ denoting potential output growth. Inserting equation (7.6) into equation (7.7) and letting $e = b/(1+b)$ then gives the following price adjustment equation:

$$dp = e(dy - dq^*) + e(1-c)\hat{q}_{-1} + (1-e)dp_{-1} \qquad (7.7')$$

where nominal rigidity can be measured by $(1-e)$ and real rigidity by $e(1-c)$.

As an illustration, assume that the growth of monetary aggregates is permanently reduced by 1 p.p. When velocity is constant $dy$ also falls by 1 point and if there is no excess supply initially price inflation will decline by $e$ points and output growth by $(1-e)$ points. In other words, the initial response to the anti-inflation policy is entirely determined by the degree of nominal rigidity. In the following year, however, real rigidities will also enter as the fall in output growth will lower $d\hat{q}$ $Q$ by $(1-e)\%$, so that the cumulative decline in price inflation amounts to $e + e(1-c)(1-e) + e(1-e)$. Continuing this example, it can be shown that if inflation is to be permanently reduced by 1 p.p. with no permanent loss of output $dp$ will have to 'undershoot' to allow $dq$ to exceed $dq^*$ and bring $\hat{Q}$ back to the initial level.[66] Moreover, it is in the second and subsequent years that the degree of real rigidity becomes important to the transitory output costs, since it is the sensitivity of $dp$ to output slack which determines how far $\hat{Q}$ has to fall to bring $dp$ into line with the change in monetary policy.

Table 7.4 shows estimates of the parameters of equation $(7.7')$ using national accounts data for the period 1960–90. As discussed in Andersen (1989), applying equation $(7.7')$ as a 'short-cut' to estimating aggregate supply curves and the degree of real and nominal price rigidities can be problematic. This may be one reason why the ranking of real and nominal rigidities differs between labour and output markets (see Table 7.5). On the other hand, the differences may reflect 'real' factors which were also apparent in the sacrifice ratios.

Overall, the range of real rigidities in the output market is much narrower than for the labour market and, except for the Netherlands, all coefficients are rather well determined. Japan again appears to have the lowest real rigidity, but otherwise the correspondence between the two measures of real rigidities is poor and the rank correlation is negative. The largest discrepancies can be observed for the United Kingdom, Finland and New Zealand, where the ranking based on the labour market parameter is very low relative to the output market measure, and for Austria and Belgium, where the reverse pattern is seen.

The nominal rigidities are somewhat closer, though again the rank correlation is not very high. In the United States and Germany both output and labour markets have a relatively high degree of nominal rigidity, while in the United Kingdom, Finland and Ireland both markets have low nominal rigidities. In Japan prices appear to respond more quickly than wages but the lag structure for Japan is uncertain since it was difficult to satisfy the homogeneity condition. For France and Denmark wages respond more quickly than prices, while New Zealand and Norway have a response pattern similar to that of Japan.

# Notes

Parts of this paper were also presented at a Reserve Bank Conference in Sydney, Australia on 10–11 July and published in *Inflation, Disinflation and Monetary Policy*, A. Blundell-Wignall (ed.), Reserve Bank of Australia, 1992. The views expressed are strictly those of the author and are not necessarily shared by the BIS. I am indebted to H. Bernard, J. Bisignano, B. Cozier, O. Risager and S. Roger for comments on an earlier draft of this paper.

1. See Coe et al. (1986), who estimate the contribution of monetary policy by a counter-factual simulation where the nominal rate of interest is kept at the pre-1980 level.

2. This can also be seen from a comparison of the GDP deflator and the private consumption deflator. While the latter fell on average by 8.8 p.p. between 1980 and 1986, the former fell by only 6.1 p.p. and the trough occurred 1 year later.

3. In Figures 7.1 and 7.3 nominal wage growth has been measured by hourly compensation in manufacturing as published by the US Department of Labor, whereas in Table 7.1 and Figure 7.2 and in the equations reported in the Appendix, nominal wages are derived from the OECD National Accounts. The former indicator is frequently used for international comparisons, but since manufacturing employment on average accounts for only 20% of total employment, it is not representative of aggregate trends.

4. The year-to-year variability of the OECD private consumption deflator fell from 3.6 to 1.0 between 1980–5 and 1985–90, or, measured by the coefficient of variation, from 0.6 to 0.3.

5. Inflation also declined steeply in the early 1950s. However, this disinflation process started from a lower initial rate (8.5–9% in 1951) and was completed in just 2 years.

6. Some countries have managed to reduce inflation without major output losses, but most of these cases refer to episodes of hyperinflation, which are typically characterized by the virtual absence of backward-looking expectations and a high degree of credibility of the policy measures taken (see Vegh (1991) and Sargent (1982)). When the initial rates of inflation are similar to those of 1979–81, inflation has rarely been reduced without major output losses (Gordon (1982)).

7. On this point see also Ball (1990–92), who argues that both lack of credibility and lags in price and wage adjustment are necessary conditions for the transitory costs. Ball in fact goes one step further by proving that a credible anti-inflation policy will be accompanied by excess demand pressures because of a substantial rise in the real money stock. A related problem has been discussed by other analysts (see for instance Freedman (1989), Scarth (1990) and Chadha et al. (1991)) but is usually referred to as the 're-entry problem'.

8. For a comprehensive review of the theoretical and empirical literature see Agenor and Taylor (1991) and Blackburn and Christensen (1989).

9. In theory a distinction should be made between *reputation* and *credibility*, with the former referring to the behaviour of the authorities and the latter to the perceived effects of the policies announced. In practice, however, it is difficult to maintain this distinction.

10. The precise definitions and measurements of real and nominal rigidities differ between authors. Taylor (1989), for instance, relates differences in output fluctuations between the United States and Japan to 'nominal' rigidities, but we interpret his results as reflecting 'real' rigidities as defined above.

11. Table 7.2 also includes an overall measure of real wage or unemployment persistence, which is further explained in the Appendix.

12. See the Appendix and the various simulations reported in Chadha et al. (1991). Note that while a high degree of real and nominal flexibility is helpful in reducing the transitory costs of anti-inflation policies, their general usefulness very much depends on the kinds of shocks to which a country is exposed. For instance, a low degree of nominal flexibility helps to reduce the effects of adverse supply shocks and there are also cases where a low sensitivity to economic slack is desirable. For further discussion see Andersen (1989).

13. Ideally unemployment should have been measured as deviations from the natural rate and not as actual rates. Moreover, recent *changes* in the rate of inflation may provide additional information about the initial conditions.

14. Large regional differences in inflation and unemployment may be another source of non-linearities.

15. See Giavazzi and Spaventa (1989), who argue that a favourable profit situation—partly the result of tax measures—was one reason for the relatively low sacrifice ratio found for Italy.

16. See in particular Fischer (1986b) and Bruno (1991).

17. A real appreciation will, of course, strengthen an anti-inflation policy stance, but if the nominal anchor is not reflected in the wage and price adjustment process it will eventually become unsustainable.

18. On the other hand, except for France in 1982, Belgium in 1982–3 and New Zealand in 1983, countries have generally not resorted to price and wage controls as a means of reducing inflation expectations.

19. Large regional differences may be another argument for adopting a gradual approach; see Freedman (1991).

20. According to Taylor (1983), the rate of inflation would only fall from 10 to 8·75% during the first 2 years of a programme of disinflation geared to a wage and price adjustment process with staggered 3-year contracts and forward-looking expectations.

21. In Denmark the growth of M1 and M2 jumped to over 25% shortly after the successful implementation of disinflation policies and remained exceptionally high over the next 2 years.

22. See Chadha et al. (1991), especially p. 19.

23. By convention, sacrifice ratios for periods of *falling* inflation are given as *positive* figures when the cumulative change in unemployment is positive or the cumulative deviation between actual and potential output growth is negative. This rule has also been followed throughout this paper.

24. Selody (1990) reports sacrifice ratios for Canada ranging from 4.7 for calculations based on actual developments during the 1981–2 recession (Howitt, 1990) to 2.0 for estimates derived from a short-run aggregate supply curve (Cozier and Wilkinson, 1990), with simulations on the RDXF macromodel yielding an intermediate ratio of 3.4.

25. The sacrifice ratio implied by Tobin's path is by no means an outlier relative to other assessments. It is very close to the 'rule-of-thumb' proposed by Kahn and Weiner (1990) and, applying an Okun-coefficient of 2.5 it is also close to the ratios reported by Gordon and King (1982) but at the lower end of Okun's (1978) range of 6–18. Our estimate of 0.85 is close to Sachs' (1985) output-based ratio of 2.5, while Dornbusch (1989), relying on 1981–8 changes in US unemployment, arrives at a *negative* figure.

26. This discrepancy becomes particularly evident when calculating the Okun coefficients corresponding to the sacrifice ratios.

27. See Jarrett and Selody (1982), who, on the basis of data for Canada, find that lower inflation tends to increase productivity gains and thus potential output growth. In a more recent study Cozier and Selody (1992) conclude that lower inflation mainly affects the long run *level* of potential output, while the effect on output *growth* is much smaller and only transitory.

28. The coefficient on the dummy variable would suggest that the sacrifice ratio for the United States is understated by 2.85 p.p. and that for Australia overstated to a similar extent. The use of a dummy variable is, of course, very ad hoc, but it leaves the coefficients of other variables virtually unchanged.

29. The high sacrifice ratio does not result from using a price deflator rather than a wage

deflator. In fact, when the sacrifice ratio is calculated for the wage changes shown in Table 7.1, it rises to more than 10, compared with 1 for the United States and 3.3 for EC countries on average.

30. When a dummy variable with 1 for ERM members (excluding Germany but including Austria) and 0 for non-members was added in Table 7.7, a negative coefficient was obtained, but it was never significant.

31. While Van Poeck (1989) includes all ERM countries, Artis and Ormerod confine their sample to Germany, France, Italy, Belgium and the Netherlands. See also De Grauw (1992) who observes that significant inflation differentials still exist between ERM countries and ascribe these to differences in the reputations of the monetary authorities. In other words, a currency link to the DM is not sufficient to 'buy' the reputation of the Bundesbank and to equalize expectations of inflation.

32. The absence of converging wage formation processes is also evident in Artis and Nachane (1990), who find that price and wage changes in other ERM countries are not cointegrated with those for Germany, either before or after 1979.

33. For all three output-based measures the actual ratios for Finland exceed the estimated values by more than one standard deviation.

34. This observation also applies to Canada, Australia and Sweden, where Y3 is biased by excess demand, rising inflation and a widening current account deficit.

35. The separate business cycle for Finland to a large extent reflects the large share of raw materials and semi-manufactured goods in exports, volatile terms of trade and a high dependence on trade with eastern Europe and the former USSR; for further discussion see Andersen and Åkerholm (1982).

36. See OECD (1986).

37. Regressing changes in unemployment on current and lagged changes in log real GDP (dy) for Finland and OECD Europe respectively produces the following results (annual data 1968–91, *t*-ratios in parentheses):

|  | $C$ | dy | dy(−1) | $R^2$ | DW |
|---|---|---|---|---|---|
| Finland | 1.70 (7.0) | −0.28 (7.1) | −0.15 (3.1) | 0.79 | 1.19 |
| OECD Europe | 0.37 (2.6) | −0.02 (1.3) | −0.02 (1.4) | 0.02 | 0.72 |

For OECD Europe the relationship is obviously not very close while unemployment in Finland is highly sensitive to output changes, with the equation implying an annual growth rate of 3.9% to keep unemployment stable.

38. Using the CPI-index, which has been affected by the decline in real property prices, inflation in Finland fell below the OECD average already in late 1990.

39. The income elasticity for Finnish exports (at 1.80) is well above that of imports (1.35), suggesting that at unchanged relative prices Finland can 'afford' a higher growth rate than its main trading partners; for further discussion see Andersen (1993).

40. Australia has also applied tax-based incomes policies as an element of the 'wage accord' whereas tax policies in Austria are strictly separated from the tri-partite negotiations. Norway and Sweden applied tax-based incomes policies in the mid-1970s but have later abandoned such policies. For further discussion see Andersen (1992).

41. Calculating means and standard deviations for respectively levels and changes of quarterly data (index 1980 = 100) for the nominal effective exchange rate gives the following results (mean ± SD):

|  | 1960–71 | 1972–7 | 1978–92 (August) |
|---|---|---|---|
| Level | 140.7 ± 16.8 | 109.8 ± 2.6 | 100.5 ± 3.5 |
| Change | −0.87 ± 5.1 | −0.45 ± 1.9 | −0.18 ± 1.8 |

Based on these calculations the average quarterly devaluations have been smaller after 1977, but the stability of the exchange rate does not appear to have increased.

42. To test the stability of money demand (M2) we applied the Engle–Granger (Engle and Granger, 1987) two-step procedure. Using real GDP (y), the rate of inflation (dlogP) and the long-term bond rate (IR) as the principal determinants, we first estimated the long run equation (annual data 1960–91):

$$\log (M2/P) = -8.54 + 1.28 \log y - 1.08 \operatorname{dlog}P - 0.033 \text{ IR}$$
$$(35.1) \quad (63.1) \quad (5.7) \qquad (6.2)$$
$$R^2 = 0.99, \text{ DW} = 1.48, \text{ SE} = 0.03, \text{ ADF} = -3.85$$

The equation appears to be stable as all diagnostic statistics reject the null hypothesis of no cointegration. As a second step the residuals (EC) of the above equation were used in estimating the error correction equation:

$$\operatorname{dlog} (M2/P) = 0.07 + 0.42 \operatorname{dlog}y - 0.019 \text{ dIR} + 0.74 \text{ d}^2\log P - 0.75 \text{ EC}_{-1}$$
$$(4.1) \quad (2.2) \qquad (1.9) \qquad (3.7) \qquad (3.8)$$
$$+ 0.27 \operatorname{dlog}(M2/P)_{-1}$$
$$(1.9)$$
$$R^2 = 0.52, h = 0.98, \text{ SE} = 0.03.$$

The coefficient on the EC term has the correct sign and is highly significant, thus again rejecting the hypothesis of no cointegration. However, when the error correction equation was estimated on the shorter period 1960–85 there was evidence of parameter instability as a Chow-test produced a significant $F$-value of 4.38. It thus appears that financial innovations and deregulations have not disturbed the long run relationship between money, income, inflation and interest rates. However, during the second half of the 1980s these changes have made short run money demand unstable and less predictable.

43. The criteria, based on economic characteristics and intended to generate an efficient resource allocation, would suggest that small and open countries with little diversification in traded goods as well as a small inflation differential against trading partners and a low degree of integration in international capital markets should choose a fixed regime. For further discussion see Heller (1978).

44. For instance, the gain between early 1974 and early 1975 was equivalent to a GDP increase of about 5% and the rise between early 1986 and early 1989 was even larger though spread over a longer period. On both occasions the terms-of-trade gains contributed to a sharp rise in output but also, with some lag, to higher inflation.

45. A terms-of-trade gain can increase the domestic rate of inflation through three channels: (i) by boosting real income relative to potential output; (ii) by encouraging firms to sell a larger share of their output in foreign markets; and (iii) by inducing additional wage claims by workers in the tradable sector which may eventually also affect wages in other sectors. Moreover, given asymmetries in the wage and price formation process a subsequent terms-of-trade deterioration is unlikely to offset the effects of the gain.

46. 'Intermargin operations' by the Bank to widen the scope for an independent monetary policy combined with the discrete exchange rate changes have probably helped to keep these memories alive.

47. Other factors complicating the evaluation of interest rate movements are the generous deductions for interest payments in taxable income and the exemptions granted interest receipts on most deposit accounts.

48. In the 1950s when prices were subject to controls and wages fully indexed to price changes, the authorities frequently increased subsidies to reduce consumer price inflation.

49. There are several differences (sample period, definitions and measurements, estimation method and the choice of additional variables) between the national estimates and those reported below. The level specification is strongly supported in the case of Finland whereas for international comparisons focusing on the process of disinflation it is preferable to rely on a first-difference specification (see the Appendix).

50. Notation: $W$, wages and salaries per employee; $U$, rate of unemployment; $P$, GDP deflator; $PC$, private consumption deflator; $Q$, productivity (measured as the ratio of real GDP to employment); $t_1$, ratio of indirect taxes less subsidies to GDP in factor prices; $t_2$, income tax, average rate; and $t_3$, employers social security contribution, average rate.

51. Solving for $W$ and leaving out all variables in first differences, the long run nominal earnings equation may be written as:

$$\log (W) = -11.4 - 0.10 \log U + 1.0 \log Q + 0.7 \log P(1-t_1) + 0.3 \log PC$$

The absence of permanent tax effects is in line with findings for most other countries; see Andersen (1992a) and the references given therein.

52. A rise in the unemployment rate from 5 to 6% will reduce short run nominal wage changes by 1 p.p. and the level of long run real earnings by 2%.
53. Hysteresis appears to be associated with wage equations estimated in first differences, see also OECD (1986), but given the superior performance of the equation including a lagged real wage term it is likely to reflect a specification error.
54. Most general wage agreements concluded in the 1970s and 1980s have included clauses calling for additional wage increases or a reopening of the negotiations if consumer prices (excluding prices of certain imported goods) rose more than expected at the time of the agreement. In most years the threshold indexation clauses have not become effective and their effect on the process of disinflation is ambiguous. On the one hand, they may advance the adjustment of nominal wages to a fall in actual or expected inflation. On the other hand, one-way threshold indexation introduces an element of asymmetry which under certain conditions may retard the process of disinflation.
55. The 1970s saw the development of an informal credit market, mainly in the form of interfirm credits. During the 1980s this market was gradually absorbed by the banks and unregulated deposits and loans expanded rapidly even though rather high minimum requirements precluded most households from participating.
56. As discussed in Tsuru (1992), the shift in macroeconomic policies in Japan led to important institutional changes in the labour market and to a significant reduction of wage spill overs.
57. One argument frequently advanced against exchange rate targets—namely, the loss of an instrument of adjustment to meet external shocks—does not seem valid in this case as the external shocks of the 1980s were mostly favourable for the ERM countries. On the other hand, the high sacrifice ratios should not be taken as proof that these countries would have been better off with monetary aggregate targets and flexible exchange rates.
58. A similar problem may occur if the key currency country, for reasons not present in other countries, is forced to tighten monetary policy and increase nominal and real interest rates. This situation could be observed in 1991–2 and has also been a problem during part of the period reviewed in this paper.
59. Rewriting the terms in $\ln U$ as $-\eta(1-\alpha)\ln U - \eta\alpha d\ln U$, the degree of long run real wage rigidity is easily seen to be $\eta(1-\alpha)$ or $1/\eta(1-\alpha)$.
60. For further discussion and evidence see Barrell et al. (1990).
61. Failure to satisfy the neutrality condition may also indicate that the market power of employees and their unions is low and that output prices should have been included in the wage equation. This argument may explain the results for the United States and Japan but does not appear particularly valid for Italy and Sweden.
62. Equation (7.4) is equivalent to their wage adjustment equation except that they enter $W$ and $PC$ in levels. We also tested the level version and found virtually the same values for $\eta$ and $\alpha$ as shown in Table 7.1. However, for most countries $\beta_3$ was close to unity and in all cases the DW-statistics were very low, implying that the dynamic structure was misspecified.
63. For the United States, Canada and Australia the inclusion of only two lagged terms in $U$ is clearly insufficient. In all three cases the addition of $U_{-3}$ reduced the $h$-statistics to below 1 while the sum of the coefficients remained close to those shown in Table 7.2.
64. In a study of the Okun's law relationship for Australia, Mitchell and Watts (1991) find that lower capacity growth and a rise in the sectoral variability of employment changes have been the major factors behind the increase in the equilibrium unemployment rate. For Canada Coe (1990) finds that the unemployment benefit insurance system has been an important source of hysteresis.
65. The following is the approach preferred by Gordon (1981, 1990).
66. See Coe and Holtham (1983) and Bispham (1984).

# References

Agenor, P.R. and Taylor, M. (1991), 'Testing for credibility effects', IMF Working Paper, No. 91/110.

Alogoskoufis, G. and Manning, A. (1988), 'On the persistence of unemployment', *Economic Policy*, No. 7, 427–69.

Andersen, P. (1989), 'Inflation and output: a review of the wage–price mechanism', BIS Economic Papers, No. 24.

Andersen, P. (1990): 'Developments in external and internal balances: a selective and eclectic review', BIS Economic Papers, No. 29.

Andersen, P. (1992), 'Taxes and labour market developments', Budget Memorandum, Annex, pp. 7–96.

Andersen, P. (1993), 'The 45° rule revisited', *Applied Economics*, **25**, 1279–84.

Andersen, P. S. and Åkerholm, J. (1982), 'Scandinavia', in A. Boltho (ed.), *The European Economy*, Oxford University Press, Oxford, pp. 610–44.

Artis, M. and Nachane, D. (1990), 'Wages and prices in Europe: a test of the German leadership thesis', *Weltwirtschaftliches Archiv*, **126**, 59–77.

Artis, M. and Ormerod, P. (1991), 'Is there an 'EMS' effect in European labour markets?', CEPR Discussion Paper, No. 598.

Ball, L. (1990), 'Credible disinflation with staggered price setting', NBER Working Paper, No. 3555.

Ball, L. (1991), 'The genesis of inflation and the costs of disinflation', *Journal of Money, Credit and Banking*, **25**, 439–61.

Ball, L. (1992), 'Disinflation with imperfect credibility', NBER Working Paper, No. 3983.

Barrell, R., Darby. J. and Donaldson, C. (1990), 'Structural stability in European wage and price systems', NIESR Discussion Paper, No. 188.

Baxter, M. (1985), 'The role of expectations in stabilisation policy', *Journal of Monetary Economics*, **15**, 343–62.

Bispham, J. (1984), 'Inflation, recession and recovery: a nominal income analysis of the process of global disinflation', BIS Economic Papers, No. 11.

Blackburn, K. and Christensen, M. (1989), 'Monetary policy and policy credibility', *Journal of Economic Literature*, **27**, 1–45.

Blundell-Wignall, A. and Gregory, R. (1990), 'Exchange rate policy in advanced commodity–exporting countries: Australia and New Zealand' in V. Argy and P. De Grauwe (eds), *Choosing an Exchange Rate Regime: The Challenge for Smaller Industrial Countries*, IMF, Katholiche Universiteit Leuven and Macquarie University, pp. 224–84.

Bruno, M. (1991), 'High inflation and the nominal anchors of an open economy', Essays in International Finance, No. 183, Princeton University.

Chadha, B., Masson, P. and Meredith, G. (1991), 'Models of inflation and the costs of disinflation', IMF Working Paper, No. 91/97.

Chouraqui, J.-C., Hagemann, R. and Sartor, N. (1990), 'Indicators of fiscal policy: a reassessment', OECD Working Paper, No. 78.

Coe, D. (1990), 'Structural determinants of the natural rate of unemployment in Canada', IMF Staff Papers, pp. 94–115.

Coe, D. and Holtham, G. (1983), 'Output responsiveness and inflation', OECD Economic Studies, pp. 93–146.

Coe, D., Durand, M. and Stiehler, U. (1986), 'The disinflation of the 1980s', OECD Economic Studies, pp. 89–121.

Cozier, B. (1991), 'Wage and price dynamics in Canada', Bank of Canada, Technical Report, No. 56.

Cozier, B. and Wilkinson, G. (1990), 'How large are the costs of disinflation in Canada ?', Bank of Canada, Working Paper, No. 90–6.

Cozier, B. and Selody, J. (1992), 'Inflation and macroeconomic performance', Bank of Canada, Working Paper, No.92–03.

de Grauw, P. (1992), 'Inflation convergence during the transition to EMU', CEPR Discussion Paper, No. 658.

Dornbusch, R. (1989), 'Credibility, debt and unemployment: Ireland's failed stabilisation', *Economic Policy*, No. 8, 173–210.

Engle, R. and Granger, C. (1987), 'Co–integration and error correction: representation, estimation and testing', *Econometrica*, **55**, 251–76.

Eriksson, T. Suvanto, A. and Vartia, P. (1991), 'Wage setting in Finland', in L. Calmfors (ed.), *Wage Formation and Macroeconomic Policy in the Nordic Countries*, Oxford University Press, Oxford, pp. 189–296.

Fahrer, J. and Myatt, J. (1991), 'Inflation in Australia: causes, inertia and policy', Reserve Bank of Australia, RDP 9105.

Fischer, S. (1977), 'Long-term contracts, rational expectations and the optimal money supply rule', *Journal of Political Economy*, **85**, 191–205.

Fischer, S. (1986a), 'Contracts, credibility and disinflation' in S. Fischer (ed.), *Indexing, Inflation and Economic Policy*, MIT Press, Cambridge, MA, pp. 221–45.

Fischer, S. (1986b), 'Exchange rates versus money targets in disinflation', in S. Fischer (ed.), *Indexing, Inflation and Economic Policy*, MIT Press, Cambridge, MA, pp. 247–62.

Fortin, P. (1990), 'Can the costs of an anti–inflation policy be reduced?' in R. C. York (ed.), *Taking Aim: The Debate on Zero Inflation*, C. D. Howe Institute, Ottawa, pp. 135–72.

Fortin, P. (1991), 'The Phillips curve, macroeconomic policy and the welfare of Canadians', *Canadian Journal of Economics*, **24**, 774–803.

Freedman, C. (1989), 'Monetary policies in the 1990s: lessons and challenges', in *Monetary Policy Issues in the 1990s*, Federal Reserve Bank of Kansas City, pp. 1–54.

Freedman, C. (1991), 'The goal of price stability: the debate in Canada', *Journal of Money, Credit and Banking*, **23**, 613–18.

Giavazzi, F. and Spaventa, L. (1989), 'Italy, the real effects of inflation and disinflation', *Economic Policy*, No. 8, 133–72.

Gordon, R. (1981), 'Output fluctuations and gradual price adjustment', *Journal of Economic Literature*, **19**, 493–532.

Gordon, R. (1982), 'Why stopping inflation can be costly: evidence from fourteen different episodes', in R. E. Hall (ed.), *Inflation: Causes and Effects*, NBER Project Report Series, University of Chicago Press.

Gordon, R. (1988), 'The role of wages in the inflation process', *American Economic Review*, **78**, 276–83.

Gordon, R. (1990), 'The Phillips curve now and then', NBER Working Paper, No. 3393.

Gordon, R. and King, S. (1982), 'The output cost of disinflation in traditional and vector autoregressive models', *Brookings Papers on Economic Activity*, No. 1, 205–44.

Heller, R. (1978), 'Determinants of exchange rate practices', *Journal of Money, Credit and Banking*, **10**, 308–21.

Howitt, P. (1990), 'Zero inflation as a long–term target for monetary policy', in R. Lipsey (ed.), *Zero–Inflation*, C. D. Howe Institute, Ottawa, pp. 67–108.

Jarrett, P. and Selody, J. (1982), 'The productivity–inflation nexus in Canada: 1963–79', *Review of Economics and Statistics*, **64**, 361–7.

Kahn, G. and Weiner, S. (1990), 'Has the cost of disinflation declined?', *Economic Review*, Federal Reserve Bank of Kansas City, pp. 5–24.

Mehra, Y. (1991), 'Wage growth and the inflation process: empirical note', *American Economic Review*, **81**, 931–9.

Mitchel, R. and Watts, M. (1991), 'Alleged instability of the Okun's Law relationship in Australia: an empirical analysis', *Applied Economics*, **23**, 1829–38.

Mundell, R. (1971), 'The dollar and the policy mix: 1971', Essays in International Finance, No. 85, Princeton University.

Murphy, C. (1991), 'The transitional costs of reducing inflation using monetary policy', in *Australia's inflation problem*, EPAC Background Paper, No.11, pp. 8.1–8.22.

OECD (various years), *OECD Economic Surveys of Finland*, Paris.

Okun, A. (1978), 'Efficient disinflationary rules', *American Economic Review*, **68**, 348–52.

Sachs, J. (1985), 'The dollar and the policy mix: 1985', *Brookings Papers on Economic Activity*, No. 1, 117–97.

Sargent, T. (1982), 'The ends of four big inflations', in R. E. Hall (ed.), *Inflation: Causes and Effects*, NBER Project Report Series, University of Chicago Press.

Scarth, W. (1990), 'Are the costs of getting to zero too high?', in R. C. York (ed.), *Taking Aim: The Debate on Zero Inflation*, C. D. Howe Institute, Ottawa, pp. 135–72.

Selody, J. (1990), 'The goal of price stability: a review of the issues', Bank of Canada, Technical Report, No. 54.

Takeda, U. (1992), 'The term structure of interest rates as an indicator of the central bank's policy stance', Mimeo, BIS.

Taylor, J. (1980), 'Aggregate dynamics and staggered contracts', *Journal of Political Economy*, **88**, 1–23.

Taylor, J. (1983), 'Union wage settlements during a disinflation', *American Economic Review*, **73**, 981–93.

Taylor, J. (1989), 'Differences in economic fluctuations in Japan and the United States: the role of nominal rigidities', *Journal of the Japanese and International Economies*, **3**, 127–44.

Tobin, J. (1980), 'Stabilisation policy ten years after', *Brookings Papers on Economic Activity*, No. 1, 19–90.

Tsuru, T. (1992), 'The spring offensive: the spillover effect and the wage–setting institution in Japan', Discussion Paper, No. 247, The Institute of Economic Research, Hitotsubashi University, Tokyo.

Tyrvainen, T. (1991), 'Unions, wages and employment evidence from Finland', Bank of Finland Discussion Papers, No. 16/91.

Van Poeck, A. (1989), 'Wage formation, labour market characteristics and the EMS', Report No. 891235, University of Antwerp.

Vegh, C. (1991), 'Stopping high inflation: an analytical overview', IMF Working Paper, No. 91/107.

Weber, A. (1991), 'Reputation and credibility in the European Monetary System', *Economic Policy*, No. 12, 57–102.

# Discussion

## John Driffill
*University of Southampton and CEPR*

Palle Andersen has given us a thorough survey of the arguments surrounding disinflation: the costs of disinflation, the role of 'credibility' of policies, nominal and real rigidities in the economy, and the effects of the initial conditions. He discusses the role of alternative nominal anchors for monetary policy: a pegged exchange rate, targets for monetary growth, or targets for inflation directly. He compares a wide variety of 'sacrifice ratios' for a number of countries. He considers the ways in which all these considerations apply to Finland.

A principal conclusion appears to be that Finland achieved a reduction in inflation during the 1980s at low cost in terms of unemployment or foregone production compared with other OECD countries. Finland began the decade with fairly low unemployment and only moderate inflation (4.8% and 11.7% respectively in 1980–1—see Table 7.3). Inflation fell in Finland slightly less quickly than in the OECD on average (see Table 7.9), but unemployment rose in Finland by considerably less. The cumulative increase in unemployment in Finland over the period from 1975 to 1989 was 1.3%, compared with the OECD average figure of 4.3% (again, see Table 7.9). Meanwhile, output grew more quickly in Finland than in the OECD. Finland enjoyed healthy growth in output per hour in manufacturing (5.4% per annum) through the 1980s, compared with other OECD countries (see Table 7.6). The 1980s appear to have been a much less traumatic period, from the point of view of economic developments, in Finland, than they were in many other European countries. Of course, Finland has suffered more severe problems in the last few years (1989–93) since its export markets in Russia collapsed, and unemployment has shot up.

A striking feature of the Finnish economy at the start of the period was the lack of any government debt outstanding (see Table 7.3). In 1980 and 1981 the government had on average net assets of 5.4% of the GDP. Even after the fiscal deficits of recent years, Finland is predicted to have a debt to GDP ratio of only 25% by 1996. At the same time, Finland had net debts abroad equal to 14.1% of the GDP in 1980–1. Presumably these are debts of the private sector, and may result from low private saving relative to investment, perhaps because Finland has comprehensive social security and national pension provisions, which discourage private saving.

One of the questions which emerges from the paper is about the supply side of the Finnish economy, in particular the labour market, and how it was possible to maintain low unemployment while having falling wage and price inflation. The relevant comparisons are on the one hand with the other Nordic countries, especially Sweden and Norway, but also Denmark, and on the other hand with larger Western European countries—Belgium and the Netherlands, the United Kingdom, Germany, France, and Italy—in which there was a much more pronounced rise in unemployment during the 1980s, and in which the labour market seems to have been much less well able to absorb a reduction in inflation without unemployment.

In Sweden and Norway, the very centralized bargaining arrangements, and the possibility of implicit or explicit collaboration between unions, employers, and government, appears to have helped to maintain low unemployment in the period. Palle Andersen notes the use of incomes policies tied to tax changes in Finland, but finds little empirical support for their having played a role in low inflation. In his conclusions, he comments on the notorious problem of cumulative distortions introduced by long-term incomes policies, but this presumably applies more to the kind of policies imposed by government with conspicuous lack of success in the United Kingdom in the 1960s and 1970s rather than the more cooperative and implicit policies pursued in a small, more centralized economy like Finland's.

The unemployment benefit system in Sweden—generous benefits for a limited period combined with active efforts to find unemployed workers jobs and/or training—is often credited with Sweden's having been able to keep down unemployment rates and having avoided the growing problem of long-term unemployment which has appeared in the United Kingdom, France, Germany, and elsewhere. Andersen notes that in Finland, notwithstanding fairly centralized bargaining, wage drift has always accounted for a substantial fraction of total wage increases. He does not appear to attribute much of Finland's successful disinflation to centralized bargaining. However, in Sweden also wage drift has been an important component of wage increases, but that does not appear to have undermined the role of centralized bargaining in holding back wage growth in the 1980s. The role played by Finland's labour market institutions and bargaining arrangements may deserve closer analysis.

There is, I think, some tension in the paper between the extensive discussion of the role of 'credibility' of disinflationary policies, and the wage equations which are estimated and form the basis of some of the measures of sacrifice ratios. Equations (7.1) and (7.2) model expected inflation as depending on current inflation and past wage growth. Similar equations are estimated and compared across countries (see Table 7.2).

The estimation procedures assume these to be structurally stable over the whole sample period. If credibility is important in wage formation, then it must depend in part on expected future policy and price expectations derived from it. Past inflation can only be a useful proxy for or predictor of future inflation if the policy regime is stable, and there is no reason to suppose that it was. Indeed, the credibility issue arises because the policies of the 1980s were a complete change from those of the preceding decade. In these circumstances, it is natural to expect that equations like (7.1) and (7.2) might not be stable over time. It would be interesting to have more extensive diagnostic statistics for such estimates. If the wage equations are not structural—invariant to policy regime—they might give a fair impression of what the sacrifice ratio was, but not of what it might have been with other (more credible?) policies. I think it would have been very useful to have other sources of information on price (and other) expectations in Finland during the 1980s with which to form at least tentative judgements about this elusive creature 'credibility'.

The Finnish experience stands in striking contrast with that of the United Kingdom in the 1980s. In the United Kingdom, a dramatic shift of policy in 1980 introduced what was intended to be a gradualist disinflation policy, but which turned out to be cold turkey, and left lower inflation but an apparently irreducibly higher level of unemployment. In Finland a gradual disinflation had been achieved by 1989 with little increase in unemployment, and it had maintained high productivity growth. In both countries the disinflationary message contained in government policy was confused by unexpectedly expansionary policies pursued in the period 1986–9. But again Finland responded with much more output growth and less inflation acceleration, reinforcing the view that the supply side, especially the labour market, is particularly important in determining the costs of disinflation.

# 8

# The Currency Band and Credibility: The Finnish Experience

## Olli-Pekka Lehmussaari and Antti Suvanto
*Bank of Finland/Suomen Pankki*

## Laura Vajanne
*Union Bank of Finland*

## 8.1    Foreword

After this paper was written, the Finnish money and foreign exchange markets experienced severe turbulence. It proved difficult to restore confidence in the foreign exchange markets, and the markka was under pressure on several occasions in the spring and the summer of 1992. The nervousness in the currency markets was partly due to the harsh adjustment process the Finnish economy was going through and the difficulties in drawing up a politically acceptable economic programme to tackle the serious economic problems. In addition, increasing nervousness in the European currency markets contributed to instability in the domestic foreign exchange markets and fuelled demands for the second devaluation of the markka within a year.

Doubts about the commitment to a fixed currency band, together with the restlessness in European currency markets, contributed to a substantial capital outflow in the early autumn 1992. As a result the Board of the Management of the Bank of Finland decided to abandon the markkas fixed parity in relation to the ECU on 8 September 1992. The change in the foreign exchange regime has not altered the objective of monetary policy—which is still price stability.

## 8.2    Introduction

Finland was one of the first countries to peg its currency to a currency basket. After the collapse of the Bretton Woods system and the system of central rates, the basket-pegging system was adopted as a guideline for exchange rate policy in mid-1973. In November 1977, the basket-pegging system was formalized by an amendment to the Currency Act (Puro, 1978). At the same time the formal currency band was introduced. According to the Act, the external value of the markka was expressed in terms of a currency index number reflecting the exchange rates of the currencies most important for Finland's foreign trade.[1]

Since 1977, the peg has been altered twice. In 1984, the Soviet rouble was removed from the currency index, and thereafter the calculation of the currency index was based on freely convertible currencies (Puro, 1984). In June 1991, the trade-weighted currency index was replaced by the peg to the ECU.

The exchange rate arrangement adopted in Finland provides an opportunity to analyse developments in the money and foreign exchange markets in the light of the recent literature on target-zone models. In the analysis, we mainly concentrate on the period after 1987 when the assumptions underlying the target-zone models can be assumed to be fulfilled in the Finnish money and foreign exchange markets.

Rather than trying to carry out a complete empirical assessment of the implications of the target-zone models with Finnish data, we apply descriptive analysis to recent episodes in the foreign exchange market in Finland and review the Finnish experience of maintaining the exchange rate within the band. We also use more formal methods in calculating the expected future exchange rate and the devaluation risk of the Finnish markka during the period when the markka was more or less constantly under severe pressure.

In retrospect it is clear that the 'fixed exchange rate test' which has been costly in many countries, proved to be extremely difficult in Finland. The Finnish experience shows, inter alia, that the difficulties of pursuing a structurally viable fiscal policy complicated the task of maintaining a stable exchange rate. In addition, the developments in the Finnish money and foreign exchange markets suggest that too much burden in the adjustment process was placed on monetary policy and too much was expected from labour market adjustment through wages.

The paper is organized as follows. Section 8.3 describes the institutional characteristics of the foreign exchange rate system and reviews developments in the money and foreign exchange markets. The section also briefly discusses the operational mechanisms of monetary policy in Finland. In section 8.4, the basic analytical framework is described and some of the weaknesses of the basic target-zone model are characterized. Section 8.5 presents the empirical findings on the credibility of the Finnish currency band. In addition, the relationship between the interest rate differential and the position of the exchange rate inside the band is examined together with a brief discussion of the problem of the causality between the exchange rate and the interest rate differential. Moreover, a signalling effect of central bank intervention on the formation of expectations on a future exchange rate is discussed and various proxies for an expected future exchange rate within the band are introduced, which are then used empirically. At the end of the section estimation results of the time-varying devaluation risk are presented. Section 8.6 rounds up the discussion with concluding remarks.

## 8.3    Descriptive Analysis

### 8.3.1    *Institutional Framework*

Since March 1962, the decision-making procedure regarding the external value of markka has been defined in the Currency Act. The Bank of Finland is responsible for maintaining the exchange rate (index) within the band, but the government is the ultimate decision-maker as regards any realignment of the band, including changes in the width of the band. The proposal for a realignment must come from the Board of Management of the Bank and it must be accepted by the Parliamentary Bank Supervisory Board. The government can either accept the proposal as it stands or reject it.

   This decision-making procedure was already applicable in the Bretton Woods era, although the central gold parity and the width of the band vis-à-vis the US dollar was set by the agreement with the IMF. Formally, the currency band was introduced by the amendment of the Currency Act in November 1977. Since then, the width of the band has been changed a few times, alternating between ±2·25, and ±3%. Since November 1988, the width of the band has been ±3%. According to the current interpretation of the law, any larger changes in the width of the band, as well as revisions to the composition of the basket, require amendments to the Currency Act (Lehmussaari, 1991; Åkerholm, 1992).

### 8.3.2    *Deregulation and Capital Movements*

Despite changes in the peg and in the width of the band, the exchange rate regime has remained formally unchanged for most of the post-war period. The role of the exchange rate and exchange rate policy have, however, undergone considerable changes.

   Figure 8.1 portrays the history of the exchange rate during the period when the formal basket peg has been in use. It reveals, inter alia, that large jumps in the exchange rate dominate the picture and that the

EXTERNAL VALUE OF THE MARKKA

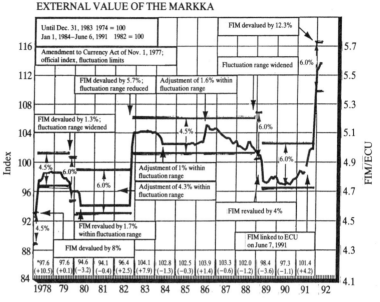

* Annual average of index. Change (%) from previous year in brackets. Old index for 1991.

**Figure 8.1** Bank of Finland currency index

upward jumps (devaluations) dominate the downward adjustments (revaluations). Some of the discrete adjustments have taken place within the band, although in the majority of cases the entire band has been adjusted. In the period up to 1985, the index was not allowed to move within the band to any significant extent, except on a few occasions when it was discretely adjusted.

As long as capital movements and domestic financial markets were tightly regulated, capital movements were slow to react to changes in monetary tightness at home relative to that abroad. As a result, monetary policy had a considerable degree of autonomy and, in addition, the exchange rate could be used as an independent instrument of economic policy.

The Bank of Finland had started the step-by-step liberalization of average lending rate controls already in 1983.[2] In late 1970s and early 1980s artificially low interest rates together with credit rationing contributed to the growth of the grey market in which financial institutions arranged loans through off-balance-sheet operations. This development started, however, to cause structural strains in the financial system and reduce the effectiveness of monetary policy which speeded up the deregulation process in the mid-1980s. As a result, bank lending rates were dismantled entirely in 1986.

In the 1970s and early 1980s, the Bank of Finland also made effective use of capital outflows, while trying to allocate capital inflows to favoured sectors. In addition, changes in exchange control regulations were often directed to support domestic monetary policy objectives. In other words interest rate policy was geared mainly towards demand management and structural objectives, whereas decisions on exchange rate policy were based mainly on maintenance of the competitiveness of the export sector (Swoboda, 1986; Åkerholm, 1987).

The early 1980s witnessed widespread circumvention of interest rate regulations and exchange controls by operators, mainly domestic firms and banks, in the forward exchange market as well as in the rapidly growing unregulated money market. The currency was subjected to a strong speculative attack in autumn 1982, to which the authorities responded by a discrete devaluation within the band. Not surprisingly, this move did not alleviate the pressure, and a few days later the markka was devalued for the second time by an upward adjustment of the band as a reaction to a large surprise devaluation of the Swedish krona.

Speculative capital outflows reappeared 1 year later, in autumn 1983. This time the Bank of Finland reacted by promptly raising the call money interest rate, which, in turn, pushed up both forward exchange rates and interest rates in the unregulated money market. This episode provided a foretaste of the interplay between capital flows, interest rates and exchange rates, as well as of their interrelationship with economic policy in general.

Some important changes regarding attitudes to exchange rate policy had already taken place before autumn 1983. Two discrete revaluations in 1979 and 1980, although small, marked the first serious attempt to depart from the 10-year devaluation cycle (Korkman, 1978; Halttunen and Korkman, 1984). A shift from 'competitiveness-orientated exchange rate policy' to a strategy emphasizing exchange rate stability was proclaimed for the first time in the programme of the new government which took office in spring 1983. The same strategy has since been proclaimed in each subsequent government programme (in 1987 and 1991), despite changes in the political composition of the government.

The tide suddenly turned in early 1984, after which stability became threatened by heavy capital inflows. Captive financial institutions invented new channels to circumvent existing regulations, and foreign investors entered the markka market for the first time in the post-war period.

In 1986, stagnation of growth, a sharp fall in oil prices and consequent decline in Finland's exports to the former USSR, together with a discrete devaluation in Norway, triggered repeated attacks against the markka. In May, the exchange rate was adjusted by a small discrete devaluation within the band. This move appears to have poured fuelled speculation even more and within a short period the Bank of Finland lost almost all its reserves. The attack was repelled by a sharp increase in the call money interest rate (to 40%) in early August, but the crisis did not recede until the end of the year, when it had already become obvious that, rather than being in the midst of a recession, the economy had already embarked on a strong cyclical upswing.

The 1986 experience speeded up the formal deregulation process. Bank lending rate controls were dismantled entirely in 1986. Deposit rates nevertheless remained administratively rigid because of the continuation of the tax exemption of interest income on bank deposits and because of the rigidity of the Bank of Finland's base rate, to which most deposit and lending rates were linked.[3] Controls on capital imports were lifted step by step during the subsequent years. The process was, however, asymmetric. While capital imports were liberalized at a rapid pace, capital exports remained more or less regulated until 1990.

The turnaround in the international business cycle in 1987, together with the domestic credit boom and bullish income expectations, led to a rapidly deteriorating external balance and to a sharp increase in asset prices in 1988 and 1989. Finland's terms of trade improved each year from 1986 to 1989, by a total of around 20%, which boosted domestic demand still further. Although central government finances exhibited growing surpluses, automatic stabilizers and attempted discretionary measures were unable to choke off excess demand.

Further monetary tightening through open market operations, which by then had become the conventional practice of monetary management, became impossible as early as in mid-1988 as the exchange rate index hit the strong edge of the currency band. In early 1989 the authorities took recourse to two unconventional measures. From the beginning of March, the Bank of Finland required the banks to make supplementary cash reserve deposits, the size of which depended on the rate of credit expansion of each bank or banking group.[4] A few weeks later, the Bank of Finland and the Government decided to revalue the markka by around 4%. Neither of these measures had a major immediate impact. The interest rate differential between domestic and foreign interest rates widened temporarily as a result of the surprise revaluation, but the rate of credit expansion by banks proved slow to diminish, despite pecuniary costs to banks brought about by the supplementary cash reserve deposits which were collected until the end of the year.

Market sentiment changed abruptly in autumn 1989, by which time it had become obvious that the economy was on an unsustainable path.

Foreign investors, in particular, who over the years had become increasingly interested in the high-yielding Finnish markka, reduced their positions as a reaction to a sequence of negative news concerning the current account and inflation developments. It appears that foreigners were better able than the Finns to distinguish 'the wood from the trees' in reading Finnish macroeconomic and political data.

The period from autumn 1989 up to the present time has been characterized by successive episodes of currency unrest and periods of relative calm, each of which would merit an in-depth 'clinical study'. The spring and summer of 1990 represent a period relative calm, but this ended suddenly as uncertainty surrounding the following year's budget and the forthcoming wage negotiations began to grow.

The uncertainty concerning the outcome of the general election in March 1991 prompted a new wave of speculation, which was resumed in late May after the decision by Sweden to switch the peg from a trade-weighted basket to the ECU. A similar move by the Finnish Parliament in early June calmed the situation for some months, but the autumn brought with it two waves of massive speculation, the latter culminating in a discrete devaluation of the markka by 12.3% on 15 November 1991.

### 8.3.3 *Operational Mechanisms of Monetary Policy* [5]

As is apparent from the discussion above, the deregulation of financial markets and the dismantling of exchange controls have resulted in a major change in the role of the exchange rate. At the same time it has changed the operational mechanisms of monetary policy. Free capital movements and free interest rate formation have broken down the traditional distinction between monetary policy and foreign exchange policy. Changes in the interest rate differential vis-à-vis foreign rates have an immediate impact on either the exchange rate or foreign exchange reserves. Changes in foreign exchange reserves affect the monetary base (amount of liquidity in the banking system) and interest rates. A change in liquidity and interest rates is quickly offset by capital movements.

Using the popular terminology, the *ultimate* target of monetary policy is price stability (low inflation). This objective has been stated in each Government programme since 1983. The exchange rate is the *inter-mediate* target. If the exchange rate (currency index) is to remain within its prescribed limits, the rate of inflation in Finland cannot for long differ from the average inflation rate for the countries whose currencies are included in the index to which the markka is pegged.

The exchange rate (within the band), the interest rate and the exchange reserves (or alternatively bank liquidity) consitute the three *proximate* targets of monetary policy. In the short term, the central bank can exert some influence on all of these through market operations, but it is not free to choose every one of them independently. For instance, an open market purchase that increases bank liquidity and thereby lowers the short-term interest rate, leads, ceteris paribus, to currency depreciation (restricted by the band) or to a decline in reserves (restricted by adequacy considerations).

This characterization was not illustrative of the operational environment in which monetary policy in Finland was conducted in the 1970s or the first half of the 1980s. Open market operations in the domestic money market could not exist before 1987, because there was no properly functioning domestic money market.[6]

Since 1987, open market operations have been the principal instrument for implementing the Bank of Finland's monetary policy (Aurikko, 1989). Initially, the Bank of Finland relied exclusively on outright open market operations. The operations affect banks' liquidity on the spot date (2 days following the trade date).[7] Since early 1991, repo or reverse repo tenders have played an increasingly important role in day-to-day liquidity management. These are arranged at frequent, though irregular, intervals in order to smooth large changes in liquidity, arising, e.g., from government loan transactions or from the expiration of earlier central bank transactions.

As the liquidity control function has been implemented through open market operations, the need for intervening spot in the foreign exchange markets has diminished. Both interest rates and the exchange rate have been allowed to react to a greater extent to pressures stemming from capital movements. Interventions in the spot market are, as a rule, unsterilized or only partially sterilized. From time to time, the Bank of Finland has resorted to swap operations in the forward exchange market. The experience of later years shows that the possibility of raising domestic interest rates by sterilizing the liquidity effects of capital imports has been reduced by the deregulation of capital movements. Forward exchange sales by the central bank during periods of currency turmoil have been relatively small in comparison to the amount of intervention in the spot market.

The significance of the call money (discount) window as a source of banks' central bank financing has diminished substantially since open market operations became available as a means of controlling liquidity.[8] Previously the call money credit facility was the banks' only source of central bank financing. At the beginning of 1986 the interest rate on call money credit was differentiated from the rate on call money deposits in an attempt to induce banks to smooth out the differences in their liquidity needs in the interbank market for overnight funds. Every bank that had access to central bank finance could obtain call money credit up to a specified quota.

In June 1989, bank-specific quotas were abolished as part of a revision of the facility. In order to induce banks to resort to the call money window only for temporary purposes and to hold their free reserves in the form of call money deposits at the Bank of Finland, the banks were obliged to maintain a positive 5-day moving average for their daily positions at the Bank. In November 1989, a monetary penalty was laid down for failure to observe the 5-day rule. Whenever the 5-day moving average of a bank's daily position was negative, the bank had to pay twice the normal rate for call money credit.

Under this arrangement, a bank's temporarily greater-than-normal level of call money credit had to be offset by making call money deposits at the Bank of Finland in excess of the normal level within the following 5 days. This increased the banks' marginal cost of call money credit, which was actually one of the main purposes of the revision. By granting small amounts of temporary call money credit at reasonable rates but making repetitive or excessive use of the facility costly, it was hoped that fluctuations in banking system liquidity would be immediately and totally reflected in short-term interest rates.

In July 1992, the existing call money facility was replaced by a new system for regulating the supply of bank liquidity. The new system differs from the previous one in that the deposit and borrowing rates are closer to market rates of interest and move in line with changes in market rates. At the same time, the new facility is expected to reduce excessive short-term volatility in the interest rates at the short end of the yield curve. The rates are tied to the current tender rate (the rate obtained in the latest tender arranged by the Bank of Finland for 1-month funds).

One further consequence of the possibility of undertaking open market operations is that the significance of cash reserve deposits in the control of liquidity has diminished. Desired changes in liquidity can be achieved at any time by operating in the money market, whereas the cash reserve deposit requirement can be adjusted once a month at best and even then by very limited amounts. The cash reserve deposits depend with a lag on the deposit base of the bank and are frozen for 1 month at a time. They allow no flexibility and therefore cannot be regarded as a part of the central bank's liquidity systems.

### 8.3.4 *Exchange Rate, Interest Rate Differentials and Foreign Exchange Reserves*

Figures 8.2 and 8.3 show movements in the above-mentioned proximate

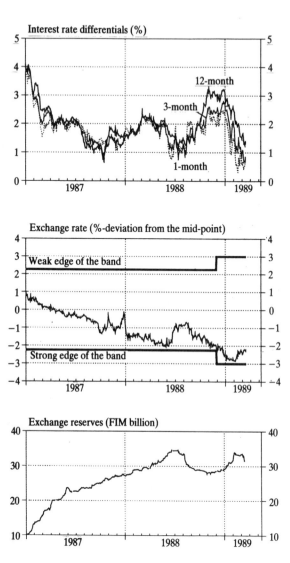

**Figure 8.2**   Proximate targets of monetary policy
(2 January 1987 – 16 March 1989)

targets of monetary policy since the beginning of 1987. Figure 2 covers the period from the beginning of January 1987 up to the revaluation on 17 March 1989. Figure 3 covers the post-revaluation period up to 14 November 1991, the eve of the devaluation. The division into two periods

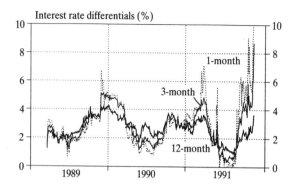

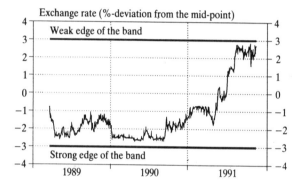

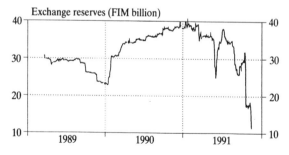

**Figure 8.3** Proximate targets of monetary policy
(20 March 1989 – 14 November 1991)

was made because there are good reasons to believe that data-generating processes differ between the two periods in a number of important respects.

Figures 8.2 and 8.3 portray the interest rate differential for the 1-, 3-

and 12-month terms, the exchange rate (external value of markka) measured as a percentage deviation from the middle point of the band, and the level of Bank of Finland's foreign exchange reserves. The interest rates differentials are measured against the weighted average of foreign interest rates and against the theoretical ECU interest rate since 7 June 1991. The exchange rate is defined in terms of the trade-weighted currency basket (theoretical ECU since 7 June 1991). An upward movement in the exchange rate indicates depreciation and a downward movement appreciation.

Figure 8.2 shows that after unrest in the currency markets in the 1986 the renewed confidence in the markka was reflected in substantial capital inflows in early 1987. As a result, interest rate differentials declined and the currency strengthened until the index almost hit the strong edge of the then ±2·25% band in June 1988. By late 1987, the interest rate differentials had shrunk to less than 2 percentage points (p.p.) from 4 p.p. at the beginning of the year. Throughout the first half of 1987, the Bank of Finland intervened in the foreign exchange market as a buyer in order to restore the exchange reserves to an acceptable level. At the same time, the Bank of Finland intervened in the domestic money market as a seller, which compensated, in part, for the liquidity effects of rising exchange reserves. Without foreign exchange intervention, the currency would have quickly strengthened to the lower edge of its band already in the first half of 1987.

From mid-1988 to the early 1991 the exchange rate fluctuated at around 2% level below the mid-point of the band while the interest rate differentials exhibited relatively large fluctuations around 2 p.p. level from the second quarter of 1987 to the autumn 1989. The exchange rate hit the strong edge of the band immediately before the widening of the band from ±2·25% to ±3% in November 1988. This move created room for some further appreciation of the markka.

On 17 March 1989, the fluctuation range of the currency index was shifted downward by about 4%. As a result the markka strengthened immediately and interest rates rose steeply by about 2 p.p. Within 2 weeks the exchange rate was again very close to the strong edge of the realigned band. The interest rate differential vis-à-vis the index currencies remained at a somewhat higher level than before the realignment.

Between March and August 1989, the Bank of Finland did not intervene to any large degree in the foreign exchange market, but it did intervene in the money market for liquidity management purposes. In the autumn the markka was under pressure on several occasions, during which the Bank of Finland lost reserves. Because of the uncertainty in the foreign exchange market the interest rate differential widened from around 2 p.p. to 4–6 p.p., which was sufficient to stop the capital outflow and to prevent a major weakening of the markka.

Confidence was restored in January 1990. Owing to the 1-month labour dispute in the banking sector in February, the decline in domestic interest rates was postponed to March/April. Heavy capital inflows contributed to the strength of the currency and brought the interest rate differential back to its 'normal' level of around 2 p.p.

The restoration of confidence proved to be temporary, however. The weakening of the economy and uncertainty about the national budget led to an expectations-driven upward drift in domestic interest rates in September and October 1990. As a result the interest rate gap widened again from 2 to around 4 p.p.

Visual inspection of the data in Figures 8.2 and 8.3 reveals that each time the 1- and 3-month interest rate differentials have shrunk to around the 1 p.p. level, the exchange rate has shown a tendency to depreciate. Such episodes are observed in late 1987, summer 1988, early 1989, summer 1989 and, again, in summer 1990. On the other hand, when the interest rate differential has stayed at its average level of 2 p.p. or above, the currency has shown a tendency to appreciate. This is especially true in summer 1987, in spring and autumn 1988, and spring 1990. These observations suggest that the interest rate differential that would have kept currency flows balanced for most of the post-1986 period up to autumn 1990 is somewhere between 1 and 2 p.p., i.e. 0·5 to 1 p.p. below the average actual outcome.

Up to 1990, the swings in the the exchange rate and the interest rate differentials exhibit negative, though not very strong, correlation. The main exceptions are early 1987, when the Bank of Finland intervened in the foreign exchange market in order to restore the exchange reserves to an acceptable level, and the period from October 1989 to March 1990, when the markka was under pressure and when the return to 'normality' was postponed by the 1-month bank strike in early 1990. Since autumn 1990, the correlation has been positive, rather than negative. Figures 8.2 and 8.3 reveal that both the day-to-day and the month-to-month volatility of interest rate differentials was greater in the period after 1988 than before, whereas the exchange rate volatility has remained roughly constant until mid-1991. A likely explanation for this development is that the increased uncertainty on the future economic development became more widespread. In addition, the discretionary measures by the Bank of Finland in the course of 1989, such as the surprise realignment of the band, the introduction of supplementary reserve requirements on banks and the changes in operational mechanisms of liquidity control aiming at limiting the banks' access to central bank borrowing, all contributed to increased interest rate variability.

Figure 8.4 depicts the interest rate differential and the exchange rate for the post-devaluation period 18 November 1991 to 31 mid-July 1992. Immediately after the devaluation, the exchange rate was slightly below the mid-point of the realigned band. More recently it has remained fairly stable at a level slightly above the mid-point. After the devaluation the interest rate differentials for 1- and 3-month terms quickly narrowed to

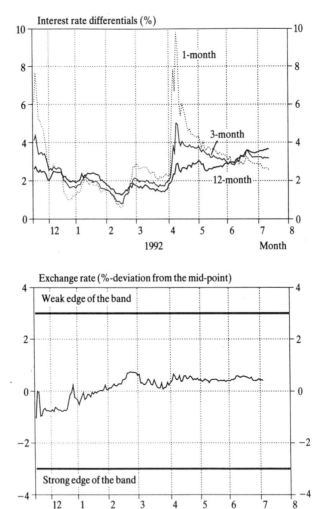

**Figure 8.4** Interest rate differentials and exchange rate

below 2% level, whereas the 12-month differential hardly changed at all compared to the level it had been prior to the devaluation. This development ended abruptly with a new speculative attack in early April 1992. A few months later, the currency once again came under pressure and yield differentials rose.

That the devaluation was a blow to credibility is not surprising. Although the real depreciation, measured as relative unit labour costs in common currency, was sufficient to restore export-sector competitiveness to a level far above its long run average, the negative impact of the devaluation on sheltered-sector employment, together with continuing concern about the sustainability of central government deficit, has increased political uncertainty, the cost of which has been reflected in higher interest rates. The Finnish experience is a powerful reminder of the high cost of losing the nominal anchor of the economy.

## 8.4    Target-Zone Models

In this section we briefly restate the standard target-zone model. Although the target-zone models have several empirical implications relevant to policy, many of the predictions of the theory are, for a number of reasons, extremely difficult to test by rigorous econometric methods. Direct testing is precluded by the impossibility of observing the so-called fundamental process, which is a composite of all factors which affect the overall macroeconomic balance. In some cases, rigorous tests are not even needed for observing discrepancies between data and the predictions of the theory. One further difficulty is that empirical testing of rational expectations models, to which category target-zone models belong, typically involves joint testing of several hypotheses (rational expectations, symmetric information, uncovered interest parity, as well as assumptions about the central banks' intervention rules).

### 8.4.1    *Basic Target-Zone Model*

The standard target-zone models start off with the asset-pricing relationship for the exchange rate (Froot and Obstfeld, 1991a; Krugman, 1991):

$$s(t) = k(t) + \alpha E_t(\mathrm{d}s(t))/\mathrm{d}t, \tag{8.1}$$

where $s(t)$ is the logarithm of the spot exchange rate (measured as units of domestic currency per unit of foreign currency). It is determined by the fundamental $k(t)$ and exchange rate expectations through the parameter $\alpha$.

This model of exchange rate determination is consistent with the flexible-price monetary model under free floating and full capital mobility. Parameter $\alpha$ represents the semi-elasticity of the demand for money with respect to the interest rate. In the monetary model, the fundamental can be defined as $k(t) = m(t) + v(t)$, where $m(t)$ is the logarithm of the money supply and $v(t)$ represents positive shocks to the velocity of money, i.e. negative shocks to money demand.

More complicated macroeconomic structures are also consistent with exchange rate determination as described by equation (8.1). In principle, the fundamental is a composite of all factors which determine the short-term IS-LM solution to the macroeconomic equilibrium. For instance, any change, such as an increase in government expenditure, or an improvement in the terms of trade, that would shift the IS-curve to the right and raise the domestic interest rate, can be interpreted as a downward shock to $k(t)$ implying, currency appreciation. The outcome will also depend on whether or not a change in some of the determinants of the fundamental affects exchange rate expectations.

The simplest characterization of the behaviour of the fundamental is to assume that it follows a Brownian motion with or without a drift:

$$dk(t) = \mu dt + \sigma dz(t) \tag{8.2}$$

If $\mu \neq 0$ the process has a drift, i.e. the fundamental has a constant rate of change. Otherwise it is driven by random shocks represented by $dz(t)$, where $z(t)$ is a standard Wiener process. In this case, $E(dz(t)) = 0$, with a constant instantaneous standard deviation $\sigma$.

Equation (8.1) can be expressed in the integral form:

$$s(t) = (1/\alpha) \int_t^\infty E_t[k(\tau)|k(t)]\exp(-(\tau-t)/\alpha]d\tau \tag{8.3}$$

where a stable (no bubbles) solution is assumed. The exchange rate depends on future fundamentals discounted by the factor $(1/\alpha)$. The conditional expectation of the future fundamental at moment $\tau$ in equation (8.3) is $E_t[k(\tau)|k(t)] = k(t) + \mu(\tau-t)$. With $\mu = 0$, the expected future fundamental is equal to the current one. Otherwise the fundamental moves according to the constant rate of drift. Taking this result into account, the exchange rate is simply $s(t) = k(t) + \alpha\mu$.

This is the solution for the exchange rate under free floating. In the target-zone regime free floating is limited to a given range. An intervention is, by definition, a policy measure which affects the $m(t)$-component of the fundamental. The target-zone for the exchange rate implies that the range of the fluctuations of the fundamental is restricted by offsetting changes in $m(t)$. By this policy rule, the stochastic process described by equation (8.2) becomes a regulated Brownian motion. In order to obtain a general solution to equation (8.1) in the presence of a target zone, let us postulate that the current exchange rate is a function of the current fundamental $s(t) = s(k(t))$. Using Ito's lemma and taking into account equation (8.2), the exchange rate in equation (8.1) must satisfy

$$s(k(t)) = k(t) + \alpha\mu s_k + \tfrac{1}{2}\alpha s_{kk}\sigma^2 \qquad (8.4)$$

In a credible target zone, the exchange rate is, therefore, a solution to the following function:

$$s(k(t)) = k(t) + \alpha\mu + A\exp(\lambda_1 k(t)) + B\exp(\lambda_2 k(t)) \qquad (8.5)$$

where $\lambda_1$ and $\lambda_2$ are the roots of the characteristic function $\tfrac{1}{2}\alpha\sigma^2\lambda^2 + \alpha\mu\lambda - 1 = 0$. The arbitrary constants $A$ and $B$ are determined by the boundary conditions. These *smooth pasting conditions* are defined as $s_k(k_u) = s_k(k_l) = 0$, where $k_u$ is the upper limit and $k_l$ is the lower limit of the fundamental. Smooth pasting conditions remove the arbitrage opportunity of making one-way bets on the exchange rate as it approaches either of the edges of the target zone.

Assuming a zero drift and a symmetric band, the current exchange rate as a function of the current fundamental is as follows:

$$s(k(t)) = k(t) - \sinh(\lambda k(t))/\lambda\cosh(\lambda k_u) \qquad (8.6)$$

where $\lambda = [2/(\alpha\sigma^2)]^{1/2}$.[9] This can be illustrated graphically by the familiar S-shaped curve (Krugman, 1991; Svensson, 1991a).

In the same manner as the current exchange rate can be expressed as a function of the current fundamental, see equation (8.6), the future exchange rate can be expressed as a function of the future fundamental (Svensson, 1991a). Assuming uncovered interest parity, the interest rate differential for an arbitrary term $\tau$ is, accordingly[10]

$$\delta_\tau(k(t)) = [E_t[s(k(t+\tau))] - s(k(t))]/\tau \qquad (8.7)$$

The term $\tau$ has a dimension of a unit of time (e.g. a month, and it determines the dimension of the interest rate (monthly interest rate).

Computation of the interest rate differential for an arbitrary maturity would be easy if the expected future exchange rate inside the band were easily computable. This is, however, not the case. The problem arises from the nonlinearity of the relationship between the fundamental and the exchange rate, which implies that $E_t[s(k(t+\tau))]$ is not equal to $s(E_t[k(t+\tau)])$, except for an infinite term, in which case the expected future fundamental is equal to its unconditional mean (i.e. the middle of the fundamental band in the absence of a drift). For all other non-zero terms the expected future exchange rate depends on the length of the term, in addition to the current fundamental.

By applying a similar kind of smooth pasting condition as above, the expected exchange rate can be expressed as a function of the current fundamental and the term (Svensson, 1991a).[11] The relationship has an S-shaped form similar to that of the relationship between the current fundamental and the current spot rate. The relationship becomes flatter and more linear as the term increases and is horizontal for an infinite term. Because the exchange rate is bounded to remain inside the (fully credible) band, the interest rate differential approaches zero as the term $\tau$ approaches infinity. In addition, the relationship between the current exchange rate and the interest rate differential is negative and becomes flatter as the term increases.

Despite elegance of the basic target-zone model, realism of the model has not obtained much empirical support. Empirical evidence from the Nordic countries and from a number of EMS countries have refuted many of the implications of the basic target-zone model.[12] In particular, empirical evidence on the U-shape of the distribution of the exchange rate and the negative relationship between the exchange rate and the interest rate differential is very scarce, which has led to a search for more realistic target-zone models.[13]

### 8.4.2   Extensions of the Basic Model

One of the weaknesses of the basic target-zone model is the assumption that the authorities intervene only when the fundamental reaches the edge of the band. There is substantial empirical evidence that movements of exchange rates within the band display strong mean reversion, which may be caused, inter alia, by intramarginal interventions. As a matter of fact, intramarginal interventions seem to be the rule rather than the exception in the majority of EMS countries. This is not surprising. After the 1987 Basle/Nyborg Agreement, the ERM participants introduced more flexible operational practices by accepting a wider use of intramarginal interventions. Some ERM countries, such as Belgium and the Netherlands, apply a voluntary band vis-à-vis DM, which is much narrower than the one implied by the ERM rules. This practice is consistent with the observations on exchange rate distributions referred to above.

These findings have led to the development of target-zone models that take intramarginal interventions into account. The implementation of potentially plausible intervention rules is, however, constrained by the fact that it is difficult, if not impossible, to find closed-form solutions similar to equation (8.6) when the fundamental follows more complicated processes. As shown by Delgado and Dumas (1992) and Froot and Obstfeld (1991b), such a solution can, however, be found in the case where the fundamental follows a mean reverting process

$$df(t) = -(1-\beta)(f(t)-f_0)dt + \sigma dz \qquad (8.8)$$

where $f_0$ is the reversion point of the fundamental towards which it would converge in the absence of stochastic shocks. In discrete time, equation (8.8) would take the form $f(t+1)=(1-\beta)f_0+\beta f(t)$. This 'partial adjustment' equation has a finite reversion point if $0<\beta<1$. The corresponding reversion point of the exchange rate is $s_0=s(f_0)$. This could be interpreted as the central bank's preferred level for the exchange rate. While accepting temporary deviations, the central bank intervenes in order to steer the exchange rate towards the preferred level, thereby smoothing fluctuations in the exchange rate.

This policy rule is equally applicable to managed floating and to target zones. In the latter regime, the presence of mean reversion in the fundamental reduces the non-linearity (S-shaped) in the relationship between the fundamental and the exchange rate (Lindberg and Söderlind, 1992). The exchange rate distribution becomes unimodal around $s_0$.

An interesting, but analytically more difficult, situation arises if the central bank does not aim at exchange rate smoothening as such, but instead aims at policy activism by changing from time to time the position of the exchange rate target inside the official band. In other words, the central bank defends a narrow unofficial band, which has soft edges and the position of which may change. Such intervention practices may play an important role in determining expectations on the future exchange rate as discussed in section 8.5.3.

The obvious difficulty in attempts to use limited policy autonomy with the help of bands within official bands is that market participants quickly learn the intervention policy rule. As a result, such intervention policy may prove to be counter-productive. For instance, when the markets have learned the unofficial band and believe that the central bank is likely to defend it for some time but not for ever, short-term interest rates may decline, even if the exchange rate is near the strong edge of the band, whereas longer term rates may actually rise because of the expectation that the defence point will shift up in the future.

Another basic assumption behind the basic target-zone model is that the currency band is fully credible. It does not, however, require any in-depth study to learn that many countries have, at least occasionally, suffered from a serious lack of credibility. Thus, an obvious extension to a basic model is to incorporate a time-varying devaluation risk (Bertola and Svensson, 1991). In addition to theoretical considerations an interesting question in this connection is whether the lack of credibility, i.e. the devaluation risk, is quantifiable in some way.

Bertola and Svensson (1991) have suggested the following procedure for measuring the devaluation risk. Let $s(t)$ stand for the log exchange rate and define $e(t)$ as its deviation from the mid-point $c$ of the band, $e(t)=s(t)-c$. The expected change in the exchange rate is thus

$$E_t(s(t+\tau)-s(t))/\tau = E_t[e(t+\tau)-e(t)]/\tau+E_t(\Delta c)/\tau \tag{8.9}$$

The first term on the right-hand side (within the parentheses) represents the expected depreciation inside the band between the dates $t$ and $t+\tau$, whereas the latter term represents the devaluation risk, i.e. the expected change in the mid-point of the band. The latter is denoted by $g(t)$. Let $\delta_\tau(t)$ stand for the interest rate differential (at term $\tau$) between domestic and foreign interest rates. Assuming uncovered interest parity, the devaluation risk can now be written as follows:

$$g(t) = \delta_\tau(t)-E_t[e(t+\tau)-e(t)]/\tau \tag{8.10}$$

The interest rate differential is observable data, but the expected depreciation inside the band is not. Several authors, including Rose and Svensson (1991), Svensson (1991b) and Frankel and Phillips (1991) have estimated the expected exchange rate inside the band. We also use the Bertola–Svensson method to assess the devaluation risk of the Finnish markka in section 8.5.4.

## 8.5   Some Empirical Results

### 8.5.1   *Simplest Test of Band Credibility*

In the following we continue our discussion of the credibilty of the currency band. The easiest way of testing the credibility is the simplest test described in Svensson (1990). The credibility of the Finnish currency band has previously been examined using this method in Kontulainen et al. (1990) and Geadah et al. (1992). Although the method can be used to identify periods when there was an acute lack of credibility, it is insufficient to make any conclusions about whether and when the band has been fully credible.

The results are presented in Figure 8.5. It presents data on the spot exchange rate as well as the computed forward exchange rate for 1-, 3- and 12-month terms. The computation is based on the following formula:

$$f_\tau(t) = s(t)((1 + i_\tau(t))/(1 + i_\tau^*(t)) \tag{8.11}$$
$$\approx s(t)(1 + i_\tau(t) - i_\tau^*(t))$$

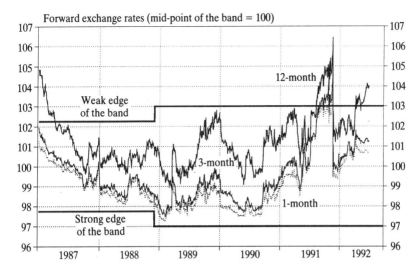

**Figure 8.5** Computed forward exchange rate

where $s(t)$ is the current spot rate, $i_\tau(t)$ is the domestic and $i_\tau^*(t)$ the foreign interest rate, and $\tau$ is the term (in years). The interest rates are expressed as straight annualized rates. The foreign interest rate is LIBOR and the domestic rate HELIBOR adjusted for a 360-day year (instead of 365 days). The spot rate is defined in terms of the currency index (since 7 June 1991 in terms of the ECU) with the mid-point of the band being indexed to 100. For the ECU-period, the market ECU spot rate and the market ECU interest rate are used instead of their theoretical (basket) counterparts.

Assuming uncovered interest parity and a credible band, $f_\tau(t)$ is between the upper and lower edges of the band. Otherwise there would be unexploited arbitrage opportunities if the band were credible. We can thus conclude that if $f_\tau(t) > s^u$, the weak edge of the band, it is perceived that there is a high probability of a devaluation, and if $f_\tau(t) < s^l$, the strong edge of the band, it is perceived that there is a high probability of a revaluation. The test is inconclusive when $s^l < f_\tau(t) < s^u$. The reason for inconclusiveness is that, while the interest rate differential reflects exchange rate expectations, uncertainty implies that there is a probability distribution around the mean. Incomplete credibility would imply that this distribution goes beyond one of the edges of the band, even though the mean may remain inside.

Examining the graphs in Figure 8.5 reveals that the computed forward exchange rates has remained inside the band for most of the time. The

12-month forward rate was above the weak edge in early 1987. From autumn 1987 to mid-1990 the 12-month forward rate fluctuated slightly above the mid-point reaching the weak edge in autumn 1989. From autumn 1990 onwards, all forward rates were on a rising trend, reflecting movements in the spot rate. In July 1991, the 3 and 12-month forward rates passed the weak edge, while the 1-month rate just hit the limit. Since the November 1991 devaluation, the computed 12-month forward rate has remained very close to the weak edge of the band, passing the limit again in April 1992.

These observations are in accordance with discussion in section 8.3. The interest rate differentials started to widen in autumn 1989, and this was more pronounced in longer maturities. The policy which allowed the exchange rate to remain near the strong edge of the band for a number of years may in itself have created expectations of a future relaxation. Although the March 1989 revaluation did not have a major impact on interest rate differentials in the short term, it may have created expectations of a future reversal, thus undermining band credibility.

Figure 8.6 depicts similar data computed for the 5-year term. For the domestic interest rate we used a 5-year government bond yield. Data are monthly up to the pegging to the ECU and daily thereafter. Because of lack of data on long-term bond interest rates in some countries whose currencies were included in the Finnish trade-weighted currency index, we used the 5-year ECU bond rate as a proxy for a basket bond yield. The currencies making up the ECU represented about 50% of the currencies in the currency index.

The 5-year forward rate for the markka has constantly been above the weak edge of the band. In 1988–90, the computed 5-year forward rate fluctuated between 110 and 115. The blow to credibility brought about by the devaluation in November 1991 is reflected in the computed forward rate, which drastically rose from around 112 to around 120 in July 1992. Part of the gap can be attributed to the poor liquidity of the bond market in Finland, which introduces a liquidity premium in to effective yields, but this does not alter the conclusion concerning the lack of long-term credibility.[14]

Comparing these observations with similar data from Denmark, Norway and Sweden reveals interesting differences and similarities (Geadah et al., 1992). The computed 12-month forward exchange rate for Denmark remained above the upper limit of the DM band of the Danish krone until 1990, but has since remained inside, although close to the weak edge. Computed for the 5-year term, the forward rate for the Danish krone has been above the the weak edge, although the gap has narrowed rapidly from year to year. In Norway the test reveals lack of credibility until early 1989, whereafter the forward rates up to the

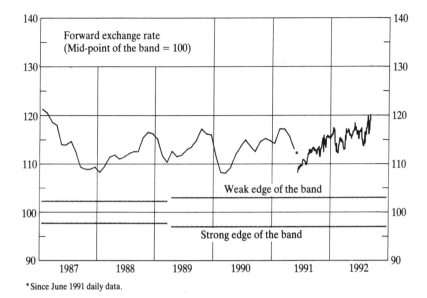

*Since June 1991 daily data.

**Figure 8.6**   Five-year forward exchange rates

12-month term have been safely inside the band. For Sweden the computed forward rates generally remained inside the the Swedish ±1·5% band until autumn 1989, since when the 12-month forward rate has been above the upper limit. The credibility problems in Sweden have thus arisen at about the same time as in Finland. The 5-year forward rate for the Swedish krona has remained outside the upper limit by a margin of around 9%. The Swedish situation has improved since 1990, whereas in Finland the course of development has been the opposite.

### 8.5.2   *Interest Rate Differential and the Exchange Rate*

One of the main implications of Svensson's (1991a) analysis of the basic model is that the interest rate differential should be a negative function of the current exchange rate. The intuition is straightforward. If the band is credible and the exchange rate is close to the strong edge of the band, the expected future level of the exchange rate is somewhere above its current level. The implied expected depreciation is reflected in the interest rate differential; the domestic interest rate is above the foreign interest rate by an amount equivalent to the expected depreciation. The same applies symmetrically for the case where the current level of the exchange rate is close to its weak edge; the implied expected appreciation drives the domestic rate below the foreign rate.

The empirical evidence on the negative correlation between the exchange rate and the interest rate differential is mixed and highly dependent on the time period examined. Svensson's (1991a) results were broadly consistent with the theory regarding the negative relationship between the exchange rate and the interest rate differentials and the term-structure of interest rates. The negative slope of the estimated linear relationship declined as the length of the term increased, and the standard deviations of the interest rate differentials were decreasing in term.

It is apparent that Svensson's results depend, to large extent, on the particular period used in estimation. As shown by Lindberg and Söderlind (1991), quite a different conclusion emerges when the data set is extended beyond the relatively short and relatively calm period used by Svensson.

The study by Kontulainen et al. (1990) used daily and weekly data on Finland covering the period from October 1987 to the eve of the March 1989 revaluation. The period was *intentionally* restricted to one which was characterized by comparatively small interest rate differentials and by the absence of major uncertainty in the market. The correlation between the interest rate differential and the exchange rate was found to be negative in most cases. In addition, the slope coefficients were all negative and significantly different from zero, as the theory predicts. The slope did not, however, decline as the term increased.

Vajanne (1991) examined the robustness of these results by extending the estimation period to include the full year 1987 and to cover all days from the March 1989 revaluation to early June 1991. In contrast to Kontulainen et al. (1990), the correlation between the exchange rate and the interest rate differential was found to be significantly positive for both subperiods and for all four terms examined.

As noted in section 8.3 there have been repeated episodes of currency unrest since autumn 1989. Thus, positive correlation is not a surprise in so far as the latter period is concerned. Positive correlation in the case of the former subperiod, which differs from that used by Kontulainen et al. (1990) only in that it is 9 months longer is, however, somewhat surprising. A likely explanation is that the Bank of Finland intervened heavily during the first half of 1987 in order to restore the official reserves to the level they had been before the 1986 upheaval.

Table 8.1 presents the summary statistics on the exchange rate and the interest rate differential for maturities of 1-, 3- and 12-months in three subperiods for Finnish data. The first subperiod stretches from 1 October 1987 to 15 March 1989, that is, to the eve of the revaluation of the

**Table 8.1**  Basic statistics (Wednesday data)

| | 1 October 1987 – 15 March 1989 | | | | 22 March 1989 – 15 May 1991 | | | | 22 March 1989 – 13 November 1991 | | | |
|---|---|---|---|---|---|---|---|---|---|---|---|---|
| | Mean | Std | Min | Max | Mean | Std | Min | Max | Mean | Std | Min | Max |
| $e(t)$ | -1.60 | 0.60 | -2.83 | -0.20 | -1.89 | 0.61 | -2.62 | 0.32 | -1.25 | 1.50 | -2.62 | 2.67 |
| $\delta(t, 1)$ | 1.63 | 0.48 | 0.38 | 2.45 | 2.93 | 1.35 | 0.83 | 7.11 | 3.03 | 2.05 | -0.26 | 17.04 |
| $\delta(t, 3)$ | 1.69 | 0.49 | 0.75 | 2.74 | 2.91 | 1.04 | 1.23 | 5.12 | 2.85 | 1.28 | 0.43 | 8.71 |
| $\delta(t, 12)$ | 1.98 | 0.56 | 0.97 | 3.18 | 2.88 | 0.64 | 1.37 | 4.23 | 2.68 | 0.76 | 1.03 | 4.23 |

*Correlations*

| | $e(t)$ | $\delta(t, 1)$ | $\delta(t, 3)$ | $\delta(t, 12)$ | $e(t)$ | $\delta(t, 1)$ | $\delta(t, 3)$ | $\delta(t, 12)$ | $e(t)$ | $\delta(t, 1)$ | $\delta(t, 3)$ | $\delta(t, 12)$ |
|---|---|---|---|---|---|---|---|---|---|---|---|---|
| $e(t)$ | 1 | | | | 1 | | | | 1 | | | |
| $\delta(t, 1)$ | -0.04 | 1 | | | 0.47 | 1 | | | 0.29 | 1 | | |
| $\delta(t, 3)$ | -0.42 | 0.86 | 1 | | 0.31 | 0.94 | 1 | | 0.09 | 0.93 | 1 | |
| $\delta(t, 12)$ | -0.60 | 0.60 | 0.89 | 1 | 0.12 | 0.72 | 0.87 | 1 | -0.39 | 0.56 | 0.79 | 1 |

markka. The second period covers the post-revaluation period up to the middle of May 1991. Finally, the third subperiod covers the data from the 1989 revaluation to the eve of the 1991 devaluation. The data used are weekly (Wednesdays).

Taking into account the previous empirical findings with Finnish data and the basic statistics presented in Table 8.1, we can conclude that for a given period the Finnish data exhibit some of the properties predicted by the basic model. In the first subperiod the interest rate differentials and the exchange rate have negative correlation. This is evident especially for the 3-month and 12-month terms.[15] For the 1-month term correlation is negligible. Negative correlation disappears after autumn 1989 when confidence became a problem. However, when the post-revaluation data are extended to include autumn 1991, the correlation is again negative for the 12-month term, but positive for the 1-month and the 3-month term.

These findings are broadly consistent with the argument presented by Bertola and Svensson (1991). If the volatility of the devaluation risk relative to the volatility of the fundamental has risen since 1989 then a positive correlation between the exchange rate and the interest differential is to be expected.

In Svensson's model with a constant devaluation risk and in the absence of intramarginal interventions, the stochastic movements in the fundamental move the exchange rate inside the band, which, in turn, affects the interest rate differential. The causality runs from the exchange rate to the interest rate differential through the expectations mechanism built in the band.

The observation of a negative correlation in itself does not establish causality. In the case of intramarginal interventions the causality may run in the opposite direction. As discussed in section 8.3.3, open market operations by the central bank affect the liquidity of the banking system, which has an impact on domestic short-term interest rates and thereby on the interest rate differential. A change in the interest rate differential, in turn, affects capital movements and thereby either the exchange rate or the exchange reserves.

In order to shed some light on this question we estimated two versions of the relationship between the exchange rate and the interest rate differential using daily data from the period of relative tranquility, that is, 1 October 1987 – 15 March 1989. We first regressed $\delta(t,\tau)$ on $e(t)$ as suggested by Svensson, and then we regressed $e(t)$ on $\delta(t,\tau)$. The results are presented in Table 8.2.

When the interest rate differential is used as the dependent variable, the constant term is around unity. According to Svensson's model, this should be interpreted as a (constant) perceived devaluation risk (% per

**Table 8.2** Interest rate differentials and the exchange rate
(daily data): 1 October 1987 – 15 March 1989

$\delta(t,\tau) = a + b\,e(t)$

|  | $\tau = 1$ | $\tau = 3$ | $\tau = 12$ |
|---|---|---|---|
| $a$ | **1.460** (8.6) | **1.097** (6.3) | **1.149** (7.1) |
| $b$ | **−0.411** (−2.8) | **−0.668** (−4.4) | **−0.698** (−4.7) |
| Dummy | **−0.677** (−1.5) | **−0.509** (−1.3) | **−0.203** (−0.5) |
|  | $R^2=0.118$ | $R^2=0.265$ | $R^2=0.395$ |
|  | DW=0.10 | DW=0.08 | DW=0.06 |
| Standard error | 0.50 | 0.47 | 0.45 |

$e(t) = a + b\,\delta(t,\tau)$

|  | $\tau = 1$ | $\tau = 3$ | $\tau = 12$ |
|---|---|---|---|
| $a$ | **−0.760** (−3.0) | **−0.519** (−2.5) | **−0.419** (−1.5) |
| $b$ | **−0.239** (−2.1) | **−0.371** (−3.9) | **−0.404** (−4.8) |
| Dummy | **−1.165** (−6.7) | **−1.026** (−6.3) | **−0.880** (−5.5) |
|  | $R^2=0.593$ | $R^2=0.660$ | $R^2=0.676$ |
|  | DW=0.11 | DW=0.13 | DW=0.12 |
| Standard error | 0.38 | 0.35 | 0.34 |

*Note*: OLS-estimation, *t*-values based on Newey-West (Newey and West, 1987) standard errors (15 lags) in parentheses. $n = 372$.

annum). Adding a dummy for the widening of the band in November 1988 reduces the constant term by around 0·5 p.p., except for the 12-month term. The slope is increasing in the term, which is contrary to the predictions of the model. One explanation for this ordering of the slope coefficients could be the intramarginal interventions and the implied soft-edged unofficial band. This unofficial band may be more credible in a short horizon (3 months) than in the longer run (12 months).

As can be seen in the lower panel of Table 8.2, it is, however, the latter regression which performs better. Therefore, the causal explanation implied by Svensson's model can be questioned. Both the causality from the interest rate differential to the exchange rate as well as the simultaneity may stem from intramarginal interventions, which should, in principle, affect both the interest rate differential and the exchange rate.[16]

### 8.5.3   *Intramarginal Interventions*

Since changes in the interest rate differential have an impact on either the exchange rate or the foreign exchange reserves, exchange rate policy can no longer be separated from domestic monetary policy. Exchange rate movements can be steered either through open market operations or directly through spot interventions in the foreign exchange markets. The choice of the type of intervention depends on, inter alia, how quickly the desired effect on the exchange rate or interest rates is needed. If an immediate impact on the exchange rate is needed, interventions are carried out in the foreign exchange market. On the other hand, if the central bank wants to steer interest rates via banks' free reserves (liquidity), open market operations in the domestic money market are normally carried out.

It is clear from the discussion in section 8.3 that intramarginal interventions have been the rule rather than the exception in Finland. As a matter of fact, there have been no interventions which have coincided exactly with the edges of the official band. In November 1988, the exchange rate went beyond the strong edge just before the band was widened from ±2·25, to ±3%. In general, the Bank of Finland has intervened when the exchange rate has reached a level which is around 0·5 p.p. from the edge of the band. This occurred on a number of occasions near the strong edge in 1989 and 1990. In late 1991, the same occurred near the weak edge of the band.

Table 8.3 gives aggregated quarterly information on the frequency and average size of daily interventions by the central bank in the spot exchange market.[17] In 1987, central bank purchases dominated sales. The years 1988 and 1989 were dominated by days when no intervention occurred (90% of all days). The third quarter of 1988 stands out as a period when repeated sales occurred, whereas purchases dominated sales

**Table 8.3**  Average frequency and size of intervention

|      |      | Number of days | | | Average amount (FIM bill) | |
|------|------|-----------|-------|------|--------|------|
|      |      | Purchases | Sales | None | Bought | Sold |
| 1987 | Q1   | 35  | 3  | 25 | 217  | 18   |
|      | Q2   | 24  | 3  | 34 | 237  | 24   |
|      | Q3   | 21  | 5  | 40 | 230  | 11   |
|      | Q4   | 9   | 8  | 47 | 168  | 141  |
| 1988 | Q1   | 6   | 1  | 57 | 212  | 3    |
|      | Q2   | 17  | 1  | 44 | 236  | 216  |
|      | Q3   | 0   | 17 | 49 | —    | 327  |
|      | Q4   | 6   | 0  | 57 | 180  | —    |
| 1989 | Q1   | 11  | 5  | 47 | 487  | 441  |
|      | Q2   | 3   | 0  | 60 | 160  | —    |
|      | Q3   | 0   | 7  | 58 | —    | 500  |
|      | Q4   | 0   | 1  | 61 | —    | 1730 |
| 1990 | Q1   | 28  | 0  | 36 | 358  | —    |
|      | Q2   | 16  | 1  | 44 | 187  | 320  |
|      | Q3   | 4   | 3  | 58 | 110  | 293  |
|      | Q4   | —   | 2  | 60 | —    | 1170 |
| 1991 | Q1   | 0   | 27 | 35 | —    | 539  |
|      | Q2   | 16  | 10 | 36 | 631  | 1397 |
|      | Q3   | 4   | 29 | 33 | 620  | 476  |
|      | Q4   | 20  | 9  | 33 | 1095 | 2996 |

in the first half of 1990. Interventions were more frequent in 1991, with sales dominating purchases both in terms of frequency and amounts transacted.

In Figure 8.7 we look at intramarginal interventions from a different perspective. Instead of the size of interventions, attention is paid to their timing as well as to the spot rate at which an intervention takes place. The figure shows the course of the actual exchange rate, $e(t)$, measured as a percentage deviation from the mid-point of the band. The two additional variables are defined as follows:

$$e^p(t) = e(t-j) \text{ if previous central bank spot purchase is on day } t-j$$
$$e^s(t) = e(t-j) \text{ if previous central bank spot sale is on day } t-j$$

The corresponding graphs in Figure 8.7 thus indicate the levels at which the Bank of Finland has stepped in, by either buying or selling foreign exchange in the spot market. The upper line indicates the level of the spot exchange rate at which the Bank of Finland has sold foreign currency in order to stop the upward movement or, at least, to resist ongoing depreciation of the markka within the band. The lower line, in turn, indicates the dates and the points at which the central bank has bought foreign exchange in the spot market.

The new variables are introduced in order to take into account the fact that, insofar as central bank interventions have a signalling effect, they should affect short-term exchange rate expectations. For instance, if an upward movement has been stopped once or twice at a certain point this

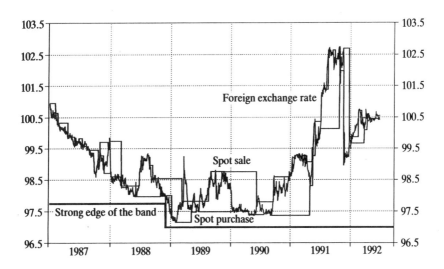

**Figure 8.7**  Exchange rate and the intervention points

is likely to increase the probability, as perceived by market makers, that the central bank will intervene at around the same point in the future as well. This is equivalent to saying that the market learns to think that there is an implicit band which the central bank will defend at least temporarily, although there may be much uncertainty about the exact level of future intervention points (soft edges of an implicit band).

There is plenty of anecdotal evidence that this signalling mechanism has, indeed, worked in the past. Although the size of central bank interventions is not known exactly, dealers, being counterparties to the central bank, know when the central bank has been in the market and at what level interventions are carried out. This is all that is needed for a signalling effect. Non-dealer participants, who are active in the market and customers of dealers, quickly learn from the latter. Because financial journalists are typically in daily touch with dealers, everyone else has a chance to learn about an intervention the next morning from financial press.

Visual inspection of Figure 8.7 confirms the observations made above. In 1987, interventions were frequent and mostly on the purchasing side, although the frequency of intervention started to diminish towards the end of the year. This indicates that the central bank was leaning against the wind by resisting the pressure towards appreciation in order to build-up exchange reserves. The three subsequent years were characterized by relatively infrequent spot interventions, while the exchange rate fluctuated near the strong edge of the official band. In summer 1991, the exchange rate shot up close to the weak edge of the band. The move was resisted by spot sales in late summer. The fact that a temporary strengthening was stopped by purchases on a few occasions probably signalled that the central bank was aiming at a point around the mid-point (=100) immediately before the pegging to the Ecu.

The data in Figure 8.7 conceal two discontinuities in the data. The exchange rate seems to jump in March 1989. This is a result of the fact that the exchange rate is measured as a percentage deviation from the mid-point. In reality, the exchange rate immediately appreciated by about 3%. Similarly, the apparent downward jump in the exchange rate associated with the November 1991 devaluation shows that the relative position of the exchange rate moved close to the mid-point of the new band after being close to the weak edge in the old one. The level of the exchange rate itself rose by 10–11%.

In section 8.5.4 below, we use this information, together with information on the total volume of interventions affecting liquidity and on the interest rate differential in order to construct a proxy for the expected future exchange rate inside the band. This proxy is then used to compute an estimate of the perceived devaluation risk.

### 8.5.4 *Devaluation Risk*

Computation of the devaluation risk as suggested by Bertola and Svensson (1991) would be straightforward, if the expected future exchange rate inside the band were directly observable. This not being the case, we have to use indirectly constructed proxies for this variable. We started by estimating the following autoregressive equation:

$$e(t+\tau) = \alpha + \beta e(t) + n(t) \tag{8.12}$$

and used the estimated coefficients for $\alpha$ and $\beta$ to obtain a proxy for the expected rate of depreciation inside the band. With this proxy and the observable data on the interest rate differential, calculation of the devaluation risk is straightforward.

We use equation (8.12) as a bench-mark. Moreover, we extend our analysis in three directions. First, we allow for the possibility that the previous intervention points may have had an effect on expected depreciation inside the band. Second, we examine the possibility that the total interventions by the central bank affect the future expected exchange rate. Finally, we want to shed some light on the usefulness of interest rate differentials in explaining the future expected exchange rate, as suggested in the section 8.5.2.

The estimation equation (8.12) is complicated by several factors as shown by Lindberg et al. (1991). First, while the sampling interval is shorter than the forecasting horizon, it results in serially correlated error terms. Second, since the expected future exchange rate within the band cannot be outside the band, the error terms must be realizations from a distribution with a finite support. Third, a wide class of exchange rate band models suggests that the error terms are likely to be heteroskedastic with a non-normal shape of the conditional distribution, mainly due to the stabilizing effect of the boundaries.

In the following we use the OLS estimation method with Newey–West (Newey and West, 1987) standard errors which allows for heteroskedastic and serially correlated error terms. The most important criteria for our results to be reasonable is whether the expected future exchange rate (or the confidence intervals) always fall within the exchange rate band. If this is not the case, the estimation method may have to be modified to explicitly take into account the restrictions the bands impose, for instance along the lines suggested by Chen and Giovannini (1992).

In addition, a few comments on equation (8.12) are in order. If $0<\beta<1$, the equation has a mean-reversion property, the reversion point being $\alpha^*=\alpha/(1-\beta)$. This property may result from mean-reversion in the fundamental, which, in turn, may reflect systematic policy rules applied by the authorities. For instance, if the central bank aims at the mid-point of the band ($\alpha^*=\alpha=0$) and intervenes accordingly, though stochastically, the exchange rate and hence the expectation tend to move in that direction (Lindberg and Söderlind, 1992).[18]

It is also important that the reversion point is inside the band. If $\beta=1$, the equation would have a unit root. The exchange rate could, in princple, move beyond the band boundaries and hence the expectation could not be anchored to any reversion point. The equation is unstable, if $\beta>1$, in which case the expected depreciation could easily go beyond the band boundaries.

In order to take the signal effect of the central bank interventions into account, we estimate the following two variations of equation (8.12):

$$e(t+\tau) = \alpha + \gamma_1 e^p(t) + \gamma_2 e^s(t) + \beta e(t) + n(t) \qquad (8.13)$$

$$e(t+\tau) = \alpha + \gamma_3 e^a(t) + \beta e(t) + n(t) \qquad (8.14)$$

where $e^p(t)$ and $e^s(t)$ are the previous buying and selling intervention points, respectively, and $e^a(t)$ is the average of the previous buying and selling intervention points, i.e. $e^a(t)=(e^p(t)+e^s(t))/2$.

The signs of the intervention coefficients are not entirely clear a priori. In principle, they should be positive. For instance, if the central bank raises the buying point $e^p$, it can be regarded as a signal that further appreciation is unwanted and hence unlikely. Similarly, if the selling point $e^s$ is lowered, it may signal to the market that the central bank wants appreciation, rather than depreciation, in the near future. On the other hand, a negative sign is also possible. For example, if the exchange rate is allowed to rise for some while and the central bank then stops the depreciation by one or more sales, this may cause the exchange rate and expectations to move back in the appreciating direction. In equation (8.13), the reaction to changes in intervention points may differ depending on the direction of the intervention. In equation (8.14) it is assumed that the reaction to intervention points is symmetric irrespective of the direction of the intervention.

Because of the lack of independently observed data on expectations we have no means to test which equation and which information set has been most important for expectations. Although we cannot choose the preferred equation by statistical criteria, we interpret the intervention points as being important for exchange rate expectations if they appear to be statistically significant in forecasting the future exchange rate.

In addition to the intervention points (as proxies for the signal effects), we augmented equation (8.12) by including total interventions $w(t)$. Total interventions cover all operations by the central bank which affect liquidity, i.e. both currency and money market interventions. To examine the possible effect of interventions on foreign exchange expectations we used a 5-day distributed lag on total interventions, $\lambda^*w(t)=\Sigma_i\lambda_iw_{t-i}$, $i=0, \ldots, 4$. We expect the coefficient of total interventions to be positive since central bank interventions increase the liquidity of the banking sector, which, in turn, tends to lower short-term interest rates and to weaken the currency.

Equations (8.12)–(8.14) were also augmented by including the distributed lag on the interest rate differential, $\lambda^*d(t)=\Sigma_i\lambda_id_{t-i}$, $i=0$, . . ., 4, to analyse the possible effect of the interest rate differential on the expectations of the future exchange rate within the band. We expect the coefficient to be negative, since within the band a higher interest rate differential should indicate expected appreciation of the exchange rate.

The estimated results for 1- and 3-month terms are presented in Table 8.4. We used daily data for the period from 2 January 1987 to 15 May 1991.[19] The discontinuity caused by the March 1989 revaluation was removed from the data by dividing the sample into two subperiods at that point. In the first subperiod, a dummy was added to account for the widening of the band on 30 November 1988.

The results of the pre-revaluation period are presented in Table 8.4. The estimated value of the rate of mean reversion in the bench-mark equation (8.12), captured by the coefficient $\beta$, is in the range 0.7–0.8. This coefficient declines to the range 0.2–0.5 when the intervention points are taken into account.[20] The parameter $\beta$ decreases when the forecast horizon is lengthened, as expected.

The coefficient of total interventions affecting liquidity $w(t)$ obtains a positive sign and is significant (at the 5% level using the $F$-test). The computed reversion point, $\alpha^*=\alpha/(1-\beta)$, is in the range $-1$ to $-2\%$ (below the mid-point). Including the intervention points in equation (8.13) shifts the reversion point upwards by around 0.5 p.p. On the other hand, the widening of the band on 30 November 1988 lowers the reversion point by approximately the same amount as the strong edge was shifted downwards, although the dummy is not significant.

The estimation results show that the signs of the intervention points are positive and of roughly equal size for both $e^p(t)$ and $e^s(t)$ over the 1-month forecasting horizon. The coefficients of the intervention points are, however, non-significant. It is interesting to note that the coefficient of the average intervention point $e^a(t)$ in equation (8.14) receives a significant coefficient. In other words, the estimation results suggest that intervention practices have been important for exchange rate expectations within the band in the sample and that the reaction to intervention points is symmetric irrespective of the direction of the intervention.

Unlike in the case of the 1-month horizon, the coefficients of intervention points for the 3-month horizon appear statistically significant.

**Table 8.4**  Expected exchange rate inside the band

| | e(t+22) | | | | | | | e(t+66) | | | | | | |
|---|---|---|---|---|---|---|---|---|---|---|---|---|---|---|
| | 1 | 2 | 3 | 4 | 5 | 6 | 7 | 1 | 2 | 3 | 4 | 5 | 6 | 7 |
| 2 January 1987 – 17 March 1989 | | | | | | | | | | | | | | |
| Constant | −0.261 (−4.9) | −0.295 (−4.5) | −0.203 (−3.8) | −0.211 (−4.5) | 0.144 (0.6) | 0.386 (5.9) | 0.323 (1.4) | −0.602 (−5.9) | −0.678 (−5.6) | −0.303 (−3.6) | −0.543 (−5.6) | −0.722 (−1.7) | −0.025 (−0.1) | −0.554 (−1.1) |
| $e(t)$ | 0.822 (11.0) | 0.82 (10.9) | 0.481 (2.9) | 0.484 (3.2) | 0.870 (12.7) | 0.483 (3.6) | 0.497 (3.7) | 0.712 (3.5) | 0.70 (3.6) | 0.210 (1.7) | 0.310 (1.2) | 0.676 (2.9) | 0.200 (1.6) | 0.324 (1.2) |
| $e^a(t)$ | — | — | 0.202 (1.3) | — | — | 0.289 (2.1) | — | — | — | 0.900 (5.1) | — | — | 0.931 (4.9) | — |
| $e^c(t)$ | — | — | 0.155 (1.0) | — | — | 0.126 (0.9) | — | — | — | −0.496 (−2.1) | — | — | −0.497 (−2.3) | — |
| $e^d(t)$ | — | — | — | 0.358 (2.1) | — | — | 0.411 (3.1) | — | — | — | 0.426 (1.3) | — | — | 0.390 (1.1) |
| $d(t)$ | — | — | — | — | −0.177** | −0.242** | −0.228** | — | — | — | — | 0.040** | −0.122** | −0.007** |
| $w(t) \times 10^{-6}$ | — | 172** | — | — | — | — | — | — | 679** | — | — | — | — | — |
| Dummy | −0.201 (−0.8) | −0.22 (−0.8) | −0.366 (−1.4) | −0.370 (−1.4) | −0.174 (−0.9) | −0.324 (−1.9) | −0.341 (−1.9) | −0.100 (−0.3) | −0.22 (−0.6) | −0.339 (−1.1) | −0.238 (−0.7) | −0.163 (−0.3) | −0.234 (−0.6) | −0.236 (−0.5) |
| ☞* | −1.45 −2.56D | | −1.07 −1.77D | −0.87 −1.59D | | | | −2.03 −2.44D | | −1.25 −1.68D | −1.32 −1.66D | | | |
| $R^2$ | 0.81 | 0.81 | 0.82 | 0.82 | 0.83 | 0.85 | 0.85 | 0.53 | 0.55 | 0.69 | 0.56 | 0.55 | 0.70 | 0.57 |
| DW | 0.14 | 0.13 | 0.12 | 0.12 | 0.20 | 0.16 | 0.16 | 0.06 | 0.06 | 0.09 | 0.05 | 0.09 | 0.11 | 0.07 |
| Standard error | 0.36 | 0.36 | 0.35 | 0.35 | 0.35 | 0.32 | 0.33 | 0.52 | 0.51 | 0.42 | 0.50 | 0.51 | 0.41 | 0.49 |

**20 March 1989 – 15 May 1991**

| | | | | | | | | | | | | | | |
|---|---|---|---|---|---|---|---|---|---|---|---|---|---|---|
| Constant | -0.480 (-2.2) | -0.488 (-2.4) | -0.796 (-0.7) | -0.411 (-0.8) | -0.054 (-0.2) | 0.521 (0.3) | 0.867 (1.2) | -0.866 (-1.6) | -0.636 (-1.2) | -2.652 (-0.6) | -2.327 (-2.3) | 0.231 (0.7) | -0.389 (-0.1) | -0.571 (-0.5) |
| $e(t)$ | 0.744 (7.5) | 0.73 (7.8) | 0.721 (6.9) | 0.735 (5.9) | 0.839 (8.3) | 0.797 (8.0) | 0.810 (7.8) | 0.497 (2.2) | 0.590 (2.9) | 0.628 (3.7) | 0.638 (3.1) | 0.678 (4.2) | 0.712 (4.1) | 0.705 (3.8) |
| $e^p(t)$ | — | — | -0.128 (-0.2) | — | 0.070 (0.1) | — | — | — | — | -0.546 (-0.3) | — | — | -0.100 (-0.1) | — |
| $e^s(t)$ | — | — | 0.038 (0.3) | — | 0.217 (1.3) | — | — | — | — | -0.404 (-2.5) | — | — | -0.176 (-0.7) | — |
| $e^c(t)$ | — | — | — | 0.042 (0.1) | — | — | 0.404 (1.2) | — | — | — | -0.838 (-1.9) | — | — | -0.338 (-0.6) |
| $d(t)$ | — | — | — | — | -0.069** | -0.110** | -0.110** | — | — | — | — | 0.219** | -0.173** | -0.173** |
| $w(t) \times 10^{-6}$ | — | -265** | — | — | — | — | — | -432** | — | — | — | — | — | — |
| ☞* | -1.87 | — | -1.44 | -1.87 | -1.87 | — | — | -1.72 | -1.63 | -1.63 | -1.63 | — | — | — |
| $R^2$ | 0.54 | 0.56 | 0.54 | 0.55 | 0.55 | 0.57 | 0.57 | 0.17 | 0.27 | 0.28 | 0.28 | 0.32 | 0.33 | 0.33 |
| DW | 0.15 | 0.16 | 0.14 | 0.15 | 0.17 | 0.17 | 0.17 | 0.07 | 0.08 | 0.08 | 0.08 | 0.10 | 0.10 | 0.10 |
| Standard error | 0.40 | 0.38 | 0.40 | 0.40 | 0.39 | 0.38 | 0.38 | 0.55 | 0.56 | 0.52 | 0.52 | 0.50 | 0.50 | 0.50 |

*Note:* OLS-estimation, $t$-values based on Newey and West (1987) standard errors (lags equal to each maturity) in parentheses.
** significant at 5% level ($F$-test).

Moreover, the coefficient of the sell intervention point obtains a negative coefficient, whereas the coefficient of the average intervention point in equation (8.14) is non-significant.

The estimated results of equations (8.12)–(8.14) modified to allow for the effect of the interest rate differential are also presented in Table 8.4 (equations (8.5)–(8.7)). The coefficient for the interest rate differential is negative and significant in all cases for 1-month and 3-month horizons, as indicated by the previous discussion.

The results for the post-revaluation period are shown in Table 8.4. The bench-mark model (equation (8.12)) gives rather similar results as for the pre-revaluation period. The β-coefficient is 0.7 for the 1-month period and 0.5 for the 3-month period. Total interventions $w(t)$ now obtain a negative sign and are significant, which is in contrast to our hypothesis.

The intervention points, both the selling and buying points as well as the average intervention point, are insignificant for forecasting the future exchange rate over 1-month horizon. For the 3-month term both the selling and buying intervention points are negative, but only the selling point $e^s(t)$ seems to be significant. Hence, it appears that intervention practices have played a minor role in the latter period compared to the first subperiod. This can partly be explained by the fact that there were only a few changes in buying and selling intervention points during this period.

The computed reversion point, $\alpha^*$, is around $-1.8\%$ (below the midpoint) and declines somewhat when the intervention points are taken into account. However, the fact that in most cases the constant term is not significantly different from zero, implies that the reversion point, if any, may have been at around the middle of the band in the latter estimation period.

Finally, when modifying the equations to allow for the effect of the interest rate differential on the expected future exchange rate, the coefficient of the interest rate differential is again significant and negative as expected.

All in all, the results of estimation regarding intervention points are mixed and difficult to interpret. Nonetheless, Figure 8.7 and empirical evidence from the pre-revaluation period support the argument that intervention practices within the band have been important in determining the expected future exchange rate. Estimation results also suggest that the interest rate differential has been an important factor in determining the expected future exchange rate within the band.

Hence, we decided to use equation (8.13) augmented by the interest rate differential to calculate the expected future exchange rate and thereby the expected rate of depreciation inside the band. The expected future exchange rate is depicted in Figure 8.8, together with the actual exchange rate.

As can be seen from Figure 8.8, the future expected exchange rate is well within the band when estimated with the OLS. The 95% confidence interval for 1-month estimation is on average ±0.7 and for 3-month estimation ±0.9 p.p. This means that the confidence intervals for

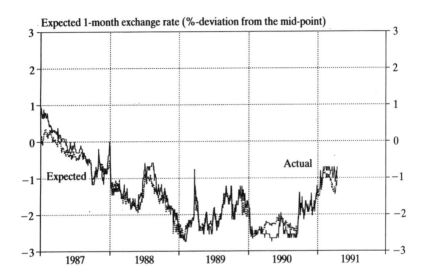

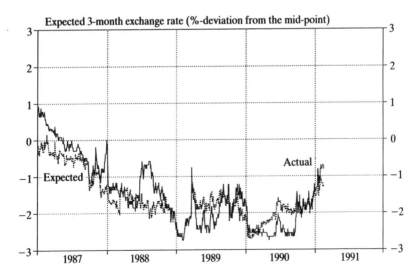

**Figure 8.8** Expected future exchange rate and the actual rate

expected future exchange rate fall also within the exchange rate band except some occasional periods when the exchange rate has been very close to the lower bound of the band.

In accordance with equation (8.10), we calculated the devaluation risk by subtracting from each observed interest rate differential the corresponding estimate of the expected rate of depreciation within the band. That is, the devaluation risk is equal to

$$g(t) = \delta_\tau(t) - (\alpha + (\beta-1)e(t) + \gamma_1 e^p(t) + \gamma_2 e^s(t) + \gamma_3 \lambda^* d(t))/\tau \qquad (8.15)$$

where $\delta_\tau(t)$ is the interest rate differential (annualized simple rates) for term $\tau$ (in years) and where the estimated values are used for $\beta$, $\gamma_1, \gamma_2$ and $\gamma_3$. The devaluation risk $g(t)$ is the product of the expected size of a devaluation and the probability intensity of devaluation.

The calculated devaluation risk for the 1-month and 3-month terms is shown in Figure 8.9. The devaluation risk is highly volatile and the volatility increases towards the end of the period.[21] It is correlated with the interest rate differential, but it is not identical with it. First, the interest rate differential is always positive, while the devaluation risk occasionally becomes zero or even negative. Secondly, it is more volatile than is the interest rate differential, and the volatility is higher for the 1-month than for the 3-month term. It is notable that zero or negative values appear in summer 1989 as well as in summer 1990, when the interest rate differential fell below 2%. The high volatility of the devaluation risk in 1988 is, in part, due to interventions or, more accurately, to the manner in which the expected future exchange rate was estimated. As noted above, the volatility of the interest rate differential should have increased in 1988, because the discrepancies between the expected future exchange rate and the current spot rate were comparatively large in that year. This did not happen, which may indicate the possibility that the central bank attempted to depress the exchange rate in order to raise the interest rate differential.

The rapid resurgence of confidence at the very beginning of 1987 after the unrest in 1986 is reflected in the data, although the devaluation risk of 4% in the middle of 1987 appears high in the light of other evidence. The steep step-by-step increase in the devaluation risk and in the interest rate differential, in autumn 1989 was connected with news concerning the budget and the trade balance, as well as with uncertainty surrounding wage negotiations. The sharp downward movement in summer 1990 is somewhat surprising given the fact that the sharp deterioration of the economic situation was more widely acknowledged than before. The profile in the devaluation risk in autumn 1990 is very similar to that of the previous autumn, except that the perceived risk continued to rise owing to the uncertainty surrounding the forthcoming general election.

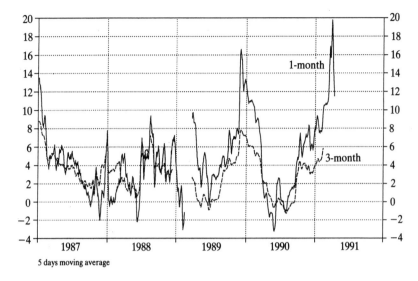

5 days moving average

**Figure 8.9** Perceived devaluation risk (% per annum)

From the end of 1987 to summer 1989, the devaluation risk for the 3-month term varied around 2–3%. In autumn 1989 and again in winter 1991, it rose to around 6%. Recall that the perceived devaluation risk is the product of the expected size of a devaluation and the probability intensity of a devaluation. A risk of 2% is hence consistent with a 10% devaluation with a probability of 20% per annum. This corresponds to a 5% probability per a 3-month period. The same devaluation risk is, however, equally consistent with a 4% jump in the exchange rate at the probability of 50% per annum, that is 12.5% per a 3-month period. In the latter case, the exchange rate could jump inside the official band, although the 'unofficial band' maintained by sell interventions in the lower half of the official band has not been credible. Part of the perceived devaluation risk calculated by our method may therefore reflect uncertainty concerning at what point the upward movement in the exchange rate would be stopped, that is the targeted exchange rate. Similarly, those cases (in autumn 1989 and winter 1991) where the perceived devaluation risk for the 3-month term rose to 6% are consistent with an expected 15% devaluation with a probability of 10% per 3-month period (40% per annum).

## 8.6    Conclusions

This paper has examined developments in the Finnish money and foreign exchange markets in the light of the recent literature on target-zone models and discussed the Finnish experience of maintaining the exchange rate within the currency band. Although the empirical evidence of the target-zone models examined by several authors is relatively mixed, the target-zone models provide useful tools in analysing developments in the money and foreign exchange markets.

When the basket peg and the currency band regime were formally adopted in Finland in 1977, the financial markets and capital movements were strictly regulated. This provided considerable room for manoeuvre in monetary policy. Although the formal deregulation took place as late as in the latter half of the 1980s, the effectiveness of capital controls and interest rate regulations had already started to erode in the early part of the decade. Since 1983, each successive government has announced a stable currency as a cornerstone of its economic policy. Despite this, the pressure against the currency has gathered momentum each time the economy has slowed.

The period since 1986 is in many respects an extraordinary phase in Finnish economic history. The year 1986 itself witnessed what, at the time, was the most powerful speculative attack against the currency. This was repelled by prompt central bank action on the interest rate front, although uncertainty subsided only after it was clear that the economy had embarked on a strong cyclical upswing. The driving forces behind the boom were constantly improving terms of trade and a boom in consumption and construction. In textbook terminology, the IS-curve shifted to the right. As these fundamentals were not counteracted by tighter fiscal policy, the pressure was towards real appreciation of the currency. Given the counter-inflationary stance of monetary policy (LM-curve unchanged or shifted to the left), there was a pressure on interest rates which led to currency appreciation until the markka strengthened to the strong edge of the band and was ultimately revalued in March 1989.

The boom aided to the most severe peacetime recession ever experienced in Finland. The pressure against the currency once again gathered momentum. The November 1991 devaluation was a blow to credibility and the currency has had to face repeated attacks since then.

Against this background the Finnish data provide a good opportunity to examine some of the implications of the target-zone models. In the empirical part of the present paper the relationship between the interest rate differential and the exchange rate was examined. The question of causality between the exchange rate and the interest rate differential was also raised and the possible effect of central bank interventions were taken into account in estimating the future exchange rate within the band. This proxy for the expected exchange rate was then used to calculate the devaluation risk of the Finnish markka.

The findings of the paper support the argument that for a given period the Finnish data exhibit some of the properties of the basic target-zone model. However, our findings support the view that causality runs from the interest rate differential to the exchange rate and not vice versa as implied by the basic target-zone model. The estimation results also indicate that intervention practices have been an important factor in determining the expected future exchange rate.

In retrospect, it would appear that the band arrangement has provided some room for monetary policy autonomy, although any quantitative assessment of its significance is most uncertain. In the post-1986 period up to autumn 1989, the average interest rate differential of around 2 p.p. helped to maintain the tendency for capital inflows, whereas capital outflows resulted when the interest rate differential fell to 1 p.p. or below. It therefore appears that an interest rate differential of between 1 and 1.5 p.p. would have kept currency flows in balance on average during the period concerned. In terms of the interest rate differential, the degree of monetary policy autonomy was about 50 basis points at most, which was not much and certainly not sufficient to prevent serious overheating of the economy.

With the benefit of hindsight, the 1991 devaluation was caused by a gradual deterioration in confidence in the economic policies pursued. The fixed exchange rate test, which, in Finland, coincided with the deepest recession in the post-war era, proved to be extremely difficult.

Monetary policy, which aimed at a stable exchange rate and low inflation, was not supported by sufficient flexibility in fiscal policy. As a result, the policies aimed at improving the economy through structual adjustment and increasing competitiveness via nominal price and cost adjustments lacked credibility. The task of economic policy-making was also complicated by the disagreement on policy options within political circles and by the fact that many of the necessary cuts in public expenditure needed support from the opposition. The lack of credible policy alternatives eventually resulted in the devaluation of the markka.

# Notes

The views expressed do not necessarily represent those of the bank of Finland or the Union Bank of Finland. We are grateful to Jarmo Kontulainen and Carolina Sierimo for their help and advice.
  1. Weights at the Bank of Finland currency index were adjusted quarterly and published in the *Bank of Finland Bulletin*.
  2. For a detailed description of the financial reform in Finland see Abrams (1989).
  3. The Bank of Finland's base rate may be somewhat misleading as a term, because the ultimate decision is made by the Bank's Parliamentary Supervisory Board. This explains its upward rigidity, which may not have been a problem in times of straight

regulation and credit rationing. The asymmetry in deregulation and the political ridgidity of the base rate probably sowed the seeds of future imbalances in the banking sector, as bank deposit rates did not rise in line with market rates and banks funded their new lending increasingly in the wholesale market (including the forward exchange market). The interest margin was further reduced later as the cost of funding had increased while but the rates on outstanding loans tied to the base rate remained at a low level.

4. Supplementary cash reserve requirements were intended to penalize aggressive lenders and to raise bank lending rates in order to reduce credit demand. The system was in force from March 1989 to the end of that year.

5. For a detailed description, see Suvanto (1990).

6. Since 1980, the forward exchange market had functioned as a substitute for the otherwise non-existent domestic money market and as a new channel for short-term capital movements, which made it possible for the Bank of Finland to utilize forward exchange market intervention as a means of controlling liquidity. Forward exhange operations were used extensively in 1983 and 1984 in order to sterilize the liquidity impact of capital inflows (cf. Lindroos, 1989).

7. In exceptional cases, the Bank of Finland has carried out money market operations in the deposit market in overnight, 1-week and 2-week maturities. These contracts differ from other operations in that their value date coincides with the trade date.

8. For a thorough analysis of the call money window, see Pulli (1992).

9. Sinh and cosh are hyperbolic sine and cosine functions, respectively. These are defined as follows: $\sinh(x) = \frac{1}{2}(\exp(x) - \exp(-x))$ and $\cosh(x) = \frac{1}{2}(\exp(x) + \exp(-x))$.

10. This holds approximately, because the expected rate of change in the exchange rate is defined as a logarithmic difference, whereas the interest rate differential is defined in terms of basis points (hundreth of a p.p.).

11. Assuming risk neutrality, the expected future exchange rate is equal to the forward exchange rate.

12. See Lindberg and Söderlind (1991) and Vajanne (1991) for the empirical findings from the Nordic target zones, and Flood et al. (1990) for the EMS countries.

13. Bertola and Svensson (1991) provide a possible theoretical explanation for these mixed empirical results. They show that depending on the relative variability between the devaluation risk and the fundamental almost any pattern of observations between the interest differential and the exchange rate can emerge. A low variability of the devaluation risk relative to the fundamental implies a negative correlation between the interest rate differential and the exchange rate, whereas the opposite situation may cause the correlation to become positive.

14. Assuming that the liquidity premium is 75 basis points in the effective yield to maturity, this would lower the computed 5-year forward rate by only 4 p.p.

15. The correlations are of the same order of magnitude when daily or monthly (every fourth Wednesday) data are used instead of weekly data (Wednesdays). The correlations are positive when the first three quarters of 1987 are included in the sample.

16. In order to assess the causality between the variables we also carried out standard Granger-Non-Causality tests for 1-month, 3-month and 12-month terms. This was done by regressing $\delta(t, \tau)$ on its own distributed lags as well as on the distributed lags of $e(t)$ and by regressing $e(t)$ on its own distributed lags and on the distributed lag of $\delta(t, \tau)$. The $F$-test was used to test the non-causality. The results indicated that the hypothesis that the interest rate differential is *not* a Granger-cause of the exchange rate cannot be rejected in any of the examined cases.

17. Daily data on foreign exchange interventions by the Bank of Finland is not published. Since April 1990, data have been published on a weekly basis in the Bank of Finland statistical review (*Financial Markets*).

18. The basic target-zone model with interventions only at the edges of the band leads to a similar relationship for longer terms (Svensson, 1991a). Intramarginal interventions tend to linearize the relationship; see Lindberg and Söderlind (1992).

19. We also estimated equation (8.12) for 1-day and 5-day horizons. Interestingly, the results were very similar to the 1-month model as regards both the rate of mean reversion and the reversion point.

20. The *t*-values for the coefficients being less than unity are around −2 in equation (8.12), while the critical level for the Dickey–Fuller test at the 5% significance level is −2.87 for this sample size (Fuller, 1976, Table 8.5.2), for which reason the unit-root cannot be rejected. When intervention points are added (equations 8.13 and 8.14) β differs significantly from unity.
21. The EMS-currency bands have gained increased credibility between 1987 and 1991 (Frankel and Phillips, 1991; Rose and Svensson, 1991; Svensson, 1991b; and Weber, 1992). In Finland, as in Sweden, credibility problems have increased during the same period (Lindberg et al., 1991).

# References

Abrams, R. K. (1989), 'The Financial Reform in Finland'. *Kansallis-Osake-Pankki Economic Review*, **1**.

Åkerholm, J. (1987), 'Fixed exchange rate policy in Finland', *Bank of Finland Monthly Bulletin*, **61**, (6–7).

Åkerholm, J. (1992), 'The exchange rate regime in Finland—Developments and experiences', Bank of Finland Central Bank Policy Department, Working Paper 2/92.

Aurikko, E. (1989), 'The Bank of Finland's market intervention', *Bank of Finland Bulletin*, **63** (4), 3–6.

Bertola, G. and Svensson, L. (1991), 'Stochastic devaluation risk and the empirical fit of target zone models', NBER Working Paper No. 3576.

Chen, Z. and Giovannini, A. (1992), 'Estimating expected exchange rates under target zones', NBER Working Paper No. 3955.

Delgado, F. and Dumas, B. (1992), 'Target zones: big and small', NBER Working Paper 3601.

Flood, R., Rose, A. and Mathieson, D. (1990), 'An empirical exploration of exchange rate target-zones', NBER Working Paper No. 3543.

Frankel, F. and Phillips, S. (1991), 'The European Monetary System: Credible at last?', NBER Working Paper No. 3819.

Froot, K. and Obstfeld, M. (1991a), 'Exchange rate dynamics and stochastic regime shifts', *Journal of International Economics*, **31**, 203–29.

Froot, K. and Obstfeld, M. (1991b), 'Stochastic process switching: Some simple solutions', *Econometrica*, **59**, 241–50.

Fuller, W. (1976), *Introduction to Statistical Time Series*, John Wiley, New York.

Geadah, S., Saavalainen, T. and Svensson, L. (1992), 'The credibility of Nordic exchange rate bands: 1987–91', IMF Working Paper WP/92/3.

Halttunen, H. and Korkman, S. (1984), 'External shocks and adjustment policies in Finland', In M. de Cecio (ed.), *International Economic Adjustment: Small Countries and the European Monetary System*, Basil Blackwell, Oxford.

Kontulainen, J., Lehmussaari, O.-P. and Suvanto, A. (1990), 'The Finnish experience of maintaining a currency band in the 1980s', Bank of Finland Discussion Paper 26/90.

Korkman, S. (1978), 'The devaluation cycle', *Oxford Economic Papers*, **30**, 357–66.

Krugman, P. (1991), 'Target zones and exchange rate dynamics', *The Quarterly Journal of Economics*, **106**, 669–82.

Lehmussaari, O.-P. (1991), 'Experience with managing the exchange rate of the markka within the currency band', *Bank of Finland Bulletin*, **65**, (3), 3–8.

Lindberg, H. and Söderlind, P. (1991), 'Testing the basic target zone model on

Swedish data', Seminar Paper No.488, Institute for International Economic Studies, University of Stockholm.

Lindberg, H. and Söderlind, P. (1992), 'Target zone models and the intervention policy: The Swedish case', Sveriges Riksbank Arbetsrapport Nr 6.

Lindberg, H., Svensson, L. and Söderlind, P. (1991), 'Devaluation expectations: The Swedish krona 1982–1991', NBER Working Paper No. 3918.

Lindroos, N. (1989), 'The forward exchange market in Finland', *Bank of Finland Bulletin*, **63** (10), 3–6.

Newey, W. and West, K. (1987), 'A simple, positive semi-definite, heteroskedasticity and autocorrelation consistent covariance matrix', *Econometrica*, **55**, 703–8.

Pulli, M. (1992), *Overnight Market Interest Rates and Banks' Demand for Reserves in Finland*, Suomen Pankki B:47, Helsinki.

Puro, I. (1978), 'The amendment of the currency act', *Bank of Finland Monthly Bulletin*, **52** (2).

Puro, I. (1984), 'Finland's currency index system and its development', *Bank of Finland Monthly Bulletin*, **58** (2), 26–30.

Rose, A. and Svensson, L. (1991), 'Expected and predicted realignments: The FF/DM exchange rate during the EMS', Seminar Paper No.485, Institute for International Economic Studies, University of Stockholm.

Suvanto, A. (1990), 'Operational mechanisms of central bank policy', *Bank of Finland Bulletin*, **64** (11), 6–12.

Svensson, L. (1990), 'The simplest test of target zone credibility', *IMF Staff Papers*, **31**, 27–54.

Svensson, L. (1991a), 'The term structure of interest rate differentials in a target zone: Theory and Swedish data', *Journal of Monetary Economics*, **28**, 87–116.

Svensson, L. (1991b), 'Assessing target zone credibility: Mean reversion and devaluation expectations in the EMS', NBER Working Paper No. 3795.

Swoboda, A. K. (1986), *Ongoing Changes in Finnish Financial Markets and Their Implications for Central Bank Policy*, Suomen Pankki A:62, Helsinki.

Vajanne, L. (1991), 'Exchange rate under target zones: Theory and evidence of the Finnish markka', unpublished manuscript. Union Bank of Finland.

Weber, A. (1992), 'Time-varying devaluation risk, interest rate differentials and exchange rates in target zones: Empirical evidence from the EMS', CEPR Discussion Papers No 611.

# Discussion

## Lars E. O. Svensson
*Institute for International Economic Studies, Stockholm and CEPR*

I find this a very informative chapter on the struggle to maintain the exchange rate band for the markka. The chapter starts with a report on the history and working of the exchange rate band up to the float in September 1992. This report gives the impression that the Bank of Finland has very actively and consciously used the scope for exchange rate movements within the band. Let me start by suggesting a simple framework in which such activism within the band can be discussed.

Why do real-world fixed exchange rate regimes have an exchange rate band instead of a completely fixed exchange rate (between realignments)? Keynes (1930, pp. 319–31), in discussing the significance of the gold points in the Gold Standard, suggested that the function of the band is to provide some monetary independence, that is, some domestic influence over the domestic (−currency) interest rate. The existence of such monetary independence in a fixed exchange rate regime with international capital mobility may come as a surprise to readers who are familiar with the standard textbook result that a fixed exchange rate regime with free capital mobility implies a complete loss of monetary independence. Let me first explain the textbook result, then go on and explain how an exchange rate band gives some monetary independence.

Consider the instantaneous equilibrium condition in the international capital market according to which the domestic interest rate of a given maturity equals the sum of the foreign (−currency) interest of the same maturity, the average expected rate of domestic currency depreciation over the maturity, and a possible foreign exchange risk premium. We can write this as

$$i_t^\tau = i_t^{*\tau} + E_t(s_{t+\tau} - s_t)/\tau + \rho_t^\tau \tag{1}$$

where $i_t^\tau$ and $i_t^{*\tau}$ denote the domestic and foreign interest rate at time $t$ of maturity $\tau$, $E_t$ denotes expectations conditional upon information available at time $t$, $s_t$ denotes the log exchange rate (the log of the number of domestic currency units per foreign currency unit), and $\rho_t^\tau$ is the foreign exchange risk premium. If (1) holds, domestic and foreign investors prefer to hold existing portfolios, and the central bank need not intervene at time $t$ to support the current exchange rate; that is, currency flows are zero. If the central bank tries to maintain a domestic interest rate at time $t$ below the right-hand side of (1), investors prefer to increase their relative holding of foreign currency assets. Then an *incipient* currency outflow starts to depreciate the domestic currency (increase the exchange rate), or, if the central bank intervenes in the foreign exchange market to prevent the exchange rate from rising, an *actual* currency outflow results; vice versa if the central bank tries to maintain a domestic interest rate above the right-hand side of equation (1).

In an exchange rate band we can write

$$s_t = c_t + x_t \tag{2}$$

where $c_t$ is the (log) central parity and $x_t$ is the (log) deviation from central parity, what I shall call the exchange rate within the band. From (2) it follows that the expected rate of currency depreciation can be decomposed into two components:

$$E_t(s_{t+\tau} - s_t)/\tau = E_t(c_{t+\tau} - c_t)/\tau + E_t(x_{t+\tau} - x_t)/\tau \tag{3}$$

these components being the expected rate of realignment and the expected rate of currency depreciation within the band.

In the textbook case of a fixed exchange rate regime there is no exchange rate band, and the exchange rate is identical to the central parity, $s_t = c_t$. Then the second term on the right-hand side of (3) is always zero. The textbook case also disregards the foreign exchange risk premium. Then, the equilibrium condition (1) can be written

$$i_t = i_t^{*\tau} + E_t(c_{t+\tau} - c_t)/\tau \tag{4}$$

If foreign exchange reserves shall remain stable there is hence no choice for the central bank but to set the domestic interest rate equal to the foreign interest rate. This is the textbook case of a complete loss of monetary independence.

With an exchange rate band, the expected rate of currency depreciation within the band is not always zero, and the equilibrium condition (1) can with (3) be written

$$i_t = i_t^{*\tau} + E_t(c_{t+\tau} - c_t)/\tau + E_t(x_{t+\tau} - x_t)/\tau + \rho_t^\tau \tag{5}$$

Let me now use this form of the equilibrium condition to explain how monetary independence can arise in an exchange rate band. Suppose that we start in an equilibrium that fulfils (5) and that the current exchange rate is at central parity, that is, in the middle of the band. Suppose now that the central bank lowers the domestic interest rate below the right-hand side of (5). This causes an incipient currency outflow which puts upward pressure on the exchange rate. Suppose the central bank does not intervene but allows the currency to depreciate and the exchange rate to rise in the band. If the investors expect the exchange rate deviation from the central parity to be temporary, the agents expect the exchange rate to revert back towards the central parity in the future. That is, the agents expected the currency to appreciate back towards the central parity, and they expected the rate of depreciation within the band, the third term on the right-hand side to become negative. The upward pressure on the exchange rate continues until the expected rate of depreciation has become sufficiently negative to equal the initial lowering of the domestic interest rate. Then, the international capital market is in a new instantaneous equilibrium, with a lower domestic interest rate and a higher exchange rate. It follows that the central bank can indeed exercise some control over the domestic interest rate, by moving the exchange rate within the band and in this way create expectations of depreciation or appreciation within the band. This is indeed the mechanism by which an exchange rate band gives some monetary independence.

This monetary independence is limited for several reasons. First, it is clearly limited by the size of the exchange rate band. A narrower band allows less scope for the expected rate of depreciation within the band to vary. Second, the control over the domestic interest rate is only temporary. Unless expectations are systematically violated, the exchange rate, once away from the central parity, must eventually be allowed to drift back towards the central parity. Put differently, over a longer period the average expected rate of depreciation must be close to zero; the unconditional expected rate of depreciation within the band must be zero. Third, only interest rates of short maturities can be effectively controlled. For long maturities the expected rate of depreciation within the band must by necessity be small, since the amount of depreciation is bounded by the width of the band and then divided by a long maturity.

Finally, even the temporary control over short maturity interest rates may disappear if the expected rate of realignment, the second term on the right-hand side in (5), is endogenous and depends on the exchange rate's position in the band. If a depreciation of the currency within the band increases the expected rate of realignment, this counters the effect of the expected depreciation within the band.

Even with all these limitations, the amount of monetary independence in a fairly narrow band may be surprisingly large. Svensson (1994) estimates the monetary independence in the previous ±1.5% Swedish exchange rate band. Compared with a situation with a zero width band, it appears that Sveriges Riksbank, by controlling exchange rate movements within the band, was able to reduce the standard deviation of the 1 month krona interest rate by about a half.

I believe this potential monetary independence, even if limited, is the best explanation of why fixed exchange rate regimes almost always have bands, or put differently, why central banks reveal a preference for non-zero bands in fixed exchange rate regimes. In any case, I think it would be very useful to apply this framework to Lehmussaari, Suvanto and Vajanne's discussion of the history of the markka band. For instance, the period after the small devaluation within the band in May 1986 may have been an example of the expected rate of realignment being sensitive to the exchange rate's position within the band. The strong markka during 1988–90 is consistent with the central bank trying to maintain a tight monetary policy and as high a domestic interest rate as possible.

The detailed discussion provided by the authors should be a useful background for a more explicit evaluation of the Finnish exchange rate policy. In retrospect, should anything have been done differently? What were the options available at critical instances? One characteristic of the Finnish exchange rate regime that distinguishes it from other countries are the changes that occurred in the bandwidth, from ±2.25% to ±3%, then back to ±2.25%, then back again to ±3%. Another distinguishing characteristic is that each revaluation was followed by a devaluation, and each devaluation was before November 1992 followed by revaluation. In addition, there were conscious changes of the exchange rate to different levels within the band. Could this activism have given investors and private agents the impression that the Finnish exchange rate regime was a rather soft one?

The Finnish experience should also be fruitful for studies of the role of institutional and political environments for monetary policy; for instance, the importance of central bank independence and the importance of political unity in exchange rate policy issues.

After the discussion of the Finnish experience the authors give an excellent summary of recent theoretical and empirical research on exchange rate target zones. The last part of the paper contains some empirical results. Let me end with a couple of more technical comments on the empirical methods used.

First, in the 'drift adjustment' estimates of expected rates of devaluation the authors add intervention variables to the explanatory variables for the regressions on expected future exchange rates within the band. I think this is an an important improvement, but I would like to add that in principle one should include all variables of the current information set as explanatory variables. In similar regressions for the Swedish krona and for EMS exchange rates domestic and foreign interest rates sometimes have explanatory power for future exchange rates within the band. Since the coefficients are sometimes of different magnitudes, it is safest to always include these separately, rather than as an interest rate differential.

Second, I find confidence intervals for the expected future exchange rates, and for the expected rates of realignment, very useful. The precision of the estimates are of independent interest, and the confidence intervals are necessary for hypothesis testing. In particular, it is important to examine whether confidence intervals for expected future exchange rates always fall within the exchange rate band. If this is not the case, the estimation method may have to be modified to explicitly take into account the restrictions the band limits impose, for instance along the lines suggested by Chen and Giovannini (1992).

# References

Chen, Z. and Giovannini, A. (1992), 'Estimating expected exchange rates under target zones', NBER Working Paper No.3955.
Keynes, J. M. (1930), *A Treatise on Money. Vol. II, The Applied Theory of Money*, Macmillan, London.
Svensson, L. E. O. (1994), 'Why exchange rate bands? Monetary independence in spite of fixed exchange rates', *Journal of Monetary Economics*, **33**, 157–99.

# Index

*Note:* 'n.' after a page reference indicates the number of a note on that page.